Scenes That Never Made It To The Screen

Morris Bright & Robert Ross

Introduction by Peter Rogers

Virgin

DEDICATION

Dedicated to our unsung *Carry On* Heroes –
Terry Scott and Peter Butterworth.

First published in Great Britain in 2000 by
Virgin Publishing Ltd
Thames Wharf Studios
Rainville Road
London
W6 9HA

Copyright © Morris Bright and Robert Ross 2000

The right of Morris Bright and Robert Ross to be identified as the Authors of this Work has been asserted by them in accordance with the Copyright, Designs and Patents Act, 1988.

This book is sold subject to the condition that it shall not, by way of trade or otherwise, be lent, resold, hired out or otherwise circulated without the publisher's prior written consent in any form of binding or cover other than that in which it is published and without a similar condition including this condition being imposed on the subsequent purchaser.

A catalogue record for this book is available from the British Library.

ISBN 1 85227 990 7

Printed and bound in Great Britain by Butler & Tanner.

Designed by Design 23, www.d23.co.uk

Contents

Introduction

By producer Peter Rogers

For many years now I have received literally thousands of letters from *Carry On* fans across the world asking whatever happened to out-takes or scenes that were taken out of my films before they made it to the big screen. Unfortunately, the footage was destroyed in the mid-1980s when the Rank Organisation decided to rationalise their vault storage space and gave the order to junk the reels of material from literally hundreds of films in their library.

Alas, scenes from the *Carry Ons* that never made it to the final cinema print were also lost at the same time. And so it looked as though I would never be able to allow the fans an opportunity to glimpse some of the missing gems from the series of films they helped to make so endearingly popular.

Then those two chaps Morris Bright and Robert Ross with whom I have built up a firm friendship over the past few years, came up with the suggestion of trying to piece together some of these long-forgotten scenes, by drawing on the original shooting scripts and pictures from the *Carry On* archives – many of which have not been seen since they were taken over 30 years ago. What started as a casual suggestion over a glass of wine in the Pinewood Studios bar has now become the volume you are holding in your hands.

Many people seemed surprised to hear that there were scenes to be taken out of a *Carry On* film in the first place. For decades I have been accused of making cheap films which utilised every inch of footage that my director Gerald Thomas got in the can. It is certainly true to say that my films were economic in production costs, but cheap! I should say not. Our production staff were some of the highest paid in the country. Just look at *Carry On... Up the Khyber*. The number of people who really thought we went to film in India was astounding. We had letters congratulating us on the scenery. Yet we filmed it in Wales! And if a scene didn't quite work in the context of the finished film or a joke was regarded too risqué by the censor, then if all else failed – including editing – the scene would be taken out. Simple as that.

There were several reasons why it may have been deemed necessary to remove a scene or some lines in a scene from the finished film. As often as not, it was to keep the pace of the film ticking along. A *Carry On* never dragged, even if some of the actors had to!

Certain films, like *Follow That Camel* or *Carry On... Up the Khyber* were positively

Keeping the British end up! The classic kilt-lifting scene from producer Peter Rogers' favourite of the film series, Carry On . . .Up the Khyber *(1968).*

epic in proportions. If we had filmed the scripts as Talbot Rothwell had written them, we would have something akin to a David Lean production on our hands! It wasn't so much that dear Talbot had overwritten, but the action scenes – such as the final blowing up of the Governor's residency in *Up the Khyber* – had little dialogue, though plenty of visual comedy, and represented several minutes of film footage. Talbot, as a writer, could only estimate how long he thought action scenes would take. In reality – particularly in the two films I have just mentioned – the action scenes made up a large part of the fun and so some of his script had to be cut back to ensure the film did not overrun. The pace had to remain brisk and the jokes plentiful. Therefore, it was with great sadness but with a relentless desire to present the film as best I could, that certain scenes were edited while Gerald and myself viewed the rushes, or even, on occasions, cut from the screenplay before the cameras began rolling.

One such example appeared in *Carry On Cowboy*. It was a funny little scene with Charlie Hawtrey whose character had become a little inebriated in the local tavern. His drunken performance of a saucy limerick tickled me, but added little to the plot and therefore was taken out. The limerick went something like this:

Charles Hawtrey as Big Heap in Carry On Cowboy *(1965).*

Big Heap: Oh, there was a Red Indian's daughter
Who everyone called Running Water
Till an arrow from high
Punctured her main supply
Now her water don't run as it oughter.

Some cuts were made because the scenes contained a mistake or continuity error, or a practical error occurred which affected the presentation of a comic moment.

In *Don't Lose Your Head* which was set during the time of the French Revolution, we had Kenneth Williams, as Citizen Camembert, fooled by the duelling tactics of Sidney James as Sir Rodney Ffing. In Talbot Rothwell's original screenplay this dialogue concerning the venue for the duel appears:

Camembert: The Garden of Fragrance it is, sir. Er...where is that?

Rodney: You can't miss it. Just by the cess pit.

Now, the whole point of the duel was that the Sir Rodney character is being very sheepish and uncertain, until finally tricking Camembert into taking one pace too many and landing him in the cess pit. That comic moment would have been lost if the audience were already aware of the punch-line moment. Sidney James, as Sir Rodney, laboured the point about making it fifteen paces instead of ten paces for the pistol duel with this dialogue:

Rodney: I wonder if you'd mind making it fifteen paces instead of ten?

Camembert: What on earth for?

Rodney: Well, fifteen is my lucky number, you see.

Camembert: Oh, this is preposterous!

Rodney: No, it's true. I was born on the fifteenth, you see and fifteen months later I had my first dolly...and fifteen months after that I had my first pony...and when I was fifteen years old there was this chambermaid and...

Camembert: (Doing his nut) All right, all right, all right! Fifteen paces! Anything to get this over with!

Pomfrit: Fifteen it is! Any advance on fifteen? Going at fifteen. Going...going...

With such an expert cast of comedy actors, it was often the case that odd words of dialogue would be changed during the filming. There were never any ad-libs allowed, but if an artiste thought a certain inflexion or change would enhance the comedy, Gerald Thomas and myself would consider it and pass it on its merits accordingly.

Perhaps the two finest performers when it came to spotting a winning joke or line were Kenneth Williams and Charles Hawtrey. There is a scene in *Carry On Cleo* where Kenneth (as Julius Caesar) returns to Rome to find his wife (played by Joan Sims) and father-in-law, Charles Hawtrey as Seneca, complaining. Caesar desperately tries to make up for his long absence by distributing gifts from his travels. The tag line is about Caesar bringing her "Stones from far-off Gaul..."

In Talbot Rothwell's original script, Hawtrey had the final line:

Seneca: And she's got Gaul stones, too, so there!

In the finished film that was changed too: "And she's got Gaul stones an'all!" to which Kenneth replies, "I had no idea!!" That was much funnier!

Sid James was another fine performer who would often see an extension to the humour within Talbot Rothwell's script. In *Carry On Doctor*, which was Sid's return to Pinewood – as a bedridden patient – after suffering from a real-life heart attack, there is a sequence concerning the raucous exploits of one Doctor Kilmore, played with typical gusto by Jim Dale. Sid's character, Charlie Roper, is reading from a scandalous report in a newspaper, detailing the rampage of the young doctor. This is how the sequence appeared in the script:

Charlie: It says here he tried to peep at one nurse sunbathing in the semi-nude, half stripped another, and attacked a third one in her bath! Blimey, he doesn't do things by halves, does he!

Now, once Sid had made his suggestions to Gerald and myself, the final line was removed and replaced with this much funnier observation:

Charlie: I wonder what he has for breakfast!

So, clearly, if the artistes had a notion to improve or amend the dialogue, we listened. However, the rumour that has been spread for many years by some members of the cast concerning the fact that jokes would be swapped like an apple for a conker at playtime is completely false. Actors like Kenneth Williams, Charles Hawtrey and Sidney James were far too professional for that sort of thing. The script was often referred to as the Bible and that was true....up to a point. Mind you, if Gerald and I approved, the script could be converted to the New Testament.

Most importantly, these suggested changes would come from artistes who were trying to enhance the film

Phil Silvers as Sergeant Knocker and Kenneth Williams as Commandant Burger in an excised scene from Follow That Camel *(1967).*

in general and not just their performance in that film. Sidney James and Jim Dale worked out a jolly bit of business for Charles Hawtrey in the French Revolution picture, *Don't Lose Your Head*. The poor old aristocrat is reclining on the block of the guillotine, when a pretty messenger girl runs up and exclaims: "I have an urgent message for you milord!" Charlie comments, "Drop it in the basket, I'll read it later!" That wasn't in the script...and the laugh went to another artiste. That was the unselfishness of the performers involved.

There were also occasions when some lines, though patently funny, were at the time deemed mildly offensive. It was one of the reasons that the original script title *Carry On* Jungle Boy was changed to *Carry on Up The*

Kenneth Williams and Jim Dale from an impassioned moment in Carry On Again Doctor *(1969).*

Jungle. Similarly, a couple of years earlier, we changed a few lines at the beginning of *Carry On... Up the Khyber* which might have unintentionally caused offence. The lines were to be spoken by Joan Sims and Sidney James as their characters Joan and Sidney Ruff-Diamond, and were to describe Kenneth Williams' character, the Khasi of Kalabar.

Joan: Oh, I say who's that brown job over there?
Sidney: Brown job?!!!

He looks across. Here sit, in splendour of trappings and dress, His Highness THE KHASI OF KALABAR and, beside him, his favourite and very beautiful, the PRINCESS JELHI.

Sidney: Brown job indeed! That's Rhandi Lal!

The lines then became:

Joan: Whose the turban job on the throne?
Sidney: You mean the Khasi! That's Rhandi Lal!

Much better!

Politics itself reared its very ugly head. I was advised that a particularly satirical dig at unions and fat cat union bosses who abused their privileged positions to take enjoyable holidays in the sun, could be a bad mistake...I agreed. As it happened, this particular scene, in *Carry On At Your Convenience*, was removed in its entirety. A great pity, for it removed the entire performance of that fine artiste Terry Scott. But that's show business.

Political satire within a *Carry On* film would never have been a good idea. The period between production and release could be several months. A general election could have been fought in the interim and any jokes included could seem very old hat indeed. This was one of the reasons I decided that the following lines from the beginning of *Carry On Again Doctor* delivered by the character of Kenneth Williams, Sir Frederick Carver, should be excised.

Carver: (Dictating a letter) Chairman, Labour Party Executive Committee, Dear Harold...I shall be honoured to carry out the proposed transplant operation on your member...and put in the member's name...and suggest he comes into hospital at Hampton Wick as soon as possible. Yours etc...Frederick Carver, OBE, KCB, FRCS, NIT. (To himself) A head transplant would be more appropriate.

There was obviously a satirical reference to Harold Wilson, the Prime Minister at the time. Yet just a few months later, in early 1970, there was a general election in which he lost to Edward Heath.

One of the main reasons for us having to remove dialogue from a film was at the insistence of the film censor. By and large, the censor and I got on very well indeed. Our arguments over certain lines like "Fakir Off"

A cast line-up for Carry On Matron *(1972). From left to right: Derek Francis, Bill Maynard, Bernard Bresslaw, Sidney James, Terry Scott, Kenneth Williams, Hattie Jacques and Kenneth Cope.*

in *Carry On... Up the Khyber* are well documented and little is heard of the fact that most problems were ironed out quickly and to everyone's satisfaction – particularly after my *Carry Ons* changed from a 'U' certificate to an 'A' certificate in the mid-1960s – allowing for slightly more adult and risqué material.

There were, however, occasions when the censor and I could not reach agreement and rather than spend large amounts of time trying to re-write or even re-shoot a scene, it was easier to cut around it, or – on some occasions – take out the whole scene altogether. You will see a large example of this later in the book – in a long scene from *Carry On Regardless* which was deemed far too rude for the audiences of 1961. Thankfully, most of the edited scenes were mercifully short, so we lost nothing from the quality and pace of the film. Two small examples spring to mind:

A particularly funny example is of a flamboyantly camp line from dear Kenneth Williams right at the very end of the horror parody, *Carry On Screaming!* Kenneth, playing the manic, undead, Doctor Watt, is chasing after the heroes of the film – Harry H. Corbett and Jim Dale among them. He is armed with a syringe and acting menacingly:

Watt: Aha! You thought you'd beaten me, didn't you? Ha, ha, ha! But you'll never get away. Oh, no! You think this is for greenfly, don't you? But it isn't see? It's filled with petrifying liquid. And it works. I've tried it on my rhubarb with amazing results!"

A family portrait from Carry On Screaming! *(1966) with (front) Kenneth Williams, Fenella Fielding and Harry H Corbett, and (back) Billy Cornelius as Odbodd Junior and Tom Clegg as Odbodd.*

Now, the censor allowed us to keep all the description dialogue about the petrifying liquid in the film, but that closing, comic comment about the rhubarb was censored. It's a shame, because it still makes me laugh on the written page, but erection gags – however subtle – weren't considered quite right in 1966!

An even more blatant example is a short preamble between the two ambulance driver characters Henry (Peter Gilmore) and Sam (Harry Locke) from *Carry On Doctor* outside the hospital:

Henry: Here come the poor bleedin' visitors!
Sam: Yep. I don't know who to feel more sorry for. Them or the poor muckers they're visitin'.
Henry: You ever in 'ospital, Sam?
Sam: Not 'alf! I 'ad mumps when I was thirty. Ooh, shocking it was. My utensils was all swelled up!
Henry: I know. Something to do with the prostitute gland.
Sam: That's right. Oh a right do that was, I'll tell you. You know, the doctor made me promise not to 'ave anything to do with my wife for six months!
Henry: Get away!
Sam: Yeh! It was a damn good job I 'ad a girlfriend or I don't know what I'd've done.

As well as being able to read scenes edited out of existing *Carry On* films, I am also delighted that, for the first time, via this book, fans of the *Carry Ons* have the chance to read the full script of a *Carry On* film that was written but never made.

Every film producer has unproduced scripts in the bottom drawer of his desk and as soon as it is announced in the newspapers that more money is to be made available for production, out they come, the dust is blown off and they are re-submitted to the powers that be – henceforward known as PTB. Mostly they are rejected and back they go into the bottom drawer. The producer, of course, is anxious to get his money back after the outlay for rights and script. In the case of the script for *Carry On Again Nurse*, which is reproduced in its entirety in this book, the case was slightly different.

Carry On Again Nurse was penned by the series' original screenwriter Norman Hudis in 1988, exactly thirty years after he had given us the first film, *Carry On Sergeant*. Yes, it had been three decades since our series of films had started and some ten years since I had made the last *Carry On* at that time, *Carry On Emmannuelle*. It was planned to reunite surviving cast members including Kenneth Williams, Charles Hawtrey, Joan Sims, Barbara Windsor and others in an affectionate tribute to our earlier films and, specifically,

Charles Hawtrey 'dragged' in for publicity for Carry On Again Doctor *(1969).*

to our earlier medical *Carry Ons*.

Unfortunately, fate dealt a cruel hand that year with the sudden deaths of Kenneth Williams and Charles Hawtrey. Making the film became almost unthinkable without them.

Now though, over a decade later, you can enjoy Norman's fine work. As problems with our National Health Service appear to rumble on, the script is as funny and as satirical as ever. And though the film was never made, our stars over the years became so much part of all our lives that I am sure you will literally be able to hear their voices delivering the lines. It's never going to be as good as having a real film to watch, but it comes a very close second place.

Carry On Again Nurse is by no means the only unfilmed *Carry On* script which adorns my desk at Pinewood Studios. I have several which either were considered not good enough by me or were put aside when the PTB decided that the *Carry Ons* had had their day and they only wanted to make films like *Jaws*. One distributor did say to me, "Now, Peter, if you presented me with a subject like *Jaws*..." This was after the success of the film in the mid-1970s. I replied: "If I'd done that, you would have turned it down." They're like sheep, you know, the PTB. There's only one gap in the hedge for them to go and that's where some other stupid sheep has gone first.

So whilst I can never rule out entirely making another *Carry On*, it could take a little time!

But in the meantime, do please sit back and enjoy *The Lost Carry Ons* – found at last!

Kenneth Williams in a publicity pose for Carry On Abroad *(1972).*

Chapter One

Cinema Parodies . . . ooh!

The art of film parody is almost as old as cinema itself. The *Carry Ons* relentlessly proved they had their innuendo-encrusted finger on the pulse of current cinematic trends and could twist serious productions into uproarious comedies. There was even opportunity to parody the *Carry On* series within the *Carry On* series itself. A cheeky Frankie Howerd was outraged at a daffodil approaching his rear in *Carry On Doctor* nearly ten years after Wilfrid Hyde-White had had his rectal thermometer replaced by a similar flower in *Carry On Nurse*.

However, the real golden age of the *Carry On* parody started with *Carry On Spying*. Basking in the initial success of the James Bond films, the *Carry On* crew became bumbling mince spies within a narrative more awash with references to earlier films. The Vienna sequence is packed with knowing nods to the 1949 classic *The Third Man*. Bernard Cribbins emerging from a manhole cover, the Café Mozart meeting place and the subtle inclusion of a cuckoo clock, all point towards the exploits of Orson Welles as the notorious Harry Lime. Classic Hollywood *Film Noirs* like *The Maltese Falcon* are also addressed with the cunning partnership of over-sized Eric Pohlmann and diminutive John Bluthal acting like a comic answer to Sydney Greenstreet and Peter Lorre.

Carry On Cleo mocked ancient Egypt and William Shakespeare historically and literally, although contemporary audiences were more concerned with the tempestuous relationship between Cleopatra stars Elizabeth Taylor and Richard Burton. *Carry On Cowboy* wallowed in memories of the Raoul Walsh comedy western *The Sheriff of Fractured Jaw* which featured frightfully English Kenneth More getting involved with glamorous Jayne Mansfield and wild ways way out west. Furthermore, the *Carry On* team embraced references to classic Hollywood westerns like John Ford's *Stagecoach* and Fred Zimmerman's *High Noon* to support the glorious, barrel-scraping puns.

The Hammer horror films from Bray studios were as much a part of the British way of life as the *Carry Ons*, and a comic look at the teeth and claw picture seemed inevitable. Despite the array of vampires, vamps, werewolves, mad monsters, mummies and mammaries on display in *Carry On Screaming!* the film was less about the Hammer tradition and more about the horror classics of an earlier age. The basic plot line of a manic doctor kidnapping women and turning them into dummies was directly lifted from the 1933 Lionel Atwill chiller *The Mystery of the Wax Museum*. That vintage terror fest had, itself, been remade as the 3D Vincent Price

A menacing Kenneth Williams as Doctor Watt in this stunning publicity shot for Carry On Screaming! *(1966).*

Tyrant Galley Master Peter Gilmore (centre) keeping an eye on his oarsmen – including Jim Dale as Horsa (far right) – as they sail up the Nile in Carry On Cleo *(1964).*

classic *House of Wax*.

The French Foreign legion, the stirring story of P.C. Wren and the cinematic exploits of Beau Geste (in the person of Gary Cooper) were all rolled out alongside Phil Silvers doing his Sergeant-Bilko-by-proxy for the desert and harem flick that was *Follow That Camel*. Memories of Peter O'Toole's finest hour as Lawrence of Arabia are evoked at every corner and Anita Harris as the seductive Corktip is a direct reference to Claudette Colbert's character of Cigarette in the 1936 Ronald Colman film *Under Two Flags*.

Historical capers came thick and fast between the contemporary forays into hospitals and holidays but the next direct parody didn't come along until the very end of the 1960s when the gang went into starkest Africa for *Carry On Up the Jungle*. Originally filmed as *Carry On Jungle Boy*, the central character was the bumbling, slow-witted Tarzan styled man of the woods played with energetic gusto by Terry Scott. The estate of Edgar Rice Burroughs wasn't happy about the idea of a comic look at their client's legendary literary creation and even Jacki Piper's scripted character of Jane was changed to June during production. However, most *Carry On* filmgoers went fully equipped with collective memories of Johnny Weissmuller's classic MGM jungle adventures or any of the many other big screen Tarzan actors, from Elmo Lincoln to Mike Henry. The concept of Valerie Leon and her female tribe of sex-starved glamour girls can be traced back to such B movie treats as *Untamed Women* (1952) and *Wild Women of Wongo* (1965).

Although notably absent for most of the 1970s (when Mel Brooks seemed to have cornered the market), parody informed the *Carry On* series until the bitter end. *Carry On Emmannuelle* was the camp answer to the hugely successful 1974 film *Emmanuelle* and its several spin-off productions. Ill-fated attempts at resurrecting the series in the 1980s threw up *Carry On Texas* and *Carry On Down Under*, having a dig at glossy soaps, *Dallas* and *Neighbours*. Even the reappraisal which did get made, *Carry On Columbus*, came hot on the heels of Ridley Scott's *1492: Conquest of Paradise* and John Glen's *Christopher Columbus – the Discovery*.

Carry On Cleo 1964

Scriptwriter: Talbot Rothwell
Producer: Peter Rogers
Director: Gerald Thomas
Production started: 13 July 1964

Our distinguished announcer, Gaumont-British Newsreel legend, E.V.H. Emmett, sets the historic scene. The Roman Empire, headed by Julius Caesar (Kenneth Williams) is conquering every known country and a load of Britons including Hengist Pod (Kenneth Connor) and Horsa (Jim Dale) give Mark Anthony (Sidney James) and his Roman boys a tough time. Captured and transported for the slave trade, our British heroes escape while Mark Anthony is hatching some double-crossing deals with the seductive Queen Cleopatra (Amanda Barrie). Camp and true love triumphs, while Mark Anthony ends up in a bath of ass's milk with his beloved Cleo.

The plot so far: Julius Caesar (Kenneth Williams) has just returned from a bit of conquering. His father-in-law, a scatty, bespectacled old sage by the name of Seneca (Charles Hawtrey) has just been discovered in his room with a tasty new blonde bimbo (Thelma Taylor). Caesar's ever nagging wife, Calpurnia (Joan Sims) is having a rant about being left during her neglectful husband's three-year crusade.

SCENE 32: INTERIOR. MAIN ROOM. DAY.

This is the all-purpose room. There is a sunken pool, banqueting table, several elegant marble chairs and divans. An ornate screen near bath.

Seneca suddenly darts into shot, pointing a quivering finger.

Seneca: Your days are numbered! Beware the ides of March!
Caesar: Oh shut up, you old faggot!
Calpurnia: How dare you speak to my daddy like that?
Caesar: Well, he gets on your nerves.
He kneels down by bath to talk to her.
Caesar: I'm sorry, dear. But I really am getting sick of listening to him and his visions and omens and stuff.
Calpurnia: I'd just like to know where you'd be without him, that's all. The name of Seneca is respected throughout Rome as a truly great sage.
Seneca: That's right. And I know my onions!
Caesar: (Turning to him) I wish you'd been in Britain! They know what to do with sage and onions there!
Seneca: You'll be wishing you were back there soon! Ha ha! You just wait till the ides of March!
Caesar: You silly old fool! You don't even know what the ides of March are!
Seneca: Is!
Caesar: Eh?
Seneca: Ides is: not ides are!
Caesar: All right, but I still say you don't know what they is!
Seneca: Are!
Caesar: Eh?
Seneca: They are: not they is. Your grammar!
Caesar: Oh, for Jupiter's sake! What are they then?
Seneca: What are what?
Caesar: Ides!!!
Seneca: Well, that's easy. They're the skins you get off animals.
Caesar: I give up. You win.
Seneca: Oh good. I think I'll open the box.
Caesar: Do anything! So long as I can just talk to Calpurnia in peace!
He turns back and bends down to bath. It is empty
Caesar: Now listen, darling...Calpurnia?
We hear the gurgle of bath water running out. He looks anxiously down into the water.
Caesar: Calpurnia!
Calpurnia: (off) What is it?
Caesar looks up. We see her come from behind screen wearing a sort of Roman bath towel robe.

Caesar: Oh, thank goodness! I thought we'd lost you for a moment.

She sits pouting on a padded divan and starts to titivate her hair. Caesar sits beside her and gives her a tentative little cuddle.

Caesar: Oh, you don't know how I've missed you, dear. Three years is a long time to go without, you know.

Calpurnia: Without what?

Caesar: Without the company of a beautiful wife.

The plot so far: Our heroes, Hengist Pod (Kenneth Connor) and Horsa (Jim Dale) have gone through the hands of slave-traders Markus and Spencius (Gertan Klauber and Warren Mitchell). Major stirrer Mark Anthony (Sidney James) has planted some very attractive seeds of what Cleo (Amanda Barrie) looks like, in the mind of Julius Caesar (Kenneth Williams). The Emperor's wife, Calpurnia (Joan Sims) is outraged at the prospect of another business trip for her husband, particularly with the pretty young blonde slave girl, Gloria (Julie Stevens) on board. That dirty old sage, Seneca (Charles Hawtrey) is also going along for the ride! The burly Captain of the Ship, Agrippa (Francis de Wolff), cousin of Caesar, has been persuaded to assassinate the Emperor, by his so-called friend Mark Anthony. The cowardly Hengist Pod is Caesar's only line of defence although, unbeknown to anyone, Horsa and his pals are rowing the galley under the evil regime of Galley Master (Peter Gilmore).

SCENE 80: EXTERIOR. DECK OF GALLEY. DAY.

Calpurnia: Well, anyway, I'm glad Daddy's going with you. He'll keep an eye on things.

Caesar looks at Seneca, who is standing next to Gloria and ogling her shamelessly.

Caesar: He's doing that already, the old...! Seneca! Say your farewell!

Seneca: Oh, right (Embracing Gloria) Bye bye...

Caesar: Not to her! She's going with us!

Seneca: I know, but it's more fun than saying goodbye to my daughter.

Caesar: Oh, come on! Let's get under way.

Seneca embraces Calpurnia.

A hale and hearty Caesar as played by Kenneth Williams in Carry On Cleo *(1964).*

Seneca: Goodbye, daughter.

Calpurnia: Goodbye, Daddy.

Calpurnia turns to Caesar.

Calpurnia: Goodbye, Julius.

Caesar: Goodbye, dear. Good...

They embrace. Calpurnia turns again and hurries away down the gangway.

Caesar: Good...riddance.

Caesar addresses Agrippa.

Caesar: How long will the voyage take, Agrippa?

Agrippa: A week or two, sir. Depending on how much wind we get.

Caesar: (At Seneca) You'll get plenty of that with him around!

Seneca suddenly stiffens, claps one hand over his eyes and stretches the other out, and makes an exclamation.

Caesar: What did I tell you? He's off already!

Agrippa: What is it, sir?

Caesar (Kenneth Williams) bids a not-so-fond farewell to Calpurnia (Joan Sims) as he departs with Seneca (Charles Hawtrey) and Gloria (Julie Stevens) in a sequence which was partially edited from Carry On Cleo *(1964).*

Caesar: Just a touch of the visions.

Seneca: It's indistinct...no, I see something now. A large area of darkness...there's lots of lines across it like rivers... there's a smell of fish...

Then he takes his hand from his eyes, sniffs at it, then smiles around.

Seneca: Oh no, sorry, it's me. I had sardines for breakfast.

Caesar: Oh dear, oh dear. Agrippa, show this girl to her quarters.

Seneca: Oh, I will!

Caesar: No, you won't! And take your fish fingers off her! She's a gift!

Seneca: I know. I said that the moment I saw her!

Agrippa: This way girl.

He takes her to door of main cabin.

Caesar: Well, gentlemen, let's get started. Where's Hengist?

Hengist: (Off) Here, sir!

He comes dashing through the door of main cabin, trips on sill again, and sprawls flat on the deck. He grins stupidly up at Caesar and his visor clangs down again.

EXTERIOR. GALLEY AT SEA. DAY.

It is well out to sea, the sails are fully set, and the oars are going in a regular movement.

Narrator: And so they sailed off, little knowing that deep in the bowels of the galley, chained to his oars, was the man who was destined once again to play a major part in their destinies.

INTERIOR. BOWELS OF GALLEY. DAY.

The Six Slaves are in two lines, three aside, at the oars. There is a 'walk' down the middle and the Galley Master strides up and down this, making with the whip and calling the strokes. As he passes Horsa and goes out of shot, Horsa takes one hand from the oar and starts fiddling with the bolt holding his chain to the seat, trying to work it loose.

As the Galley Master starts back he quickly puts his hand back on the oar again. The Galley Master gives him a slash with the whip in passing.

Galley Master: Come on, put your back into, scum!

HORSA watches him out of shot, then hisses...

Horsa: You...oarsmaster!

And goes back to working on the bolt.

INTERIOR. MAIN CABIN. DAY.

There is a heavy side to side rolling motion. Caesar, Seneca, Hengist and Mark are seated at the table having a meal, which is being served by Gloria. Caesar looks miserable and is obviously a poor sailor. Gloria goes to him with a bowl of what looks like stew.

Gloria: Will you have some, My Lord?

Caesar: Oh, I don't know, dear. What is it?

Gloria: Delicious, My Lord. Peacocks' tongues and alligator brains in aspic.

Caesar: (Making a face) No, thank you.

Gloria: (To Seneca) For you, My Lord?

Seneca: Well, I wouldn't mind a nibble, I must say. *He leers at her as she serves him. Suddenly she straightens up with a little squeal.*

Caesar: That will be quite enough of that.

Seneca: I only wanted to see what was for afters.

Mark: (Wickedly) Here, did I ever tell you about the feast Cleopatra threw for me on her barge?

Caesar: Please, don't mention throwing.

Gloria: You are not well, My Lord.

Caesar: Just a little sic transit, Gloria.

Seneca: Oh, that's rather good. Sic transit, Gloria, you must remember that.

Mark: That was a real do! First there was locust soup, which was like bits of grasshoppers floating in pond water...

Caesar: Ooooh...

Mark: Then we had the *pièce de résistance* – stuffed camels' humps...

Seneca: Sounds delicious!

Mark: It was. Then there was bags of sweet wine and then there were some of these belly dancers.

Seneca: Oh, I've never tried those. What are they like?

Mark: Not to eat! To entertain! One of 'em did a dance with seven veils. They called her Salami.

Seneca: I thought salami was one of those long thin things covered in skin.

Mark: She was.

Francis De Wolff as Agrippa (2nd right) listens to Seneca's 'fishy' tale in Carry On Cleo *(1964).*

Carry On Emmannuelle 1978

Scriptwriter: Lance Peters
Producer: Peter Rogers
Director: Gerald Thomas
Production started: 10 April 1978

The seductive Emmannuelle Prevert (Suzanne Danielle) comes to England to join her impotent husband, French Ambassador Emile Prevert (Kenneth Williams) and sexually works her way through most of the male population. Even the respected downstairs staff including Lyons (Jack Douglas), Leyland (Kenneth Connor) and aged boot boy Richmond (Peter Butterworth) get in on the act. A snubbed lover, Theodore (Larry Dann) finally lifts the lid on Emmannuelle's affair and she returns to the loving arms of her husband and their extensive, newly-born, family.

The plot so far: Sexually permissive Emmannuelle Prevert (Suzanne Danielle) is travelling to England on Concorde. She has already made a less than subtle advance towards the steward and now has designs on a fellow passenger, a nervous, bespectacled Englishman by the name of Theodore Valentine (Larry Dann). Although remnants of this scene made the final print of *Carry On Emmannuelle*, almost all of the dialogue as scripted was abandoned.

SCENE 6: INTERIOR. W.C. CLOSET ON CONCORDE. NIGHT.

Theodore closes the W.C. door behind him and finds himself nose to nose with Emmannuelle. There's scarcely room for one, let alone two.

Theodore: (Nervously) Ah... excuse me, I didn't know this was...taken...(tries to open the door again)...I'd better...go.

Emmannuelle takes his hand away from the door.

Theodore: I mean...I wasn't...sure. I mean...how do you...do?

Emmannuelle puts her fingers to her lips and shushes him. Then she starts to help him out of his suit coat, which takes some effort, as his long arms flail about, knocking into walls, cabinet and plastic cups. When his coat is off, he holds it up by the loop, trying to turn around, not sure where to hang it. But Emmannuelle takes it from him, leans forward so that her whole, soft, voluptuous frame is pressing against him and then hangs it on the door peg behind him.

He grins helplessly, impressed with her cleverness. He seems to be using his awkwardness to delay the inevitable.

Her hands go up to his necktie. She tries to unknot it. But can't. So he helps and tugs at it, frantically. When it suddenly unknots, the back of his hand collides with her cheek. He is horror-struck and tries to rub the smack off...

Emmannuelle: (With a charming French accent) Is okay. I like a little stuff that is roughs.

Theodore: Oh. (With a giggle) Oh.

She unbuttons his shirt and her fingers seem to tickle him a bit.

Theodore: (More giggles) I've always been (with a mad laugh) ticklish.

She admonishes him with a motherly gesture. She pulls his shirt out of his trousers and then peels it off him entirely.

Theodore: Oh. (Another giggle) Oh. (takes the shirt)

He has a rather thick singlet on underneath. Emmannuelle looks at it and shakes her head with disapproval. It has a large hole in it.

Theodore: (With a nervous laugh) My mum calls it air-conditioning.

Emmannuelle tut-tutting, tries to remove his singlet but it's very tight. So she puts both her hands inside the large hole and tugs, ripping the singlet wide open in front. It falls off his shoulders and on to the floor.

Theodore: (A bit peeved) My mum won't...like that.

She shushes him again. Now her hands go to his trousers. She quickly unbuttons his belt. He looks panic-stricken.

Theodore: Oh no!

She unzips his trousers.

The sequence during which Emmannuelle (Suzanne Danielle) flirts openly with the Indian Emigration Officer

Suzanne Danielle (Emmannuelle) seduces Larry Dann (Theodore) aboard Concorde in Carry On Emmannuelle *(1978).*

(Dino Shaffek) remains almost entirely intact, although the following scenes were removed. In the final print, Emmannuelle's line to the Emigration Officer ("He is Ambassador") cuts to our first sighting of her husband Emile Prevert (Kenneth Williams). In the original script these edited scenes and Emmannuelle's dialogue with butler Lyons (Jack Douglas) precede the introduction of Emile.

SCENE 9: INTERIOR. CUSTOMS BAGGAGE AREA. AIRPORT. DAY.

Emmannuelle approaches the customs bench with her suitcase. A young Custos Officer to her as she puts the luggage down on the bench.

Customs Officer: Have you anything to declare?

Emmannuelle: No. (Opens her coat) Would you like to search me?

Customs Officer: I don't think that will be necessary.

Emmannuelle: I may have something hidden in my bra.

Customs Officer: (Embarrassed) You're not wearing one.

Emmannuelle: (Feigning surprise) So I am not.

Theodore wheeling his luggage by on a trolley, unhampered by a customs inspection, stops behind Emmannuelle. He clears his throat to attract her attention.

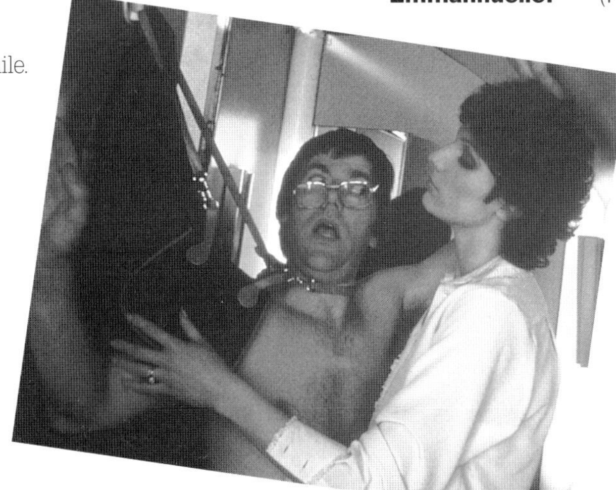

(Above) Happy Families! The cast gathers for the last scene. (Below) Director Gerald Thomas embraces his 'Emmannuelle'.

Emmannuelle turns, gives Theodore just a cursory glance, then turns back to the Customs Officer. Theodore looks hurt, hesitates, then wheels his trolley towards the exit.

EXTERIOR. TERMINAL BUILDING. AIRPORT. DAY.

A Middle Aged Man is hailing a taxi. The taxi pulls up and the Man opens the door. Emmannuelle enters frame.

Emmannuelle: (Stepping in the taxi) Thank you.

Man: That's my taxi.

Emmannuelle: So kind of you to share it with me.

Man: How far are you going?

Emmannuelle: As far as you wish.

She pulls the man into the taxi.

EXTERIOR. LONDON STREET OF STATELY MANSIONS. DAY.

Emmannuelle's taxi lumbers down this tree-lined street of imposing two- and three-storey residences fronted by iron railings and grand gateposts. It turns left into a short driveway fronted by a tall iron fence and hedge. The windows are all steamed up. Emmannuelle climbs out with her suitcase and smiles into the interior of the taxi.

Emmannuelle: Thanks for the ride.

Carry On Cowboy 1965

Scriptwriter: Talbot Rothwell
Producer: Peter Rogers
Director: Gerald Thomas
Production started: 12 July 1965

The infamous western settlement of Stodge City is over-run with baddies ever since the swaggering Rumpo Kid (Sidney James) murdered the befuddled old Sheriff Earp (Jon Pertwee). His sharp-shooting daughter, Annie Oakley (Angela Douglas) has vowed vengeance, while bumbling British sanitation engineer, Marshal P. Knutt (Jim Dale) has been mistakenly taken for the new Sheriff by the corrupted Judge Burke (Kenneth Williams). With a little help from his friends, Knutt clears up the city and unwittingly allows the Rumpo Kid to escape into the sunset with seductive saloon signer Belle (Joan Sims).

The plot so far: The Rumpo Kid (Sidney James) has turned Stodge City into a haven for gun-slingers and chorus girls. In order to cover his crooked racket of cattle rustling, the Kid determines to aid Marshal P. Knutt (Jim Dale) and his attempts to prevent another night raid of the ranch of Colonel Sam Houston (Sydney Bromley). The Kid assigns a couple of his gang, Short (Simon Cain) and Curly (Peter Gilmore) to help with the subterfuge and frame Knutt as the cattle rustler.

SCENE 86: EXTERIOR. BEAR PASS. NIGHT.

Resume Knutt, Curly & Short.

Knutt: Well...where are all the rustlers?

Curly: (Drily) Reckon just the sight of you must've scared 'em off, Marshal.

Knutt: (Pleased) Oh. Yes, I suppose so. Well, what do we do now?

Curly: Reckon the best thing we can do, Marshal, is to leave you here to look after them steers while we ride for some help.

Knutt: Just what I was going to suggest.

Curly gives Short a knowing wink and a nod and they turn their horses round and gallop off. Left alone, Knutt turns towards the cattle, which are mooing quite a bit.

Sidney James as the Rumpo Kid in Carry On Cowboy *(1965).*

Knutt: There, there, it's all right. Nobody's going to rustle you tonight. Shh, quiet now, quiet.

He gets, or rather slithers, awkwardly off his horse and goes towards the cattle to make friends, stops on a step and makes a face and looks down disgustedly at his boot.

Knutt: Urr. Dirty moocows!

EXTERIOR. THE OPEN RANGE. NIGHT.

We see Sam and Rumpo leading a posse of Cowhands at a gallop towards us, all heavily armed.

As they near camera, Rumpo holds up his hand and they slither to a stop.

Rumpo: (Pointing) There they are, Colonel!

Sam: Yeh! All right, men, let's get 'em!

And as they spur on...

EXTERIOR. BEAR PASS. NIGHT.

Knutt is sitting on a boulder, carefully wiping off his boot with a wedge of grass. We hear the thunder of hooves and plenty of shooting and he ducks flat as bullets whistle over his head. The posse gallops into view and

Little Heap (Bernard Bresslaw) tries to spring his father Big Heap (Charles Hawtrey) from jail in this excised scene from Carry On Cowboy *(1965).*

forms a circle around him. MEN with hard, vengeful faces.

Knutt looks up at them.

Knutt: (Tentatively) Oh, Colonel Houston?

Sam: That's me.

Knutt: (Brightly) I've got your cattle.

Sam: You can say that again! Where's the rest of your gang?

Knutt: Gang? What gang?

Sam: Man doesn't go around rustling cattle on his own.

Knutt: Oh! (Gets up and laughs) You're got it wrong, Colonel. I didn't rustle them. I just happened to find them here.

He looks round at the grim faces and his laugh starts to falter.

Knutt: I'm the new Marshal of Stodge City.

Sam: Yeah? Where's your badge?

Knutt: Badge? Oh yes, I took it off. I didn't want to be a good target, you see.

He fishes it out of his pocket and Sam snatches it from him.

Sam: That's Sheriff Earp's star. Still got his name on the back.

Knutt: Yes, it was, but I hadn't got one, you see, so...

He falters, realising that this sounds pretty thin. Then he suddenly spots Rumpo.

Knutt: Oh, it's Mister Rumpo! You can tell them, can't you? That I'm the new Marshal...

Rumpo: (Sadly) Well, you certainly fooled all of us. I really thought you were a Marshal. I'm very disappointed in you.

Knutt: But I am! Judge Burke will tell you. If we go and see Judge Burke he'll tell you!

Sam: You ain't getting' as far as any judge mister! We got a quicker way of dealing with cattle thieves around here!

And as some of the Posse close in on him... Mix to...

EXTERIOR. THE HOUSTON RANCH. NIGHT.

Knutt, absolutely petrified, sitting on his horse, hands tied behind his back and a dirty big noose around his neck. A circle of silent grim-faced men around. Knutt is

immediately below a big branch of the hanging tree which is about fifteen feet from the ground.
Rumpo has the coil of rope belonging to the noose in his hands.

Rumpo: Do you mind if I do this, Colonel? As an honest law-abiding citizen of Stodge and old friend of Sheriff Earp, I consider it my duty.

Sam: Your privilege, sir.

The plot so far: Knutt (Jim Dale) has asserted his authority in town, Annie Oakley (Angela Douglas) has shot the saloon barman Charlie (Percy Herbert) in the mistaken belief that it was the Rumpo Kid (Sidney James) and the continually intoxicated Indian brave, Big Heap (Charles Hawtrey) is locked up in the sheriff's cell. Desperate to release the Indian, who knows far too much of his crooked plans, the Rumpo Kid is figuring out ways to break into the cell. Big Heap's slow-witted, hulking son, Little Heap (Bernard Bresslaw) is aiding and abetting. At least the coast is clear – Knutt's night's sleep is being disturbed by a never-ending stream of females, Annie, Belle (Joan Sims) and Dolores (Edina Ronay), all intent on using their charms for their own ends.

SCENE 130: EXTERIOR. SHERIFF'S OFFICE. NIGHT.

Rumpo is holding a coiled lasso. He gives one end of it to Little Heap.

Rumpo: Right, let's go. Tie that to the cell door.

Little Heap: Why we no use-um dynamite?

Rumpo: Because, like you, it makes too muchum noise! Now go on!

Little Heap goes in with end of rope.

INTERIOR. SHERIFF'S OFFICE. NIGHT.

Little Heap tiptoes elaborately across to the lock-up and ties end of rope to one of the door bars. This will give us time to appreciate the fact that Knutt has left the key in the lock.

EXTERIOR. SHERIFF'S OFFICE. NIGHT.

Rumpo has his horse backed up to the door and is tying the other end of the rope to the rear of his saddle. Then he gets on the horse.
Little Heap comes out.

Little Heap: Okayum!

Rumpo gives a giddyap yell, digs his spurs in.

EXTERIOR. MAIN STREET. NIGHT.

The horse starts across the street at a gallop. It gets about halfway before the rope gets taut, and then saddle and rider are neatly whisked off and land, still in riding position, in the dust, while the horse goes on.
Rumpo is sitting on the saddle.

Rumpo: Funny. It's worked every time I saw someone else do it!

Little Heap comes into shot.

Little Heap: (Helpfully) Doorum not open.

Rumpo: I know doorum not open. (Getting up) All right, get the dynamite!

Rumpo (Sidney James) locks up Marshal P. Knutt (Jim Dale).

Carry On Up the Jungle 1970

Scriptwriter: Talbot Rothwell
Producer: Peter Rogers
Director: Gerald Thomas
Production started: 13 October 1969

A collection of British eccentrics travel through the perilous jungles of Africa with Lady Evelyn Bagley (Joan Sims) desperate to track down her long-lost husband, Walter Bagley (Charles Hawtrey) and son. Great white hunter Bill Boosey (Sidney James) is at hand with his bumbling tracker, Upsidasi (Bernard Bresslaw), while Professor Inigo Tinkle (Frankie Howerd) and Claude Chumley (Kenneth Connor) are more concerned with tracing the rare Oozulum Bird. Lady Evelyn's son has grown up to be the clumsy Jungle Boy (Terry Scott) and takes a fancy to mild-mannered secretary June (Jacki Piper).

In the original Talbot Rothwell script (in which he describes himself as Great White Hunter), the lecture of Professor Inigo Tinkle (Frankie Howerd) is much longer than the final version retained in the film. Clearly there was a sense of urgency in getting the flash-back, jungle-based action started almost immediately. Here is the entire opening sequence reproduced for the very first time.

Terry Scott as Jungle Boy.

SCENE 1: EXTERIOR. A LECTURE HALL. DAY.

A Victorian building, somewhere in London. A couple of people wearing clothes of the period stroll up and look at a poster outside...

It reads:

ROYAL BIRDWATCHING SOCIETY
A LANTERN-SLIDE LECTURE BY
PROF. INIGO TINKLE
1st August 1873 at 3pm

INTERIOR. THE LECTURE HALL. DAY.

Tinkle, wearing morning suit of the period, standing on the platform beside a lantern slide screen, holding some notes and a pointer.

Tinkle: Friends, colleagues...Royal Bird Watchers.

GENERAL SHOT of the audience, as from his point of view as he goes on...

Tinkle: It is a great honour for me today to be invited to tell you the incredible story of my last expedition.

Resume Tinkle, as he taps with the end of the pointer on the platform.

Tinkle: If I may have the first slide please?

And, turning towards screen.

Tinkle: This, ladies and gentlemen, is darkest Africa!

And immediately all the house lights go out, leaving them in pitch blackness. We hear Tinkle shout...

Tinkle: Not that dark!!

And a sepia-coloured slide showing a rough map of the central part of Africa appears on the screen. There is

Frankie Howerd (Tinkle) in the deleted lecture scene from Carry On Up the Jungle *(1970).*

sufficient light from it to light Tinkle.

Tinkle glares out at the back of the hall.

Tinkle: Thank you!

Then, using the pointer...

Tinkle: Here is the starting point of our expedition – and here our ultimate goal – the Interior!

He taps with the pointer on the floor again. The slide changes to one of an African native holding a paint pot and paintbrush.

Tinkle: Oh, and that is an interior decorator. Yes, that slide shouldn't have been there. The next one please!

Taps again and the slide changes to one of the safari party, posed rather like a wedding group, smiling at the camera. Seated on two chairs, centrally, are Lady Evelyn Bagley and Jane. Evelyn is a middle-aged, but still very sex-minded widow, wearing a woman's safari kit of the period. Jane, her maid, although being in fact, an extremely attractive and curvaceous girl, manages to conceal it with frumpish shapeless clothing, and wire-framed glasses. In other words, at this stage she looks uninteresting and undesirable.

Standing behind them in a line are Claude Chumley, a stocky little character, wearing khakis and holding a tripod box camera, Tinkle himself, wearing immaculate safari kit, BIll Booosey, a rugged weather-beaten character, wearing the traditional Great White Hunter clobber and toting a couple of enormous guns. And finally his Tracker, Upsidasi, a great hulking coloured brute.

Tinkle: Ah yes, and here we have all the members of our ill-fated safari.

Camera tracks in to CLOSE SHOT of slide as the pointer indicates each character.

Tinkle: (Over) Lady Evelyn Bagley – who joined

the safari for reasons which I shall disclose later. And her personal maid, Miss Jane. This is Mr Claude Chumley, my assistant and photographer. And this is the leader of the safari, the Great White Hunter William Boosey. Known affectionately throughout Africa as Rattlesnake Bill, because he was always on the job. And finally, his faithful Tracker Upsidasi a member of the fearless Banga Tribe, wearing the traditional sausage skin.

Camera pulls back to bring Tinkle into shot as he taps with his pointer again and the slide changes to one of Jungle Boy standing on the open platform of his tree-top house. Looking arrogantly out over his jungle domain, he wears a leopard skin loincloth, with a hefty hunting-knife at his waist, and he has a magnificent head of shoulder-length hair.

Tinkle: Ah yes, and this is the man who was later to have such a dramatic effect on our expedition – Jungle Boy! A man with a remarkable history. Lost as a mere babe in the jungle, he was found by a friendly boa constrictor...suckled by a short-sighted hippopotamus...and grew to maturity never having seen another human being. He is photographed here in his tree-top home high in the branches of a giant rhubarb tree. You can't see it now, but there's another slide later showing all of his rhubarb.

He taps the stick again and the slide changes to one of the safari on the trail. Upsidasi leading, then Boosey, Tinkle, Evelyn, Chumley, and finally Jane.

Tinkle: And here we are, two weeks out on safari, already deep into the interior and...

His voice goes into echo-chamber effect...

Tinkle: Already treading ground no white man had ever trod before...

The plot so far: With our intrepid adventurers deep in the heart of the jungle, Bill Boosey (Sidney James) and Upsidasi (Bernard Bresslaw) have set up camp in a clearing. Much sexual banter and mistaken entrances within tents is the result as Boosey tries to gulp down a shy mouthful of whiskey and unsuccessfully chat up the female members of the group. Claude Chumley (Kenneth Connor) is wandering around with his binoculars while a roving gorilla (Reuben Martin) keeps his eye on things. Lady Evelyn Bagley (Joan Sims), clearly attracted to the sophisticated charm of Professor Tinkle (Frankie Howerd) heads for the safety of his tent while the bird-watcher is enjoying a magazine featuring birds of a far more interesting variety.

SCENE 44: INTERIOR. TINKLE'S TENT. DAY.

Tinkle sees Chumley out of the way, then brings out a copy of La Vie Parisienne with a pretty sexy cover and settles down.

EXTERIOR. THE JUNGLE CLEARING. DAY.

EVELYN's tent, as she comes out and looks around at the deserted clearing, sees her chance and, putting on a distressed face, goes to Tinkle's tent.

Evelyn:: Professor! Professor!

INTERIOR. TINKLE'S TENT. DAY.

As she comes in, TINKLE hastily stuffs the magazine away and gets to his feet.

Tinkle: Lady Bagley, what ails you? You look full of ail!

Evelyn: It's those awful drums, Professor. I'm so frightened!

Tinkle: But they're stopped!

Evelyn: What? So they have! How very clever of you to notice, Professor.

Tinkle: Oh, one trains oneself, you know. I remember once writing a paper on extra-sensory aural perception or lug'holes akimbo.

Evelyn: I don't know what it was, but I was lying in my tent and I suddenly had this acute feeling of foreboding.

Tinkle: Oh I know, I get it here often. It's something to do with the water, I think.

She seizes the opportunity to put her arms around him and snuggle close.

Evelyn: Oh, I'm such a weak woman.

TINKLE answers with difficulty, grimacing under her bear-rug.

Tinkle: I wouldn't say that! My ribs...!

Evelyn: (Relaxing somewhat) Oh, I'm sorry. Is that better?

Tinkle: Thank you. Now, try and compose yourself, dear. You're all of a tizz-wazz. I can feel your wazz tizzing from here!

Evelyn: I can't help it. It's being close to you like this. Don't you feel it too? Something between us?

Frankie Howerd (Tinkle) and Joan Sims (Evelyn) getting 'in-tents' in this missing Jungle scene.

Tinkle: What? Well, yes, now you come to mention it, there is...oh, it's my water-bottle!

And, it is, slung around his waist, hanging down the front. As he shifts it out of the way...

Evelyn: No no, professor, not that. It's something

else. Something...primitive! Something that makes my heart pound...my blood race!

Tinkle: Oh well, you should have said! Oh yes well, I know exactly what you need, my dear.

Evelyn: I was hoping you would say that.

Tinkle: Oh yes. Salt tablets!

And as, to her intense disgust, he turns to ferret in his medicine case...

Tinkle: Nothing like 'em, you know. Get rid of excess liquid, open the pores. I live on them!

He finds bottle of tablets and offers them to her.

Evelyn: (close to tears) No thank you!

And flounces out. Tinkle looks after her in surprise.

Tinkle: Funny woman! Doesn't know what she wants!

Shakes his head and lies down again.

Picks up magazine then, on a sudden thought, puts it down again.

Tinkle: Unless she wanted...? Oh no, she couldn't have. She's much too much of a lady. About three stones too much.

Back to magazine, then thinks again.

Tinkle: But on the other hand...? Oh no, not in broad daylight, surely? It has been known! Oh dear!

And reaches for the bottle of salt tablets and starts shovelling them into his mouth.

EXTERIOR. AREA OF JUNGLE. DAY.

To see the three beaters "beating" at the bush with Upsidasi and Boosey following. The three beaters suddenly come to a halt with warning cries, pointing ahead.

Upsidasi and Boosey come to a halt and Boosey fumbles his rifle up ready.

A tense moment as the bushes ahead are agitated, then they part and a very tired pathetic-looking man in tropical kit staggers into view. For a moment he and Boosey look at each other, then a smile lights the exhausted man's face and he asks appealingly, weakly...

Man: Doctor Livingstone, I presume.

Boosey: No. Bill Boosey.

The man slumps again.

Man: Oh. Sorry to have troubled you.

He starts to move on, then stops and turns back. Almost in tears...

Oh, if you should happen to run into Mr Livingstone, tell him Stanley would like to meet him, would you?

And totters off.

Boosey looks after him, shakes his head.

Boosey: Oh dear oh dear, even in darkest Africa!

The plot so far: Captured by the notorious Nosha tribe, Bill Boosey (Sidney James), Lady Evelyn (Joan Sims), Chumley (Kenneth Connor) and Tinkle (Frankie Howerd) find themselves on the menu. But luckily the stunning Leda (Valerie Leon) and members of her delectable Lubi Dubi tribe are on the verge of rescuing our British heroes. Note that as with the character of June being called Jane in the original script, Professor Inigo Tinkle is quite clearly called Indigo in the original script.

Sidney James as great white hunter Bill Boosey.

Jungle cast shot (left to right): Jacki Piper, Terry Scott, Bernard Bresslaw, Kenneth Connor, Sidney James, Frankie Howerd, Joan Sims and Charles Hawtrey.

SCENE 108: EXTERIOR. NOSHA VILLAGE. DAY.

The stew pot is now steaming nicely and the Noshas are all waiting expectantly. The Chief now appears and takes his place on the throne.

Boosey: Well, this looks like it.

Tinkle: Lady Bagley...Evelyn. Now that we are near to the end, I would like to disclose my first true feeling towards you.

Evelyn: Yes, Professor? What was it?

Tinkle: Revulsion!

Evelyn: (Shock) Oh!

Tinkle: You see, I was brought up to despise women. My father only spoke to my mother four times during their entire married life – and I and the other three children were undoubtedly affected by this.

Evelyn: Yes, I do understand, Indigo.

Tinkle: Ah, but you don't! The fact is, the revulsion turned into passion, then outright ardour. As the poet said...the ardour they fall...

Evelyn: Why, Indigo. Are you proposing to me?

Tinkle: Yes, I suppose I am. Oh, I know I'm not much. Just an everyday sort of man...

Evelyn: What more could a woman want?!

The Chief calls out an order. The Witch Doctor raises his carving knife and walks across to the four prisoners and comes to a stop, obviously wondering which to have first.

Boosey: Here we go. One for the pot!

The plot so far: Having been rescued from certain death, Lady Evelyn (Joan Sims) discovers that her long-lost husband Walter (Charles Hawtrey) is now called Tonka, King of All Lovers and rules over the all-woman Lubi Dubi tribe. Leda (Valerie Leon) tries to retain the status quo but a new Queen in the scenario causes concern and the King's chosen conquest, Nerda (Edwina Carroll) is rejected.

SCENE 123: EXTERIOR. VILLAGE SQUARE, AFRODISIA. DAY.

It has been made ready for the Mating Ceremony. Three little closed booths have been set up in front of the steps, with a semi-circle of wooden images like totem poles, representing the goddesses of Love, Fertility etc.

Lubi Women of various shapes, ages and sizes, sit cross-legged in a semi-circle behind these. Leda stands wearing a ceremonial gown. Walter, also wearing a ceremonial head dress, is seated on his throne and, beside him, on another smaller throne, is Evelyn. She is looking pretty grim. A very pretty young Lubi runs up, throws herself impulsively down in front of Walter and kisses his hands. Evelyn glares at Walter, and he looks a bit embarrassed.

Nerda: Oh master! King of Lovers! I am the chosen one for tonight and I hope I shall prove worthy of you!

Walter: (Very conscious of Evelyn) I'm sure you will, dear. You look very worthy to me. Now run along, there's a good girl.

He shushes her away and gives Evelyn an embarrassed little laugh.

Walter: Quaint little thing.

Evelyn: What was all that about?

Walter: I don't know, my dear. I think she must have mistaken me for someone else.

Leda: (Helpfully) No, master. That was Nerda, the one you selected to mate with tonight.

Evelyn: Well, you can think again. From now on, I've decided there's going to be some changes around here!

(Top left) Kenneth Connor as Claude Chumley holding his equipment. (Bottom) Director Gerald Thomas and Frankie Howerd discuss the Jungle script.

Walter: Oh, I do change them regularly.

Evelyn: I know all about that! But from now on, father of countless, you're going to be husband of one!

Walter: Oh. Well, I just thought I ought to take part in one more ceremony, dear, just to show the other chaps what to do.

Evelyn: From my experience, they know!

Walter: Ah yes, but it's a very complicated and difficult ritual...

Evelyn: Not when I knew you, it wasn't! Now get on with it – and leave yourself out!

Walter: Oh very well, dear. (To Leda) Have the women been selected?

Evelyn: I've done all that!

Walter: Oh. I hope you've chosen well, dear?

Evelyn: (Grimly) Don't worry, they're going to get exactly what they deserve!

Walter gets to his feet. The gong is beaten, and Leda acts as cheer-leader for the assembled Lubis.

All: Mate! Mate! Mate! Mate! Who do we appreci-ate? Ton-ka!!

Walter: Thank you, dear subjects. As you all know, the gods have seen fit to send back to me my first mate – your new queen, Evelyn.

Evelyn preens herself, visibly and gives a steely smile around. There is a low moan from the LUBIs.

Walter: To mark this auspicious occasion, I have decided not to take part in the ceremony myself today...

Evelyn: Or any other day!

Walter: But I hope and trust that you will give our three newly-arrived men the same enthusuastic support and co-operation you have given to me in the past.

All: Ton-ka! Ton-ka! Stick it up your hon-ka!

WALTER nods to one side and sits.

Carry On Screaming! 1966

Scriptwriter: Talbot Rothwell
Producer: Peter Rogers
Director: Gerald Thomas
Production started: 10 January 1966

Bung's Office (left to right): Harry H. Corbett, Peter Butterworth and Jim Dale get spooked in Carry On Screaming! *(1966).*

Mysterious goings on in Hocombe Woods have baffled Detective Sergeant Sidney Bung (Harry H. Corbett) and Detective Constable Slobotham (Peter Butterworth) but when window cleaner Albert Potter (Jim Dale) reports the disappearance of his girlfriend Doris Mann (Angela Douglas) all roads lead to a horrific conclusion. The undead Doctor Watt (Kenneth Williams), his vampish sister Virula (Fenella Fielding) and their hulking butler Sockett (Bernard Bresslaw) are a right load of hammer rejects, turning innocent young girls into shop window dummies.

The plot so far: Bumbling romantic Albert Potter (Jim Dale) has gleefully taken his sweetheart Doris Mann (Angela Douglas) into the woods, only to investigate a noise and return to find her gone. Unbeknown to him, the monstrous Odbodd (Tom Clegg) has kidnapped her. The panic stricken Potter takes his mystery to the dogged law enforcers Bung (Harry H. Corbett) and Slobotham (Peter Butterworth) who creak into action. The interrogation sequence, the vast majority of which appears in the film, was in fact, much longer in the original script.

SCENE 19: INTERIOR. BUNG'S OFFICE. NIGHT.

Bung: So you took her into Hocombe Woods. How far did you go?
Albert: Oh, not far. I've only known her for a year.
Bung: (To Slobotham) Don't put that down!
Slobotham hastily scratches it out.
Bung: What I meant was, how far did you get into the woods?
Albert: Not very far. Just to this little clearing I know.
Bung: Aha! Then what did you do?
Albert: Well, I took my coat off and we sat down on it and...
Bung: (The sharp detective) One moment! Why did you take your coat off, Mr Potter?
Albert: Oh! Well, there's a lot of stinging nettles there, see, and they can ruin your evening.
Bung: All right, all right. I know all about that.
Albert: Oh, you've sat on some too, eh?
Bung: Just tell me what happened.
Albert: Oh! Well, we were having a bit of a cuddle when Doris thought she heard someone in the bushes, so I went to have a look round like and when I got back there she was – gone!
Bung: I see. And what time was that, do you know?
Albert: Ten o'clock. I know that because I'd just looked at my watch.
Bung: And it said ten.
Albert: Oh, no. It said twenty to three. It always does. It's bust, you see.
Bung: Then how do you know it was ten o'clock?
Albert: Because I always look at my watch at ten. It's a habit I've got into. Funny, isn't it?

Bung: If you ask me, Mr Potter, you've got a lot of funny habits. Do you happen to remember what Doris was wearing?

Albert: Oh yes, a sort of frilly white blouse thing, with a dark blue jacket and a long blue skirt.

Bung: (To Slobotham) Did you get that down?

Albert, having closed his eyes in an effort to remember the clothes, now opens them, startled.

Albert: Course not! I told you, we...

Bung: I was talking to my assistant.

Slobotham: Don't worry, sir, I've got it all down.

Bung: Good. And that's all you can tell us, Mr Potter?

Albert: Yes. That is...well, there is something. I found this where she'd been sitting.

And he brings out a handkerchief, puts it on the desk, carefully unwraps it to show the Thing's finger. Slobotham gets up and crosses to have a closer look.

Bung: Hallo, hallo, hallo. What have we here then?

Slobotham: I'd say it was a finger, sir.

Bung: I know It's a finger. Is it one of hers, Mr Potter?

Albert: Course not. What sort of girls do you think I go out with?

Bung: (Sternly) I'm not paid to think, Mr Potter.

He gets up, doing some deep thinking and paces up and down. Slobotham slides into his chair, the better to examine the finger.

Bung: Not one of her, eh?

He paces some more, then comes to a staggering conclusion.

Bung: Then it must be someone else's.

Slobotham: (Enthusiastically) Ah! Now you're getting somewhere, sir.

Albert: You mean some thing else's! That didn't come off anything human, that didn't.

Slobotham: He may be right, sir. There's no blood coming from it. There should be some blood!

Bung: It doesn't mean to say it isn't human just because it hasn't got a bleeding finger.

He turns back towards his desk and sees SLOBOTHAM examining the finger with a dirty great magnifying glass.

Bung: What're you doing?

Slobotham: Looking for prints, sir.

Bung: Slobotham, only you could look for a fingerprint on a finger!

Slobotham: Oh! Yes, of course, sir.

Bung: And get out of my chair.

Slobotham leaps out of the chair.

Bung: Right. Now take that along to the Lab. I want a full report on it by morning.

Slobotham: Yes, sir.

He picks up the finger in the handkerchief.

Bung: And on your way, stop at the desk and see if anyone has reported the loss of a finger this evening.

Slobotham: Of course, sir. Why didn't I think of that?

And he goes out. Albert jumps to his feet impatiently.

Albert: Look, shouldn't we be out there looking for Doris instead of messing about here?

Bung: (Smugly) All in good time, Mr. Potter. This isn't the first case I've handled of this sort, you know. Look at these!

He indicates a pile of files on his desk.

Bung: All young women who have disappeared in this area.

He flips the files over one by one, reading off the names quickly.

Bung: Olive Ketch. Maud Bracewell. Evelyn March. Grace Shaw!

The door opens and Slobotham rushes in, excitedly.

Slobotham: We're on to something, sir! Two people reported the loss of a finger this evening!

Bung: Aha! Who were they?

Slobotham: (Consulting notebook) A Mr Snere of forty-two, Roper Street. A dog trainer, sir.

Bung: Oh! And...?

Slobotham: A Mr Frank Baker of Thistle Street. Grocer's assistant.

Bung: Grocer's assistant, eh?

Slobotham: Yes, sir. On the bacon counter.

Bung: Oh! Well, it was worth a try.

DISSOLVE TO:

EXTERIOR. COUNTRY LANE. NIGHT.

At the point where Albert picked up his tandem earlier.

Carry On Screaming! *ghouls Kenneth Williams and Fenella Fielding turn on the gruesome camp for publicity.*

It is still a pretty murky night.
We hear the noisy approach of an automobile and suddenly a 1900 vintage car comes out of the swirling mist and comes to a shuddering, shaking stop. Albert and Slobotham are passengers, Bung, at the wheel, obviously switches off, climbs out, then notices that the motor is still noisily and laboriously turning over. As of long practice, he reaches out for the starting handle, gives the side of the car a bash with it and the motor subsides.

Bung: Now, Mr Potter, I'd like you to show me where you and the young lady were.

Albert: It's through here.

And he starts towards a gap in the bordering hedge. Bung turns back on Slobotham, who is about to tag alone.

Bung: No, you stay here, Slobotham.

Slobotham: By myself, sir?

Bung: Why not? You're not frightened, are you?

Slobotham: (The liar) Oh, no. No, of course not, sir. I just thought I might be more use to you there. I feel there's something horrible about this business, sir. I have a nose for that sort of thing.

Bung: I know all that, Slobotham. You always smell something horrible. But I'd rather you stayed here.

Slobotham watches miserably as Bung follows Albert through the gap.
The owl hoots and he jumps. Then smiles nervously.

Slobotham: Just an owl. Well, whatever he says, I don't like that.

The plot so far: Having searched in vain for clues, the trio come across the only house in the Hocombe Wood vicinity, the sinister Bide-a-Wee Rest Home. Shown in by the butler Sockett (Bernard Bresslaw) who mysteriously insists that the master of the house, although dead, will see them shortly, Bung (Harry H. Corbett), Slobotham (Peter Butterworth) and Potter (Jim Dale) begin to investigate. Potter is terrified when a mummy case is opened to reveal a mummy.

Dr Watt (Kenneth Williams) is attacked by his mummy (Denis Blake) in Carry On Screaming! *(1966).*

SCENE 34: MIDDLE-CLOSE SHOT OF OPEN MUMMY CASE.

Inside it, swathed in bandages (but with legs wrapped individually for later action) a giant figure with fierce glassy eyes and a black beard.

Bung: It's only a mummy!

Albert: A mummy – with a beard?

Bung: They didn't do it only to women. Men got pickled too.

Slobotham: (The know-it-all again) Not picked actually, sir. Embalmed is the correct term. The body was immersed in spirits of wine, after stopping up all the orifices of the body with wax, then completely wrapped in tarred bandages.

Bung: I wish someone would stop up your orifices!

We hear Doctor's voice.

Watt: Ah, gentlemen, I see you are admiring my pharaoh.

They turn. Watt stands just inside the doorway, smiling. He crosses to them.

Watt: He was the founder of the fourth dynasty, you know. King Rubbatiti.

Bung: Very interesting, sir.

Watt: Yes. I've often thought how interesting it would be to get him living again. I bet he could tell us a few things, eh?

This with nudges to Bung's ribs.

Watt: All those barge orgies on the Nile. No wonder they kept finding things in the bullrushes.

Bung: No doubt, sir. Would you be the master of the house?

Watt: That's right, yes.

Bung: I only ask, sir, because your butler informed us that you were dead.

Watt: Oh, you don't want to take any notice of him. He's related to the Dracula family and you know what a batty lot they were.

Bung: Oh yes, sir. I remember Count Dracula. Had up for fraud.

Watt: Really?

Bung: Yes, sir. He was overdrawn at every blood bank in the country.

Watt: I'm not surprised to hear it. Never did like him. Those teeth! I'm sure they were false.

Bung: Yes, sir. Well, now to come to the purpose of our visit. We're police officers and we're trying to find a young lady's whereabouts.

Watt: Her whereabouts?

Bung: Yes, sir. And we were wondering if you could help?

Watt: No. Beyond advising her to use stronger elastic in future.

Bung: No, sir. The young lady disappeared. In this vicinity.

Watt: Oh, I beg your pardon.

Albert comes forward eagerly.

Albert: Her name was Doris. Doris Mann. She was a friend of mine.

Watt: Mann? Doris Mann? Would she be a rather pretty girl?

Albert: Yes! With long brown hair!

Watt: And beautiful brown eyes?
Albert: (Very excited) Yes! And long slender neck?
Watt: And little dimples in her cheeks?
Albert: Yes, yes!
Watt: Sorry, I don't know her.
Albert: Oh!

The plot so far: With only the dismembered finger of Odbodd as a clue, Bung (Harry H. Corbett) and Slobotham (Peter Butterworth) eagerly await the lab report from eccentric Doctor Fettle (Jon Pertwee). The memorable cameo from Pertwee was clearly severely edited from a much longer, more comical turn in the original shooting script. Indeed, the familiar "wrong homo…" observation when comparing the finger to illustrations in the Origins of Man book is not included in the Rothwell script at all.

SCENE 44: INTERIOR. BUNG'S OFFICE. DAY.

Slobotham is sprawled in Bung's chair behind the desk, feet up on it, catching up on his lost sleep. The door opens and Bung comes in and sees him.

Bung: Get out of my chair!!

Slobotham starts awake, slips off the chair and lands in a heap on the floor, then scrambles to his feet.

Slobotham: Beg your pardon, sir. I must have dropped off.
Bung: Never mind that. Where's the report on the finger?
Slobotham: Doctor Fettle has it, sir.
Bung: Good. Where is he?
Slobotham: In the lab, sir.
Bung: Oh! Well, let me know as soon as he comes out.
Slobotham: The laboratory, sir.
Bung: Well, why didn't you say so? While I'm seeing him I want you to bring in Mr. Potter. You know where he lives?

Slobotham quickly pulls out his notebook and shuffles through it.

Slobotham: Yes, sir! "St. Michael's Home for Fallen Women", 33…Oh no, sorry, sir, that's my aunty. Ah! Here we are…
Bung: Never mind! Just go and get him!
Slobotham: Yes, sir!

He starts for the door as BUNG turns to go out himself and they get caught in the doorway.

Bung: Do you mind?

Slobotham backs quickly out of the way and BUNG goes out.

CORRIDOR. POLICE STATION. DAY.

BUNG goes down to door at end of short corridor, clearly marked "Forensic Dept." He opens it and goes in.

INTERIOR. LABORATORY, POLICE STATION. DAY.

It is a smallish room, full of benches piled with the paraphernalia associated with Forensic medicine.
At one of the benches, cluttered with bits of pieces, is Doctor Fettle, an excitable crazy character with a slightly demented look. He is peering into a microscope.
BUNG crosses to him.

Bung: Morning, Doc.
Fettle: Ah, Bung! This should interest you! Take a look!

Bung looks into microscope.

Bung: What are they?

Dr Fettle (Jon Pertwee) gets his finger out in this missing scene.

Dr Fettle (Jon Pertwee) and Bung (Harry H. Corbett) discuss a misleading clue.

Fettle: Particles of canvas found on that camper who was murdered last week.

Bung: What do they show?

Fettle: They show he was assaulted with intent. (Crazy laugh) Within tent!

Bung: Very amusing, Doc. But right now I have something more serious to worry about. That finger I sent along to you...

Fettle: (Getting serious) Ah yes – exhibit digit! Very interesting that! Very interesting!

Bung: You found out something?

Fettle: Naturally. I subjected it to a number of exhaustive tests and found that it was composed of molecular sus scrofa, or pig meat, encased in a thin membrane of vascular epidermis or skin. Somewhat akin to a common or garden sausage.

Bung: That's extraordinary?

Fettle: There's no doubt about it. You have only to look at it yourself...where is it now?

He rummages amongst the stuff and comes up with something about the same size as the finger, with a label attached.

Fettle: Ah! There you are.

BUNG takes it, looks at it, sniffs at it.

Bung: It is a sausage!

Fettle: What?

He takes it back, examines it, takes a bite out of it.

Fettle: By jove, you're right! It must have been the one I brought in for my supper last night. I could have sworn it was in the roll I...oh!

Bung: Doc! You haven't eaten the finger!

Fettle: I sincerely hope not! I have a very sensitive stomach and...

He finds the finger on the bench.

Fettle: Oh no, here it is. That's a relief.

Bung: Oh, Doc! I've been waiting all night for a report on that!

Fettle: I'm sorry, but how do you think I feel? Up all night analysing a banger!

Bung: Well, how soon can you tell me something?

Fettle: (Examining it) Well, that's hard to say. I...By jove, this is remarkable!

Bung: What is?

Fettle: Unless I'm very much mistaken, this digit came from a man known as Homo Garguantoso.

Bung: Oh, an Italian.

Fettle: No, no, no. A species of man which existed up to some five hundred years ago in Central America.

Bung: Impossible!

Fettle: I'm positive. Now where's that book?

He finds a big book amongst others on a shelf.

Fettle: Ah, here we are. "Origins of Man!" There he is! Homo Garguantoso!

Bung looks at the page he points to.

CLOSE SHOT of the page

It is taken up with a drawing of a Thing looking just like old Odbodd, only here he wears a loin cloth and carries a crude spear.

Bung: (Over) The fingers look the same.

Resume Bung and Fettle

Fettle: Oh that's him all right. Extinct now of course.

Bung: Doc, are you saying that that finger came off something that's been dead for five hundred years?!!

Fettle: Oh yes, dead as a doornail. I don't know if you're ever seen a dead doornail? Frightening!

Bung: But...how could it have stayed whole like that? I mean, what about decomposition?

Fettle: I told you, decomposition is pig meat encased in...oh no, sorry, that was the sausage, wasn't it?

Bung: You must be wrong, Doc. It must have come off something that was living last night at least!

Fettle: Well, of course I could ascertain if it was living cell tissue by subjecting it to an electrical charge...

Bung: Well, do that, will you, Doc?

The door bursts open and Slobotham and Albert rush excitedly into the room. Albert is now wearing his window-cleaning outfit.

Slobotham: Sir! Oh there you are! Sir, we've got a lead!

Albert: It was put through my letterbox this morning!

Bung: What? What was?

Albert: Listen!

He produces a piece of paper and reads off it.

Albert: (reading) "If you want to know what happened to Doris Mann, I can tell you. I am the cloakroom attendant at the one by the Park and you can see me any time at my convenience."

Bung: Let me see that!

He snatches the piece of paper and studies it.

Slobotham: Do you think it's genuine sir?

Bung: I don't know. Unusual notepaper...perforated at both ends...could be! Come on!

Left to right: Bung (Harry H. Corbett), Slobotham (Peter Butterworth) and Albert (Jim Dale) are hot on the trail.

Chapter Two

Can I Do You Now, Sir?

"If I can help someone as I go on my way," was a sentiment immediately picked up on by the *Carry On* team. The essence of public service and social institutions were at the core of the early films from scriptwriter Norman Hudis. Whether it be the police force, schoolteachers or friendly army sergeants whipping a motley crew of raw recruits into shape, the ensemble community feel of post-war Britain was neatly brought into play. Of course, the major institution which ran throughout the history of *Carry On* was the hospital. The first medical, *Carry On Nurse*, was the second film in the series and fully set the seal on the series' longevity. Daffodils would never quite be the same again… Ten years later, the glories of *Carry On Nurse* were resurrected in the tongue-in-cheek homage, *Carry On Doctor*. Its alternative titles included *Nurse Carries On Again* and *Death Of A Daffodil*. Eighteen months later, *Carry On Again Doctor* was rushed into production, with Jim Dale being put through his paces, Kenneth Williams turning on the camp superiority once more and everybody's favourite warm-hearted matron, Hattie Jacques, crusading through the wards. She was rewarded with her own, headlining film, *Carry On Matron* – a film which saw the final series contribution from Terry Scott and the first from Jack Douglas.

However, it wasn't just medical business which saw the *Carry On* team giving their fellow man a helping hand. In *Carry On Regardless*, released in 1961, Sid James set up an agency which was literally called Helping Hands. A full decade before the Goodies, these guys – including Bill Owen, Charles Hawtrey, Kenneth Williams and Kenneth Connor – set out to do anything, anywhere for anybody who needed them. That resulted in a string of relentlessly funny sketches featuring everything from pet chimp walking to acting as a bouncer at a saucy strip club. Elements of this agency-based, sketch format *Carry On* were revived for the 1970 film, *Carry On Loving*, in which Sidney and Sophie Bliss (Sidney James and Hattie Jacques) ran the Wedded Bliss Agency with a variety of clients from a murderous Peter Butterworth to a work-obsessed Kenneth Williams looking for a partner in marriage.

The result may have been farcical and frantic whenever the likes of Sid James, Terence Longdon, Charlie Hawtrey or Liz Fraser tried to help, but at all times, the *Carry On* team had their heart in the right place!

The Helping Hands Agency staff in Carry On Regardless *(1961).*

Carry On Regardless 1961

Screenwriter: Norman Hudis
Producer: Peter Rogers
Director: Gerald Thomas
Production started: 2 January 1961

The Helping Hands Agency gets staffed by seven refugees from the labour exchange, who are sent out on a variety of assignments, including walking a chimpanzee for an owner stuck at home with the flu, making an errant husband jealous in order to try and make him appreciate his wife more, and demonstrating new gimmicks at the Ideal Home Exhibition. The agency is run by Bert Handy (Sidney James) with able help from his pixie-like assistant Miss Cooling (Esma Cannon). Together they try and keep their employees in control. Among them, the snooty Francis Courtenay (Kenneth Williams), jittery Sam Twist (Kenneth Connor) and vivacious Delia King (Liz Fraser). All seems to be going well until the agency's landlord (Stanley Unwin) demands more rent and all the stops are pulled out to try and save the day and the Agency!

A startled Gabriel (Charles Hawtrey) arrives at the home of Mrs Riley (Eleanor Summerfield).

The plot so far: This scene was deemed too rude by the censors who pointed to the film's 'U' certificate and said: "No way!". The scene was actually filmed, but never made it to the big screen. It is based round the latest Helping Hands assignment – for one of the female members of the agency to go and sit with a Mrs Riley (Eleanor Summerfield) and make a note of everything she says in her sleep. However, because the filing system of Miss Cooling (Esma Cannon) has been disturbed, all the jobs go to the wrong people. The naive Gabriel Dimple (Charles Hawtrey) unwittingly turns up for the post.

Mrs Riley: Where have you been? Come in! I'm dying to get to bed!

Before he knows where he is, she's yanked him into her flat where she does a double-take.

Mrs Riley: Aaagh! Who are you?
Gabriel: Madam – let me go!
Mrs Riley: Not until you give me an explanation.
Gabriel: Of what?
Mrs Riley: Your presence.
Gabriel: I was sent, by Helping Hands. (Referring to paper) Flat 43. Mrs Riley.
Mrs Riley: (Astonished) There's been a mistake!
Gabriel: I agree.
Mrs Riley: (Decisive) But never mind! Stay!
Gabriel: Why?
Mrs Riley: I'm in the mood.
Gabriel: Are you...?
Mrs Riley: I know I am.
Gabriel: Oh, do you...?
Mrs Riley: That's why I'm so keen to get to bed.
Gabriel: Mrs Riley!!!
Mrs Riley: There are nights when I know it's going to happen – at its most effective.
Gabriel: You don't say...

Helping Hands! Mrs Riley manhandles Gabriel into her bedroom.

Mrs Riley: I've got it!
Gabriel: I should think you have!
Mrs Riley: What does it matter what you are?
Gabriel: It takes all sorts to make a world – yes...
Mrs Riley: Mr Pimple...
Gabriel: Dimple.
Mrs Riley: You'll be able to do your part from the wardrobe!
Gabriel: You flatter me, madam. You...Eh?!
Mrs Riley: Of course! Oh, what a relief? I – I don't want to waste my mood.
Gabriel: No – of course not...
Mrs Riley: And with you in the wardrobe – we can observe the proprieties and achieve the result we both want so much.
Gabriel: M-Madam – I think I ought to warn you – I've led rather a sheltered life and...Whoop!

Dragged upstairs to bedroom...

I don't quite understand...I mean...You see...

Mrs Riley: What d'you mean you don't understand?
Gabriel: Madam – what possible good can I be to you in the wardrobe?!
Mrs Riley: Plenty – with a notebook.
Gabriel: A notebook?!
Mrs Riley: Do you have one?
Gabriel: No madam I do not. One way and another, I seem to be singularly ill-equipped for this job. I really think I'd better go...Whoop! (she grabs him)
Mrs Riley: Don't! I'm desperate!
Gabriel: I'm sorry, madam, but there's clearly been the most awful mistake.
Mrs Riley: Oh, not too awful really – though I did ask for a woman.
Gabriel: A woman?!
Mrs Riley: Well – If you were in my shoes – wouldn't you. (Gabriel yammers) Oh really – man – woman – what difference does it make so long as you use your ears?
Gabriel: (wriggling a finger in each) I can't be hearing right!
Mrs Riley: Oh do help me! I do it every single night. And the awful thing is – I don't know what comes out. That's why I need a Helping Hand.
Gabriel: And an 'elpful ear?
Mrs Riley: Exactly!
Gabriel: Preferably a woman?
Mrs Riley: Naturally.
Gabriel: But you'll settle for me?
Mrs Riley: In this emergency – yes. My husband's away for three days – and I may not be so hot the other two nights – so you will get into the wardrobe won't you?
Gabriel: Mrs Riley, I have to confess that I have not comprehended a word you've said – but my imagination boggles!
Mrs Riley: Not – understood? Didn't anyone tell you?
Gabriel: No. They did not.
Mrs Riley: Oh! (Giggles) That's embarrassing.
Gabriel: To say the least
Mrs Riley: You must think...
Gabriel: Oh I do!
Mrs Riley: Poor man (Advancing) I must explain.
Gabriel: From a distance! (She halts he's still ultra-suspicious) Well?!...

Carry On Loving 1970

Screenwriter: Talbot Rothwell
Producer: Peter Rogers
Director: Gerald Thomas
Production started: 6 April 1970

Sidney Bliss (Sidney James) and Sophie (Hattie Jacques) run the Wedded Bliss Agency, happily trying to bring together some of the most unsuited couples to be joined together in holy disharmony. In fact, though they pretend otherwise to their clients, Sidney and Sophie are not even married themselves – the whole organisation, complete with its false computer meant to team up ideal partners, is a con. Completely unaware, into the business come various clients including. the naïve and virginal Bertie Muffett (Richard O'Callaghan) who more by fluke than planning gets teamed up with the sexy model Sally Martin (Jacki Piper). Then there's independent businessman Terence Philpot (Terry Scott) who finds love in the most unexpected quarters with busty bombshell (Imogen Hassall). Meanwhile at the local Marriage Guidance Council, unmarried and sexually naive Percival Snooper (Kenneth Williams) is dishing out useless advice to anyone who cares to listen. He ends up at the Agency after Sophie visits for advice. He proposes to her – much to the chagrin of his loyal and trusting housemaid Miss Dempsey (Patsy Rowlands) who has spent many years 'doing' for him around the house, but not in the bedroom.
The proposal is the shock Sid needs. He finally asks Sophie to marry him and a big wedding party is thrown where all the unhappy couples come to celebrate with their matchmakers and end up involved in a huge pie fight! And everyone lives happily ever after!

The plot so far: Sophie Bliss (Hattie Jacques) is convinced that Sidney (Sidney James) is having an affair with one of their clients, Esme Crowfoot (Joan Sims). She decides to employ the services of a private investigator to track his movements. Back from an investigating assignment, James Bedsop (Charles Hawtrey) is debriefing his client Mr Thrush (Norman Chapell).

Charles Hawtrey as the 'Bombay Bond', James Bedsop, in Carry On Loving *(1970).*

SCENE 35: INTERIOR. BEDSOP'S OFFICE. DAY

It is a somewhat seedy set-up, quite obviously Bedsop is not in the Bond class. Bedsop, seated at his desk, wearing a Sherlock Holmes cap, making a report to someone. During his opening lines, CAMERA TRACKS BACK to show a middle-aged Man seated in the chair opposite the desk – a Mr Thrush

Bedsop: Acting on your instructions, Mr Thrush, I kept observation on your house after you left for work on the morning of May 10 at approximately 0752 hours...that of course means eight minutes to eight...

Thrush: Yes yes, I know. Get on with it!

Bedsop: Patience, Mr Thrush, please! It's most important that you understand everything absolutely clearly. Right then. (Back to report) At approximately 08 ten hours... that's ten past eight...I observed Mrs Thrush appear at the front bedroom window, wearing a pair of black lace panties and a worried expression.

Incompetent private investigator James Bedsop (Charles Hawtrey) is wanted on another case.

Thrush: What? You mean – she had nothing up top?

Bedsop: I was coming to that. Above the black panties Mrs Thrush was clad in a pink bathcap. I kept close observation on Mrs thrush at the window – along with a number of passers-by. She stayed at the window for three and a half minutes – looking absolutely delightful I must say – then disappeared.

Thrush: Three and a half minutes! That's just like her. It's a wonder she don't stuff 'em in a glass case and put 'em on exhibition. What happened then?

Bedsop: I'm coming to that, Mr Thrush. Frankly, I was at a loss to understand the motive behind her sudden disappearance from the window until at 08 fifteen hours – that's a quarter past eight – I detected the sound of a cistern flushing. From this I rapidly deducted that Mrs Thrush was having a...

Thrush: Oh for goodness sake! Do we have to go through all this?

Bedsop: Mr Thrush! It is the painstaking attention to every detail that makes a good private inquiry agent!

Thrush: All right, all right, go on then.

The telephone goes.

Bedsop: Excuse me.

He brings out a handkerchief and carefully picks up the receiver with it.

Bedsop: James Bedsop, private inquiry agent. ...Oh hallo! Yes, of course I remember you, Mrs Bliss. We met at that wedding, when I was guarding the presents...yes, it was a pity about that...no, they never did find the bride again. Such a nice girl too.

SCENE 36: INTERIOR. SOPHIE'S OFFICE. DAY.

SOPHIE at the phone.

Sophie: Mr Bedsop, I phone you because I want someone followed...Mr Bliss actually...yes, my husband, that's right.

SCENE 37: INTERIOR. BEDSOP'S OFFICE. DAY.

RESUME BEDSOP at the phone.

Bedsop: Oh! (Getting pad and pencil) Well, if you'll describe him for me, Mrs Bliss?... (Starting to write) Rotten – cheating lying – bar...no, no, Mrs Bliss. A physical description please! Yes... (Writing down) Yes...yes...

SCENE 38: INTERIOR. SOPHIE'S OFFICE. DAY.

SOPHIE just finishing off her description.

Sophie: ...and the general appearance of an ancient and dissipated walnut. And I can tell you where he will be at seven thirty this evening – the Parkway Hotel cocktail bar.

SCENE 39: INTERIOR. BEDSOP'S OFFICE. DAY.

Bedsop: (writing)...Parkway hotel cocktail bar. Right, just leave it to me, Mrs Bliss. Check, roger, over and out!

He replaces the receiver, carefully dusts off his fingers with the handkerchief, and turns back to Thrush.

Bedsop: Sorry about that, Mr Thrush. Now where were we?

Thrush: In the loo!

Bedsop: Oh yes, that's right. To proceed – at approximately 08 forty-nine – that's eleven minutes to nine – the milkman arrived at the front, rang, and was admitted by Mrs Thrush.

Thrush: Ah!

Bedsop: At 09 fifteen – that's a quarter past nine – the front door opened and the milkman left. At 09 twenty-one...

Thrush: He was in there all that time?! What was he doing?

Bedsop: I was coming to that. At 09 twenty-one – that's...

Thrush: Twenty past nine, yes!

Bedsop: Twenty one minutes past nine. At 0921 the paperman arrived at the front, rang, and was admitted by Mrs Thrush.

Thrush: The paperman...?!

Bedsop: That's right. At 09 forty-five – that's a quarter to ten – the front door opened and the paperman left. At 09 fifty-two – I observed the arrival of the dustcart. The three dustmen went up to the front door, rang, and we were admitted by Mrs Thrush. At ten thirty-five, the front door opened and the dustmen left.

Thrush: Three of 'em! What were they all doing in there?

Bedsop: I'm coming to that. At ten forty I decided that a personal investigation was necessary, so I approached the front door, rang, and was admitted by Mrs Thrush. At approximately eleven ten I left the house, having got what I wanted.

Thrush: What? What, for heaven's sake?

Bedsop: Well, I don't know what all the others got, but I had the most delicious bacon and eggs and coffee...

Inept marriage guidance advisor Percival Snooper (Kenneth Williams) prepares to greet another hapless couple.

The plot so far: The unmarried Marriage Guidance Counsellor Percival Snooper (Kenneth Williams) thinks he has cracked the cause of the problem in the Roxby's marriage and invites Mr Roxby (James Beck) and Mrs Roxby (Yutte Stensgaard) back into his office for a chat.

SCENE 74: INTERIOR. SNOOPER'S OFFICE. DAY

Snooper, grinning complacently, is at the door, inviting someone to come in.

Snooper: It's all right, you can come in now, Mr Roxby.

A worried-looking Man of about 50 comes in.

Snooper: Do sit down.

He leads him to chair beside another in which sits Mrs Roxby, a very pert, lush-looking little blonde of about 22. As Snooper goes round to his own chair...

Snooper: You'll be pleased to hear that I've had a jolly good session with your wife here.

Roxby: You and others.

Snooper: I knew if I could get her alone for long enough that I'd get something out of her.

Left to right: Yutte Stensgaard and James Beck as Mr and Mrs Roxby listen to Kenneth Williams as Snooper in this deleted scene from Carry On Loving *(1970).*

In a manner of speaking, of course.

Roxby: Well, it'll have to be good, I can promise you.

Mrs Roxby: See what I mean? He doesn't trust me.

Snooper: All right, leave this to me, Mrs Roxby. (Referring to notes) Now then Mr Roxby, it seems that you started to have suspicions about your wife last month when you came home unexpectedly and found her in bed with another man.

Roxby: Well, wouldn't you think it a bit funny?

Snooper: Not in the circumstances, no.

Roxby: Eh? What circumstances?

Snooper: Well, to recap. You went away on a business trip, got through earlier than you expected, and sent your wife a telegram to say you were coming home.

Roxby: Yes, yes.

Snooper: But – when you arrived home and went upstairs – there they were.

Roxby: Yes yes yes. Well?

Snooper: Well, as I told you, I was convinced that if I could talk to her alone, Mrs Roxby would have a satisfactory explanation.

Roxby: Well, what?

Snooper: Simple. She didn't get the telegram.

And sits back, beaming, well satisfied with himself.

Mrs Roxby: (to Roxby) You see? It was all your fault.

Roxby sits there, astounded, hardly able to believe his ears, and unable to find his tongue.

Snooper: Well, I'm glad we got that sorted out. (Getting up) I expect you'd like to go out for a celebratory lunch or something, eh?

Mrs Roxby gets up.

Mrs Roxby: He can if he wants. I've already got a date with someone.

Snooper: Come along, Mr Roxby. And next time, take a tip from me, and use a telephone!

He gets the bewildered Roxby to his feet and steers him towards the door. And calling to one side...

Snooper: And the next please?

Carry On Again Doctor 1969

Screenwriter: Talbot Rothwell
Producer: Peter Rogers
Director: Gerald Thomas
Production started: 17 March 1969

Joan Sims (Ellen Moore) and Kenneth Williams (Carver) in the missing appendix scene from Carry On Again Doctor *(1969).*

Ace surgeon Frederick Carver (Kenneth Williams) has his eyes on wealthy female patient Ellen Moore (Joan Sims) whom he hopes will fund his idea for a private health clinic. Meanwhile Doctor James Nookey (Jim Dale) is working in Casualty when the girl of his dreams turns up on a trolley following a fall. He and Goldie Locks (Barbara Windsor) hit it off immediately but after he refuses to commit to her, she leaves for Italy. After getting drunk and smashing up half of the hospital, Nookey gets sent by Carver to a clinic on a remote island run by bigamist drinker Gladstone Screwer (Sidney James). On the island, Nookey discovers a marvellous slimming potion and returns to set up his own clinic in England. He suddenly finds himself with many friends and enemies, all trying to cash in on his success. Nookey is reunited with Goldie when she books in to the clinic to lose some weight. No one is prepared for the potion's side-effects – it turns women into men. Order is restored in time for Nookey and Goldie's marriage.

The plot so far: It is early in the film and Doctor Frederick Carver (Kenneth Williams) has come to pay a visit to wealthy patient Ellen Moore (Joan Sims) following his removal of her appendix. Carver's visit is not purely professional – he has other ideas on his mind.

SCENE 14: INTERIOR. MRS MOORE'S ROOM. DAY.

Ellen Moore is a middle-aged woman, with a carefully cultivated posh accent that slips at moments of stress. She is sitting up in bed wearing an expensive bed-jacket, and the room is filled with flowers, large boxes of chocolates and other signs of opulence. She gives Carver a big smile as he comes in.

Carver: My dear Mrs Moore...and how are we today?

Ellen: Oh, I feel wonderful, Mr Carver! I'd no idea having one's appendix out could be so exhilarating. You know I feel ten years younger.

Carver: Splendid, splendid!

Ellen: (Coyly) Be honest now, do I look like a woman of forty?

Carver: You really feel as young as that?

Ellen: (Taken aback) No, that's what I am.

Carver: (Recovering quickly) Of course, I was only joking. Well well, so you go home today, eh?

Ellen: Yes, and I shan't be sorry. This bed's all right, but I do miss my slap and tickle.

Carver: Your...?

Doctor *cast shot (left to right): Charles Hawtrey, Kenneth Williams, Hattie Jacques, Sidney James, Joan Sims, Jim Dale and Barbara Windsor.*

Ellen: Slap and tickle! They're my Siamese. They always sleep on my bed.

Carver: Oh yes of course.

Ellen: Not that I'm not grateful to you for all you've done. They told me you were a wonderful surgeon.

Carver: Oh well, I suppose I am a cut above the rest.

And they laugh gaily at his little joke

Ellen: In fact, I've been thinking...(Sexily) I'd like to show my appreciation in some way.

Carver: Oh, now now, Mrs Moore. Just because you're a widow, I shouldn't take advantage of you...

Ellen: Oh, I don't mind being taken advantage of now and then.

Carver: Well, since you mentioned it, there is something I would like to do...

Ellen: (Hopefully) Yes?

Carver: For many years now I've had a dream – of something that would bring hope and comfort to thousands of suffering people...a Frederick Carver Foundation!

Ellen: (Disappointed) What's that – some sort of corset?

Carver: No, no, no! A private Clinic! But, alas its such a costly project. Fifty thousand or more...?

Ellen: Oh. I wasn't thinking of showing that sort of appreciation. Not financially. I don't do that sort of thing.

Carver: Now don't be modest, Mrs Moore. What about the Medical Mission you founded in the Beatific Isles?

Ellen: Oh well, that was different. My husband died out there and I wanted to show my gratitude. I mean, for the way they looked after him...

Carver: Quite, quite.

Ellen: But a woman like me has to be careful, you know. There's been so many men after me. For my money, I mean.

Carver: Of course – what else? I mean, what else would unscrupulous men be after?

Ellen: Exactly. Mind you, I'm not mean. I'm always ready to listen to an honest business proposition.

Carver: I'm sure you are. We must discuss it sometime when you're out and about. In the meantime...

Ellen: Oh don't go yet. Have you forgotten? You said – that before I left here – you'd show it to me.
Carver: I beg your pardon?
Ellen: My appendix! You promised to keep it for me.
Carver: Oh your appendix! Oh, you don't want to bother with that old thing. No second-hand value, you know...
Ellen: (Suspicious) You haven't...haven't got rid of it?
Carver: (Obviously has) Of course not! I've kept it in a bottle. I thought I'd quietly bury it. In a pet's cemetery of course.
Ellen: Oh no, I must see it first.
Carver: Oh. Very well then...I'll get it...
And goes out.

Ellen Moore (Joan Sims) inpects exactly what Dr Carver whipped out while she was on the operating table.

SCENE 15: INTERIOR. HALL, NURSING HOME. DAY.

Fosdick is waiting patiently in a chair as Carver comes out and closes the door behind him.
Carver: Miss Fosdick! Quickly, what happened to Mrs Moore's appendix?
Fosdick: You took it out, sir.
Carver: I know I took it out! But what did I do with it afterwards?
Fosdick: I really don't know, sir. Have you looked through your pockets?
Carver: Oh yes...(and actually starts looking) What am I doing? I don't go around with my pockets stuffed with offal, woman!
Fosdick: Well, I really don't know, sir.
Carver: Oh, this is awful! I'll have to get another from somewhere!
Then looks hard at Fosdick's stomach and starts to smile. Fosdick steps back, reading his thoughts, hands involuntarily going to guard her midriff. Carver shakes his head.
Carver: No, there isn't time.
Matron comes into the Hall.
Matron: Oh, Mr Carver. Will you be staying for some lunch? It's chicken.
Carver: No thank you, I have to get back to...
And, as an idea strikes him...
Chicken? Has it been cooked yet?
Matron: Why, no.
Carver: Good, I'll have a piece!
And goes quickly down hall to rear door, passing a very surprised Matron.

SCENE 16: INTERIOR. MRS MOORE'S ROOM. DAY.

Ellen looks up as the door opens again and Carver comes in, smiling, and holding something behind his back.
Ellen: Have you got it?
Carver: Yes. There you are.
He hands her a glass flask, sealed, and quickly makes his exit...
Ellen: Thank you.
He goes. Ellen, still smiling, holds the flask up to have a good look at her "appendix". Her smile fades.
We see that the flask is filled with clear liquid and in the liquid is an obvious "parson's nose".
Ellen looking at it rather suspiciously.
Ellen: I wonder why it's got a bit of string tied round it.

Carry On Doctor 1967

Screenwriter: Talbot Rothwell
Producer: Peter Rogers
Director: Gerald Thomas
Production started:
11 September 1967

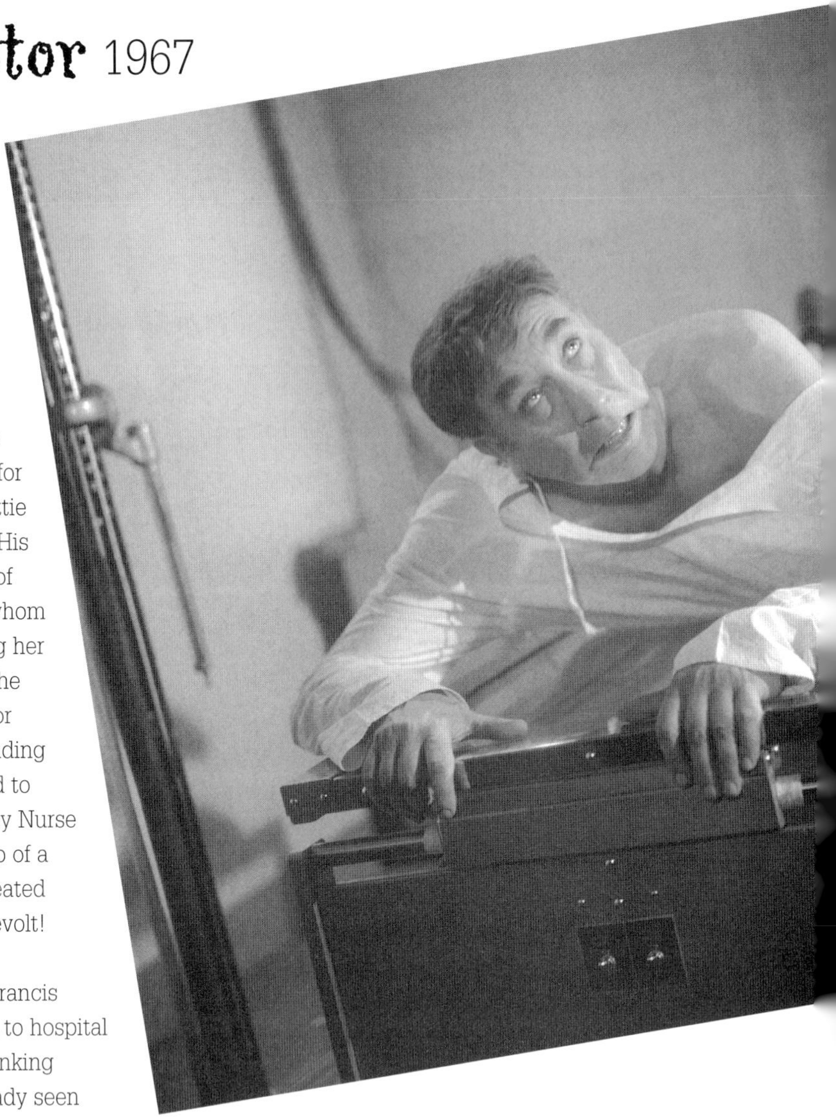

Doctor Tinkle – Tinker in the script – (Kenneth Williams) presides over the wards of the local hospital with a firm hand. All around him the nurses, doctors and patients harbour secret desires and hidden passions for each other – none more so than Matron (Hattie Jacques) who is in love with Tinkle himself. His stern demeanour is disrupted by the arrival of Nurse Sandra May (Barbara Windsor) with whom Tinkle had a brief fling when he was treating her for tonsillitis some years earlier! She raises the blood pressure of all around, including Doctor Kilmore (Jim Dale) who is dismissed after ending up in a bath with another nurse, having tried to thwart what he believes was a suicide bid by Nurse May, who was merely sunning herself on top of a roof. The patients think Kilmore has been treated unfairly by Tinkle and Matron and stage a revolt!

The plot so far: It is early in the film and Francis Bigger (Frankie Howerd) has been admitted to hospital following a fall during one of his positive thinking lectures. Doctor Kilmore (Jim Dale) has already seen him, accidentally sticking a hypodermic syringe into his backside. Now Matron is on duty and wants Doctor Tinkle to give his professional opinion on the case. It also allows her another chance to be near to the man she secretly loves....

SCENE 21: INTERIOR. HOSPITAL LOBBY. DAY.

Matron is waiting by the Lift as it comes down. Kilmore, in white coat, is in the Lift, and greets her cheerily as the doors open.

Kilmore: Good morning, Matron.

Matron: (Cold as ever) Oh, Doctor Kilmore. You're assigned to outpatients clinic this morning.

Kilmore: Oh no, not again? Can't one of the others do it for a change?

Matron: The others are needed for more important work, Doctor.

Kilmore: Oh, have a heart, Matron. How about Maternity? I'd be good at that.

He uses his hand to point as a gun.

Kilmore: Stand and deliver.

Matron is not amused.

Matron: Outpatients, Doctor Kilmore. And if you don't like the assignment you'd better

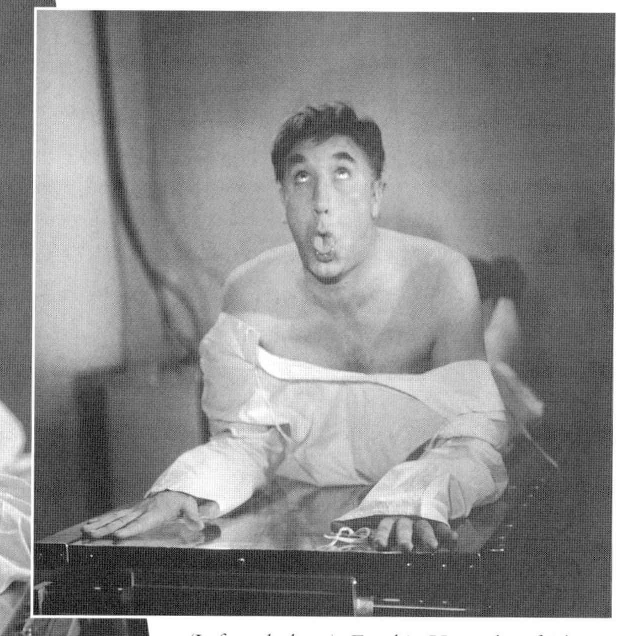

(Left and above): Frankie Howerd, as faith healer Francis Bigger, gets more than he bargained for during an explosive X-ray in Carry On Doctor *(1968). (Below) Archetypal nursing figure, Hattie Jacques, as the fearsome matron in* Carry On Doctor.

see Doctor Tinker. He decides on trainee doctor's capabilities.

With which she sweeps into the lift. Kilmore makes a face and mutters...

Kilmore: Yeh, with your help.

A Nurse hurries up to him.

Nurse: Doctor Kilmore, can you come to outpatients right away? There's a man with a nasty boil.

Kilmore: (sighs) Where?

Nurse: He didn't say. But he won't sit down.

Kilmore: I knew it. On the flip side! Lead on Lady Guinevere, and hand me my lance!

SCENE 22: INTERIOR. UPPER CORRIDOR. DAY.

As Matron comes out of the lift and starts along the corridor. She comes to a stop as she hears odd noises. A series of sharp cries of pain interspersed with thumps and maniacal laughter.

She looks across at a door plainly marked OPERATING THEATRE and her eyebrows climb in surprise. Yep, the noises are coming from there all right. She crosses to the door and peers in.

SCENE 23: INTERIOR. OPERATING THEATRE. DAY.

Quite a large room with the operating table centre. Otherwise plenty of floor space.

Matron is at glass window of door, peering in.

She sees Dr Tinker and Henry, the ambulance driver, engaged in some Judo. Tinker wears the traditional robe, but Henry just wears a floppy pullover and his uniform trousers. Tinker is doing all the throwing and Henry provides all the yells. Tinker is a thin weedy character, and a physical fitness enthusiast. One feels that stocky Henry could tear him apart if he wanted, but it obviously wouldn't be politic.

Tinker throws Henry heavily again and Henry yells as he hits the floor.

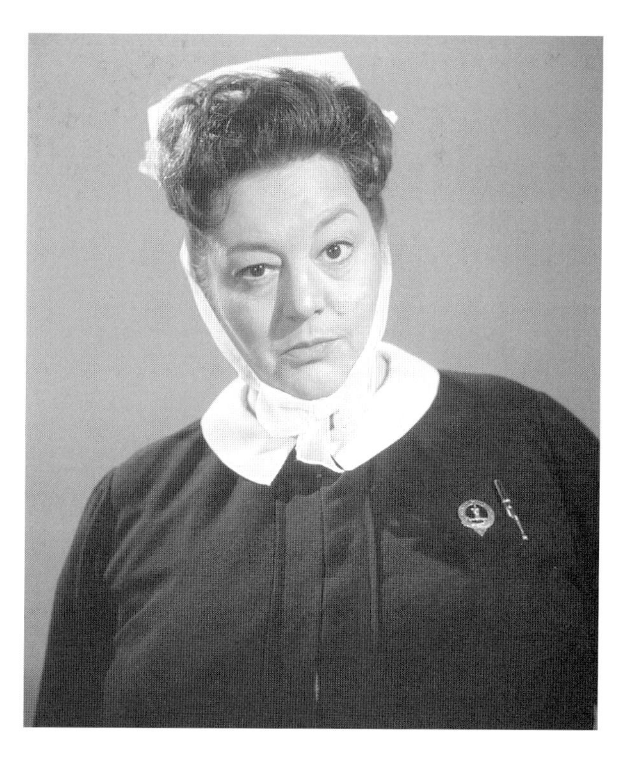

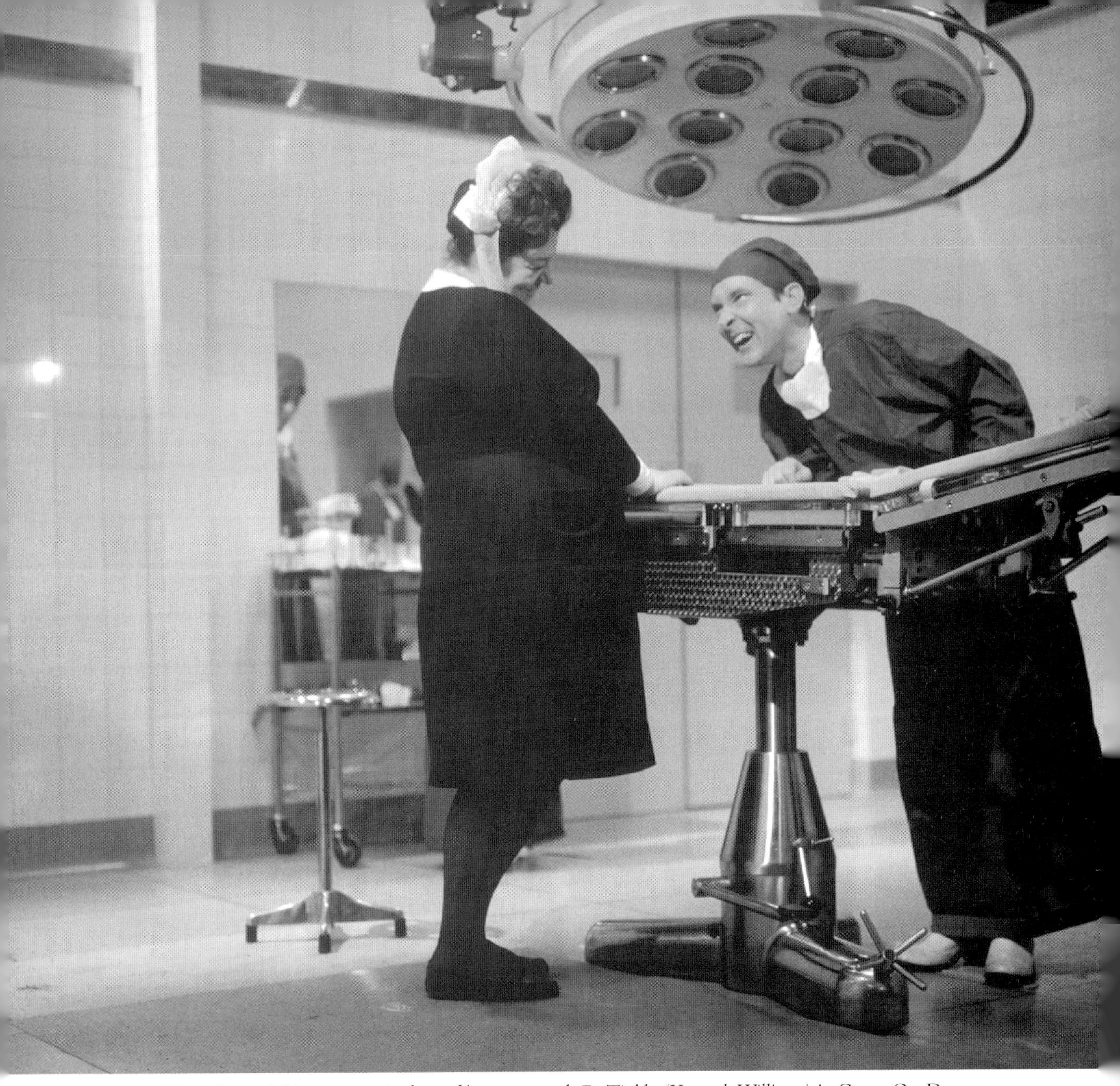

Matron (Hattie Jacques) feigns coyness in front of her secret crush Dr Tinkle (Kenneth Williams) in Carry On Doctor.

Tinker: Aha, got you again, Henry. You'll have to move quicker than that, you know.

Henry gets to his feet, obviously very fed up with the whole business.

Henry: 'Fraid you're too good for me, Doctor. I've had enough.

Tinker: Oh don't be like that. You're out of condition, that's your trouble. Too much of the old beer and bounce, eh?

Henry spots Matron coming in behind him and gives him a warning signal. Tinker turns.

Tinker: Ah, good morning, Matron. And how are the old hormones? All under control?

Matron: (Gushing) I'm very well thank you, Doctor Tinker.

Tinker: Yes, but don't let's talk shop. We

borrowed the old ops room for a spot of judo. Marvellous thing for developing the body, you know, Matron.

He pulls back one sleeve and exhibits his puny arm.

Tinker: Look at that muscle! Feel it!

She does so, gladly. Anything to make contact with the man she adores.

Matron: Why, it's wonderful, Doctor.

Tinker: Hard as a button.

Henry: And about the same size too.

Tinker: What was that, Henry.

Henry: It's about time I went, Doctor.

Tinker: All right, run along.

Henry bolts for the door. Tinker calls after him.

Tinker: See you here tomorrow morning! Bright and early!

Henry: Not if I see you first.

And escapes.

Tinker: You ought to take it up yourself, Matron. You never know when you may have to defend yourself.

Matron: (Coyly) Oh, I don't think anyone's going to attack me, Doctor.

Tinker: No, perhaps you're right.

He goes to a wall mirror and starts smoothing his hair, full of admiration for himself.

Matron: There's a casualty I think you ought to see, Doctor. Back injury. I had to get Doctor Kilmore to see him last night, I'm afraid.

Tinker: Oh well, never mind. We may still be in time to save him.

He obviously shares Matron's opinion of Kilmore. Matron titters appreciatively.

Tinker: But there, we mustn't be too hard on Kilmore, matron. We can't all be brilliant. Some of us have it and some of us don't.

And he obviously thinks he has it.

Matron: (Dutifully) Well of course, we couldn't hope for them all to be as brilliant as you, Doctor.

Tinker: Quite. Well. I'll do the rounds just as soon as I've changed, Matron.

Matron: Very good, Doctor.

Kenneth Williams in a wonderful publicity shot for Carry On Doctor *(1968).*

For a moment she admires him at the mirror and we hear her thoughts...

Matron: (Thinks) What a wonderful man he is. And God, how I love him!

And overcome by emotion, turns and goes out quickly. TINKER, at mirror, humming jauntily, smoothes an eyebrow, gives himself an admiring look, and...

Tinker: (Thinks) God, But I love you.

Chapter Three

1066 And A Bit Of The Other!

Carry On legend Jack Douglas believes that, "the *Carry Ons* always worked better when we were in historical costume…in fact, the further we went back the funnier it became. Apart from going back to 1492 of course!" The fascinating element of the *Carry On* series is that, now, the contemporary set films like *Carry On Nurse* and *Carry On Camping* can also be seen to be social historical remnants of what Britain was like during the twenty-year period in which the films were made.

However, the very first time that *Carry On* ventured into the realms of history books for comic ideas was with the script from the new writer on the block, Talbot Rothwell. The first treatment that Rothwell sent to producer Peter Rogers was for a comedy based on the Captain Hornblower books of C.S. Forester. Originally entitled *Poop-Decker RN*, Rogers was happy to turn it into a *Carry On* film, initially called *Carry On Up the Armada*. Thanks to displeasure from the British Board of Film Classification, this title was changed to *Carry On Sailor* and ultimately released as *Carry On Jack*. Its realistic, beautifully costumed and historically geared style was a turning point for the series. Whether it was hysterical history or historical parody, the *Carry Ons* were seldom out of historical costume for the rest of the decade.

The French Revolution provided futile ground for Talbot Rothwell's innuendo with the tale of daring English aristocrat Sir Rodney Ffing ("with two Fs"), played by the raucous Sidney James, attempting to rescue ill-fated French nobility from the clutches of the guillotine in *Don't Lose Your Head*. However, the *Carry On* series reached its universally accepted zenith with the classic investigation of British rule over Victorian-era India in *Carry On…Up the Khyber*. With pantomime-sized heroes and villains, the *Carry On* team ripped asunder the pomp and circumstance of God-on-our-side British righteousness to expose a crumbling, fiercely patriotic and

Kenneth Williams as the Khasi of Kalabar in Carry On . . . Up the Khyber *(1968).*

Director Gerald Thomas (centre) is joined by cast members of the 1971 entry, Carry On Henry, *(left to right) Sidney James, Barbara Windsor, Joan Sims and Julian Holloway.*

ultimately rewarding sense of misguided national pride.

British history back on home turf proved the perfect, right royal way to celebrate the 21st *Carry On* film, when that much-married monarch, King Henry VIII was given the innuendo treatment. An even more notorious historical figure, the dreaded highwayman Dick Turpin, was celebrated with Rothwell's final screenplay, *Carry On Dick*, although the basic idea of a crook hiding behind the pious garb of a village vicar was gleefully lifted from the 1963 Patrick McGoohan film *Dr Syn*. Historically important in terms of the series, *Carry On Dick* marked the final appearances of both Sidney James and Hattie Jacques. Their absence was greatly felt with the wartime military farce *Carry On England* which revisited the ethos of the first film, *Carry On Sergeant*, by turning back the clock to somewhere in England, 1940.

On television, the Christmas specials wallowed in historical settings, while all thirteen episodes of the 1975 series *Carry On Laughing* were costume romps…from the court of Queen Elizabeth I to the weary atmosphere of the Battle of Hastings.

When the *Carry Ons* finally returned to the cinemas, it was with *Carry On Columbus*. The writer Dave Freeman firmly set his innuendo-packed mind on a celebration of the 500th anniversary of the discovery of America. This time round, history didn't get the funny bone tickled…but that's where we came in…

Carry On Henry 1971

Scriptwriter: Talbot Rothwell
Producer: Peter Rogers
Director: Gerald Thomas
Production started: 12 October 1970

The secret life of the much-married King of England, Henry VIII (Sidney James) is revealed in a recently discovered manuscript from one William Cobbler…of course, it's all cobblers, as Thomas Cromwell (Kenneth Williams) and Cardinal Wolsey (Terry Scott) suffer the King's frustrations and obsessions with Queen Marie (Joan Sims) and Bettina (Barbara Windsor). Despite interventions from the King's loyal taster, Sir Roger de Lodgerley (Charles Hawtrey) and the corrupted anti-royalist Lord Hampton of Wick (Kenneth Connor) the sex-mad King comes out on top!

The plot so far: King Henry VIII (Sidney James) has been idle, girl-chasing and corrupted for far too long and Thomas Cromwell (Kenneth Williams) is happy to back a plot against the monarch. The cunning Lord Hampton of Wick (Kenneth Connor) and his trusty band of anti-royalists are approached to take part in an abduction backed by the King – to save him from wedding night activity with Marie (Joan Sims). Naturally, the plotters intend to take full advantage of the King's compliance in this 'mock' abduction. Wick's gang includes the gun powder obsessed Fawkes (Bill Maynard). Talbot Rothwell's script has often been castigated for including Fawkes many years before his attempt to blow up parliament. However, it is clear in this sequence, severely edited in the final film, that Fawkes is not Guy of that name but an earlier incarnation of the explosive family. Rothwell, the consummate historian, covered the joke and was only let down by over-eager editing.

SCENE 21: INTERIOR. A CELLAR. NIGHT.

Lord Hampton of Wick and three other heftily-built Plotters, including one called Fawkes, are huddled around a table on which a lantern burns. It is all very cloak and dagger stuff.

The plotters discuss the downfall of the king in this edited scene from Carry On Henry *(1971).*

Hampton: Right, gentlemen, we are agreed that for the good of England, Henry must go. But how is it to be accomplished?

Fawkes: (eagerly) I've had one idea, Lord Hampton. You see, I have these barrels of gunpowder and if we could smuggle them into Parliament when he goes to open the next session...

He starts to fizzle out under their baleful looks.

Fawkes: ...and blow the lot up...?

Hampton: An excellent notion, Fawkes...but you overlook one small detail. We all sit in Parliament.

Fawkes: Oh yes.

Hampton: No, we must attack this problem more cunningly. What, for instance, are the King's great weaknesses?

Plotter: That's easy. Women.

Hampton: Correct. Well then, how can we attack him through a woman?

Fawkes: (After a pause) Well, if we could find one who's flat-chested and then stuff her bodice with gunpowder and...and...

Hampton: Oh for heaven's sake, Fawkes! Forget about your damned barrels of gunpowder!

Fawkes: (Sulkily) Well, I feel I ought to do something with them...

Hampton: Leave them to your heirs! Let them find something to do with them!

There is a discreet knock at the cellar door. Hampton lifts a finger to caution silence, then goes to the door.

Hampton: Who's there?

Cromwell: (off) I, Thomas Cromwell

Hampton: Cromwell! Quickly!

The Plotters quickly produce embroidery samplers and start needling like crazy as Hampton opens the doors and admits a cloaked Cromwell.

Hampton: My Lord Chancellor, this is indeed an honour.

Cromwell: Yes...having a meeting, Hampton?

Hampton: Just the usual Friday night sewing circle, milord.

Cromwell crosses to look the samplers over.

Cromwell: Umm, interesting.

Hampton: You like the designs?

Cromwell: (Casually) Yes, but not as much as those you have on the King's life.

Hampton: What? My Lord, I...I don't know what you talk about...

Cromwell: Really? Then you won't be interested to learn that he has expressed a wish to be forcibly abducted tonight.

Hampton: He's what?

Cromwell: Purely to suit his own ends of course. I thought you might like the job.

Hampton: Well of course, I would be honoured. But what of the Palace guards?

Cromwell: He has already removed them.

Hampton: I see. And after he's been abducted...?

Cromwell: That's up to you of course. Accidents will happen. For example, the house to which you take him might be accidentally blown up with gunpowder...

Fawkes: (Excitedly) I told you! I knew it would come in useful one day!

Cromwell: Well, milord?

Hampton gives him a long look, then smiles and shouts:

Hampton: Roll out the barrels!...

The plot so far: King Henry (Sidney James), greatly displeased with the garlic-loving Queen Marie (Joan Sims) is keen to secure another wife to bear his desired son and heir. Cardinal Wolsey, wary of the Pope's disgust of divorce but equally keen to retain his high position at the court of good King Hal, happily shows off the latest regal options from across Europe. Sidney James, apt at crafty cockney banter from a lifetime in film and television, took to this scene with aplomb. Dismissing each female in turn in terms of used car salesman knowledge, this is a priceless scene which, sadly, only survives in these shots from the studio and the original screenplay.

Cromwell (Kenneth Williams) joins Lord Hampton (Kenneth Connor) and Guy Fawkes (Bill Maynard) as the plot unravels.

SCENE 43: INTERIOR. HENRY'S APARTMENT. DAY.

Half a dozen portraits of aristocratic-looking Ladies are ranged in a line on a series of easels. Henry is studying them carefully, going down the line for all the world like a man buying a new car, with Wolsey in close attendance, acting like a showroom salesman.

Wolsey: Now this one should suit your Majesty quite well. Anna-Marie. She'd make an excellent Queen, I feel.

Henry: Umm, I don't know. Bit on the big side. What make?

Wolsey: The Schleswig-Holstein's.

Henry: No, no, I don't like German stuff. All right for a while but they don't build 'em to last.

Wolsey: Let's face it, your Grace, you hardly need one to last.

Henry: Let's skip the jests eh?

He goes on to the next one

Ah, now this looks a bit more like it. Nice bodywork...

Wolsey: Sophia of Lombardy, sire.

Henry: Oh, an Italian job. All show and no go. No thanks.

And on to the next – a striking dark beauty.

Henry: Ah! Now there's one I wouldn't mind trying.

Wolsey: Donnabella of Spain, sire. Very nice, but not new, I'm afraid.

Henry: Oh, second-hand, eh? Even so, I won't have to bother running her in, will I? No... How many previous owners?

Wolsey: Er, two sire. Alphonse of Portugal. And (rather hesitantly) King Francis of France...

Henry: Francis! Oh no, I'm not having one of his cast-offs. I know him. He flogs them into the ground.

Wolsey: Well, there's no immediate hurry to

Woolsey (Terry Scott) assists Henry (Sidney James) in his search for a new wife in a recently discovered scene from Carry On Henry *(1971).*

choose one, your Grace...

Henry: What do you mean – no hurry? If I have to wait around much longer there won't be any point getting married again!

Wolsey: I appreciate that, sire, but there's still no confession...

Henry: What? He's been on the rack for six days now!

Wolsey: I know. Truly admirable fortitude...

Henry has reached the last portrait and is eyeing it appreciatively. It is of a young and pretty GIRL.

Henry: Who's this then?

Wolsey: Oh, just an English one, I'm afraid, sire. Katharine Parr.

Henry: Not bad. Put her on the short list.

There is a knock at the door

Henry: Yes?

The door opens and a Servant comes in.

Servant: Your Majesty, the French Ambassador is here desiring immediate audience.

Henry: Is he!

He gives Wolsey a worried look. Wolsey looks a bit uncomfortable.

All right, we'll receive him.

The Servant withdraws.

I don't like the sound of this. What can he want?

Wolsey: I know not, sire. Unless...he has somehow got wind of what has happened.

Henry: Could be. You know the French. Always getting wind.

Carry On Dick 1974

Scriptwriter: Talbot Rothwell
Producer: Peter Rogers
Director: Gerald Thomas
Production started: 4 March 1974

The mild-mannered Rev. Flasher (Sidney James) is, in fact, none other than the notorious highwayman Dick Turpin. Along with his gang, Harriet (Barbara Windsor) and Tom (Peter Butterworth) he robs the rich to give to the poor. The finest brains of the Bow Street Runners are on his trail with Captain Desmond Fancey (Kenneth Williams) and Sergeant Jock Strapp (Jack Douglas) to the fore. Finally trapped in his church with law-enforcers surrounding the building, Turpin makes a daring escape and crosses the border with his criminal cohorts in tow.
The plot so far: Dick Turpin (Sidney James) has been robbing the stage coaches of the rich and noble in order to gather quality merchandise for his popular church bazaar in aid of the poor community. He has been using the invented illness of old Mrs Giles (Patsy Rowlands) to cover up for his late night highway raids but the suspicions of Turpin's housekeeper, Martha Hoggett (Hattie Jacques), are heightened when a healthy Mrs Giles and her randy old husband (George Moon) attend the jumble sale. This sequence was severely edited in the final print, eliminating much of the already tiny role for Patsy Rowlands. It is also interesting to note that in Talbot Rothwell's original script, the character of Dick Turpin is referred to as Dick Twurpin – an added joke or a rejected ruse to avoid problems over using the name…

Dick Turpin (Sidney James) has the last laugh in the highwayman comedy Carry On Dick *(1974).*

SCENE 242: INTERIOR. THE CHURCH HALL. DAY,

Villagers are all around the half-empty stalls, still fighting over the goods. Others are making their way out, laden with clothing.

SCENE 243: THE SAME.

We see Martha, serving at a clothing stall. A very ancient but apparently sprightly old lady – Mrs Giles – fights her way through to Martha, holding a gay silk gown, and proffering money. Behind her is an equally sprightly old man, Mr Giles.

Mrs G: I'll have this please, Miss Hoggett!

Martha: Why Mrs Giles! I'm pleased to see you've recovered from your indisposition.

Mrs G: What indisposition? Nothing wrong with me!

Martha: But... I understood from the Rector that you were confined to your bed.

Mrs G: (Laughs) Me? I don't dare get into bed

And indicates Mr Giles

Mrs G: He'd have me with child afore I could snuff the candle

Mr Giles cackles delightedly, displaying toothless gums, and obviously gooses her, because she gives a sudden squawk.

Mrs G: Stop that, you old devil!

Martha: But the Rector said you were sinking fast!

Mrs G: (Very tickled) Oh dear. There's only one thing sinks fast in this house, and he's (Mr Giles) got it!

And they go off cackling, leaving a very puzzled Martha.

Martha (Hattie Jacques), Rev Flasher (Sidney James) and the Squire (Michael Nightingale) at the Church bazaar – from which the edited section is reproduced here.

Follow That Camel 1967

Scriptwriter: Talbot Rothwell
Producer: Peter Rogers
Director: Gerald Thomas
Production started: 1 May 1967

Cricket-loving gent B.O. West (Jim Dale) is disgraced on the pitch by ruthless and cunning rival in love, Captain Bagshaw (Peter Gilmore) and journeys to join the French foreign legion with faithful manservant Simpson (Peter Butterworth). His childhood sweetheart, Lady Jane Ponsonby (Angela Douglas) discovers that B.O. was framed and attempts to trace him. Meanwhile, in the hot desert sands, bombastic Sergeant Ernie Nocker (Phil Silvers) lies his way through the box of medals of Commandant Burger (Kenneth Williams) before our heroes defend the flamboyant Sheikh Abdul Abulbul (Bernard Bresslaw) and return home to another English cricket match.

The plot so far: Having drugged and seduced Lady Jane (Angela Douglas), the wicked Sheikh (Bernard Bresslaw) is pursued by B.O. (Jim Dale), Simpson (Peter Butterworth) and Nocker (Phil Silvers). He is discovered in his desert empire and while B.O. and Nocker take refuge in the Sheikh's harem, Simpson (in heavy Arab disguise) creeps around outside.

SCENE 90: INTERIOR. SQUARE TENT. DAY.

As Nocker goes to the flaps and peers out, and turns back quickly.

Nocker: Look out! There's one coming.

He looks round quickly, spots the piece of wood, picks it up, hands it to BO with an illustration as to how to

Charles Hawtrey getting the hump during the filming of Follow That Camel *(1967).*

use it, then picks up the floor covering. They station themselves either side of the entrance flap. They've only a second to wait. It parts and Simpson nips in. Nocker flings the covering right over his head, pinioning his arms. BO deals the covered head a useful clout. Simpson gives a slight muffled yell, then slumps. Nocker lets the body down.

Nocker: Nice work! Let's get his clothes!

He whips the covering off and BO removes the head-dress, then realises who it is.

BO: Simpson!

Nocker: What?! It can't be! He must have a double.

BO: But it is!

Nocker: Then I must have a double!

And takes a good swig out of his flask. BO cradles Simpson's head and pats at his face.

BO: Simmy! Simmy! It's me! BO!

Simpson's eyes open and he looks round dazedly.

Simpson: What...what happened?

BO: I'm afraid I hit you, Simpson.

Simpson: (Wounded) You raised your hand to me, Sir?

BO: Well, I couldn't help it! What were you doing creeping around in that...that sheikh's clothing!

Simpson: (Coldly) I was endeavouring to help you, Sir!

Nocker: Some help!

BO: I'm sorry, Simpson. I should have realised. But how did you know we were here?

Simpson: I was worried about you, sir. I've been following you ever since you crept out of the barracks.

BO: (Touched) Oh, Simpson. You needn't have done that. There's nothing to worry about really.

Nocker: Listen to him! We're going to lose them one by one and he says there's nothing to worry about!

Simpson: Lose what one by one?

Nocker: Never mind. If I told you, you'd only get offended again. Come on, let's all get out of here!

The plot so far: With the Fort protected by merely a handful of men – B.O. (Jim Dale), Nocker (Phil Silvers), Burger (Kenneth Williams) and Simpson (Peter Butterworth) – the Sheikh (Bernard Bresslaw) is preparing for a celebration while the legionnaires discuss their plans.

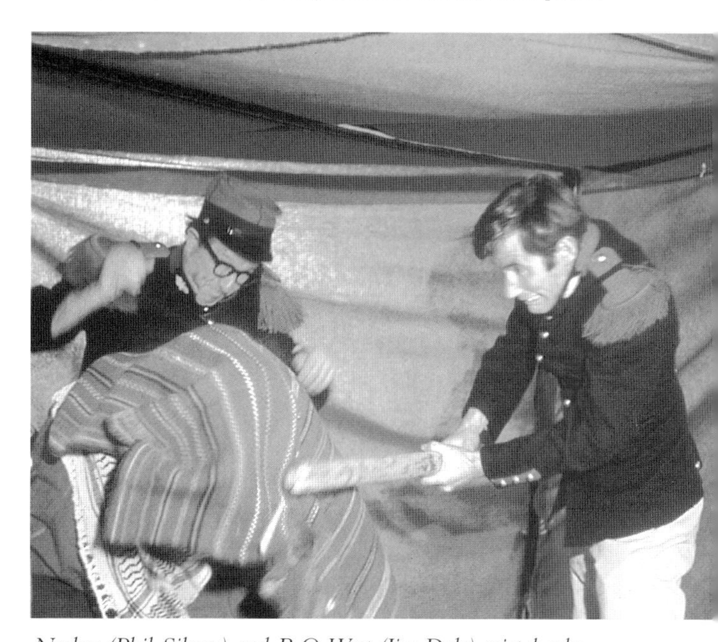

Nocker (Phil Silvers) and B.O. West (Jim Dale) mistakenly attack Simpson (Peter Butterworth) in this excised sequence from Follow That Camel *(1967).*

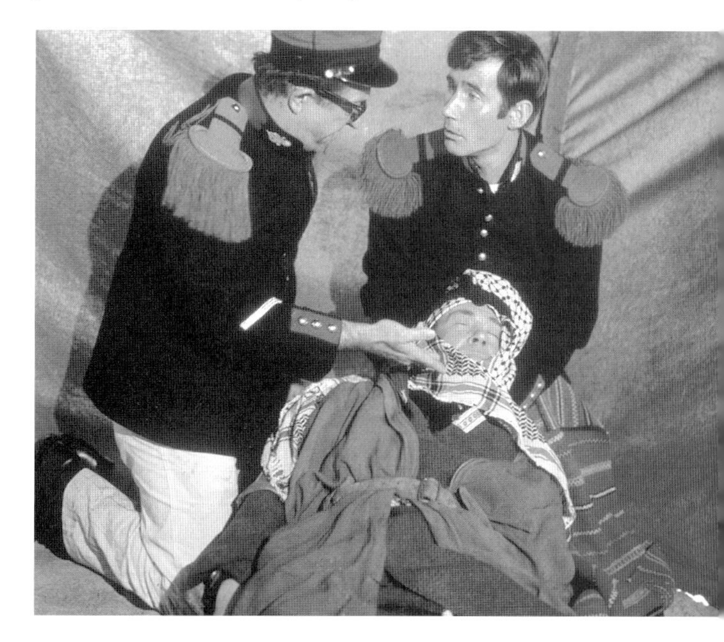

SCENE 155: EXTERIOR. FORT COMPOUND. DAY

The Fort is of familiar construction. A square affair with high walls surrounding the compound and buildings. Steps leading up to firing platform around inside of walls. Double gates, now open, below the firing platform. We are shooting from the Compound through the open doors as the Relief Force staggers in and heads straight for the big open water trough set against the buildings at the rear.

They all collapse into it, head-first.

The Boys, as their thirst's quenched, turn from the trough and look around.

PANNING SHOT, as from their POINT OF VIEW. Dead Legionnaires litter the firing embrasures, firing platform, steps, and even the Compound. One nearby corpse is obviously an Officer.

The Boys take in the awful sight.

Then, after a stunned silence...

Bo: Are we too late?

Burger: I cannot say. What day is it?

Nocker: (Consults diary) The day the third crescent of the moon enters the fourth phase of Orion.

Burger: What?

Nocker: Wednesday!

Burger: Oh. Yes, we are too late. Poor devils!

He goes to the Officer, lying with pistol still in his hand. Nocker joins him and looks at the face-down officer.

Nocker: Who was it?

Burger: The Commander...Capitaine Charles Derrière

Nocker: Oh of course. Old rear-end Charlie.

Burger: Look after them, Sergeant.

Nocker: Yes, sir!

QUICK DISSOLVE TO:

SCENE 156: EXTERIOR. THE FORT. DAY

CAMERA SLOW PANS along eighteen mounds of sand close to wall of Fort. They have rifles upended in them, or wooden crosses. At the end, BO, Clotski are heaping the last shovelfuls of sand onto the last mound, under Nocker's supervision. The job is finished and he goes up to Burger, who stands silently nearby.

Nocker: That's the lot, sir. Seventeen.

Burger: Do the last honours, please Sergeant.

Nocker produces a little book from his pocket and takes up a position near the last mound. He takes his kepi off and the others follow suit and bow their heads. It is a solemn moment.

Nocker: (Gravely) We who survive to fight another day pay the last honour to our gallant comrades who have fallen on the field of battle with the time-honoured salute of the glorious French Foreign Legion...(Opens book and reads) Nous sommes tout droit, Jacques! (Slams book shut) Okay, let's get some grub.

Burger: One moment, Sergeant.! You said seventeen dead.

Nocker: That's right, sir.

Burger: There are eighteen graves here!

Nocker: Oh, we must have dug one too many, sir.

With which the one from last mound stirs and Simpson's fed-up face appears from the sand. In a tired voice...

Simpson (Peter Butterworth) finds himself up to his neck in it in Follow That Camel *(1967).*

Fort and lost – Burger (Kenneth Williams) and Nocker (Phil Silvers) count the cost of battle in Follow That Camel *(1967).*

Simpson: I've been trying to tell you that for the last half hour!

QUICK DISSOLVE TO:

SCENE 157: EXTERIOR. THE FORT. NIGHT.

Picturesque shot of the Fort in moonlight. Suddenly we hear Arab-style music – strings and pipes start up and VOICES raised in a weird chanting.

SCENE 158: EXTERIOR. FIRING PLATFORM. FORT. NIGHT.

The BOYS are all at the embrasures, listening to the music which sounds more distant from here.

Simpson: It's coming from over there, behind the dunes!

Burger: The Riffs!

Nocker: How about that! The whole garrison wiped out and they give us selections from the Desert Song!

Burger: Nein, I have heard this sort of music before. It is for a wedding celebration!

BO: Oh, is that all.

Burger: Ja. It means that the chief is taking another wife.

BO: And good luck to him! He's got twelve already and...another wife! Number thirteen! Jane! Oh no!

Simpson: Don't panic, sir, it may not be too late. (To Burger) Is it...is it...A Before of After Celebration?

Burger: Before. The song is to wish the Chief an abundant harvest. It is called the Song of the Oats.

BO: My god, let's hurry before he gets his plough out!

Carry On Jack 1964

Scriptwriter: Talbot Rothwell
Producer: Peter Rogers
Director: Gerald Thomas
Production started: 2 September 1963

Bumbling midshipman Albert Poop-Decker (Bernard Cribbins) is assigned to the ship of Captain Fearless (Kenneth Williams) but is press-ganged aboard before he can report for duty. Fellow press-gang recruit Walter Sweetley (Charles Hawtrey) seems to be his only ally as his high position has been taken by Sally (Juliet Mills), disguised as a man and on the look-out for her childhood sweetheart, pirate Roger (Peter Gilmore). The Spanish Armada acts as the historical backdrop for all the low-jinks on the high-seas.

The plot so far: Incompetent Captain Fearless (Kenneth Williams) has foolishly welcomed a pirate ship alongside his vessel and seen his crew overrun by cut-throats. Adrift in an open boat with Albert (Bernard Cribbins), Walter (Charles Hawtrey), Sally (Juliet Mills) and a cow, the hunger rages, minds drift and the conversation gets surreal. Only remnants of this lengthy script made the final print of the film but here, reproduced for the very first time, is the unedited and very funny sequence.

SCENE 86: EXTERIOR. THE OPEN BOAT. DAY.

FEARLESS has his leg up on a thwart and it is fairly heavily-bandaged now. Albert turns away from the cow. His voice is tense and carefully controlled.

Albert: There's...there's no more milk, sir.

A moment's silence while the drama sinks in.

Fearless: No more milk? There must be. You're just trying to frighten us. You're not pulling the right things.

Albert: (equally hysterically) I tell you it's empty, empty. When I pull, it just goes "ooh"!

Hapless mariners (left to right): Bernard Cribbins, Juliet Mills, Charles Hawtrey and Kenneth Williams in Carry On Jack *(1964).*

Fearless: It's holding it back, that's what it's doing. It's deliberately holding it back for itself!

Sally: Steady sir. Don't you see why? It's had no fodder.

Fearless: I don't care if it had no mother. I want my milk.

Sally: Pull yourself together, sir.

Fearless: How many days have we been afloat now?

Sally consults the inside of the boat where marks on the wood indicate days. There are six strokes.

Sally: Six.

Fearless: Six. And no sign of land. What are we going to live on? What are we going to eat?

Walter: I've got a ship's biscuit.

Fearless: (In ecstasy) A ship's biscuit! How delicious! Well, where is it? Get it out, man.

Walter takes off his seaboot and puts his hand inside. We see that there is a darned great hole in the sole. He brings out the flat square biscuit.

Walter: They're better than cardboard, you know.

He sees them looking at it distastefully, and offers it to Fearless.

Walter: Don't you want it?

Fearless: No, thank you. You have it.

Walter: What, after where it's been? No, thanks.

He chucks it over the side. They slump into dejection. Sally looks over at Albert anxiously.

Sally: Albert?

Albert: Yes?

Sally makes strange signs and gestures to Albert who doesn't understand what she is getting at. She repeats them and still he doesn't understand. She goes over to him and whispers.

Albert: How?

Sally: It doesn't matter how. I wasn't born yesterday.

Albert: Neither was I, but...there isn't a place. It's too open.

Sally: All you have to do is create a distraction.

Albert: You'd be doing that.

Sally: Oh, stop arguing and hurry.

(Top and bottom) The castaways bemoan their fate in this scene, heavily edited for the final print of Carry On Jack *(1964).*

Albert: But...all right...I...

He suddenly turns to the bow shouting...

Albert: A sail! A sail!

Walter and Fearless both crowd up to the bow while Sally backs away out of the picture.

Walter & Fearless: Where? Where? Etc.

Albert: There. Over There. Look. A big one with two masts and white sails with black crosses on...and it's painted yellow.

Fearless: I can't see anything.

Albert: Yes, you can see a man standing on the quarter deck. He's a Chinaman, you can see his whiskers, hanging down, and...and...

Sally comes up behind him, taps him on the shoulder and gives him an "okay" sign.

Albert: Oh, no. Sorry, it was just a seagull.

FEARLESS and WALTER give him very funny looks.

DISSOLVE

SCENE 87: EXTERIOR. SKY. DAY.

A shot of the full sun blazing down out of a cloudless sky.

DISSOLVE

SCENE 88: EXTERIOR. OPEN BOAT. DAY.

There are now fifteen strokes on the woodwork. They are all sprawled out weakly, even the cow. There are weak murmurs of "Food...food...food..." Suddenly we hear the buzzing of a fly. Albert's eyes open and follow the flight of the fly.

Albert: Food! Food!

The flight and buzzing stops. Albert keeps his eyes riveted on the spot, the fly has settled on Fearless' bandaged foot. He reaches for an oar, stealthily gets to his feet, and brings the oar down with a great whack on the foot. There is a howl of anguish from Fearless. Albert grovels about the floor of the boat.

Albert: Missed it! I missed it! A great big fat juicy fly. Nothing to beat 'em done slowly over a candle. With a touch of the Hollandaise!

Sally: Albert! Albert, control yourself!

Albert comes out of his frenzy.

Albert: I'm sorry, but I can't stand this much longer. It's driving me insane. D'you hear? I just can't stand it.

Walter: You know what your trouble is, don't you?

Albert: What?

Walter: You're hungry.

Albert: Aah! Where's that oar? I'll murder him!

He goes to clobber Walter with the oar, but Sally stops him.

Sally: No! (To Fearless) Sir, we can't go on like this. We've got to have food.

Fearless: There's only one thing I can think of. Captain Coe's epic voyage in an open boat...seventy-three days...six of them set out...only three got home.

Albert: What did they live on?

Fearless: The three that didn't.

They all look at one another as his meaning sinks in. Finally Sally puts it into words.

Sally: How do we decide which one is to be first?

Albert: We'll draw for it.

He brings out a packet of playing cards and shuffles them.

Walter: (Sudden brainwave) Just a minute, what about the cow?

Albert: (After dramatic pause) I'll draw for her.

Fearless: Oh, no, you don't.

Albert: Why not?

Fearless: Don't you dare touch a hide of her hair – hair of her hide. She's mine. She's a pet, she's not for eating.

Albert: But we're all starving.

Fearless: So am I. So is the cow. Besides, I'm a vegetarian.

Walter: Since when?

Fearless: I always have been.

Sally: I saw you gnawing on a bone only the other day.

Fearless: That was for my teeth, to keep them white and sharp. It's very good for them you know. Once a week I go to the galley and get a great big shinbone and gnaw on it. Mind you, I scrape all the meat off first, all the fat and gristle.

Walter: Stop! I can't stand it.

Albert: (To Walter) Give me your knife, Walter.

Walter hands Albert his knife. Fearless jumps up and starts grappling with Albert.

Water, water everywhere . . .castaway crew (left to right): Walter (Charles Hawtrey), Captain Fearless (Kenneth Williams), Albert (Bernard Cribbins) and Sally (Juliet Mills).

Fearless: No, no, I forbid it.

Albert: Out of my way, sir.

Fearless: Kill me first! Kill me and eat me! Eat me! Look, I'm succulent and tasty.

Albert: You're a nit.

Fearless: I've never...

Sally: Oh Albert! You mustn't talk to the Captain like that.

Albert: I'm sorry, Captain, but you're a nit and I'm going to carve a chunk off that cow.

Fearless: No, no, carve a chunk off me. Look, look at the poor defenceless thing's face. How could you harm a poor mute beasts?

Albert: Easily!

Fearless: I don't believe it. I don't believe that a fine upstanding young man like you, brought up in the comfort of a good home, protected by a fond, devoted mother...

Albert: (Weakening) Keep my mother out of this.

Walter: Don't let him wear you down, Albert.

Albert: I won't. Out of my way

He pushes Fearless aside and strides towards the cow, followed eagerly by Walter and Sally. Albert stops, uncertain what to do next.

Walter: I bags the hoof. Cow heel, lovely. Go on, Albert. What are you waiting for?

Albert: I can't do it.

Walter: What? Why not?

Albert: She really does remind me of my mother. Soft and gentle and harmless.

Walter: Here! Give that knife to me.

Albert: No.

They struggle. The knife drops to the floor.

Walter: Pick it up, Sally. Pick it up.

Sally picks it up but as Walter comes towards her, she drops it over the side and it sinks.

Walter: What did you want to do that for?

Sally: Albert is right.

Walter collapses in tears. Fearless embraces Albert.

Fearless: Well done, Albert. I knew you had it in you.

Albert: That's the trouble. I've got nothing in me. I'm starving.

He also collapses in tears. Sally comforts him and is soon crying herself. Fearless goes to the cow and sobs on its neck.

Carry On... Up the Khyber 1968

Scriptwriter: Talbot Rothwell
Producer: Peter Rogers
Director: Gerald Thomas
Production started: 8 April 1968

India 1895: The natives are revolting and the imperial British ruling classes are none too pretty either! Sir Sidney Ruff-Diamond (Sidney James) and his good lady wife, Joan (Joan Sims) are in charge of the British concern much to the turbaned chagrin of the Khasi of Kalabar (Kenneth Williams). With his army headed by the "beautiful warrior" Bungdit Din (Bernard Bresslaw) a plot is hatched to over-throw the British. Blackmail, corruption, jealously and underpants all inform the plot, while the final attack on the British embassy merely highlights the stiffness of the stiff-upper lips of Ruff-Diamond and his men.

The plot so far: The alternative title for the film, *The British Position in India*, is revealed as an even funnier, more risqué joke within the pages of Rothwell's original script. The title reads: 'Carry On... Up the Khyber. A Sikh-making Saga of the North-West Frontier Dramatized from the best-selling Book "The Handyman's Kama Sutra" otherwise known as "The British Position in India."' So now you know! Within the narrative, Private Jimmy Widdle (Charles Hawtrey) has been approached by the Indian Burpa Bungdit Din (Bernard Bresslaw). Dropping in a dead faint, the warrior lifts up the Private's kilt and reveals a pair of woollen underpants, an item of clothing forbidden to the dreaded 'devils in skirts'. Bunghit Din dutifully takes this item of clothing to his leader, the Khasi (Kenneth Williams) and victory in the Indian struggle against British supremacy is within his grasp. His naïve daughter, Jelhi (Angela Douglas) fails to understand the importance of the underpants but in this scene, remnants of which remain in the finished film, the Khasi explains.

SCENE 11: INTERIOR. AUDIENCE ROOM, KHASI'S PALACE. DAY.

This (as we shall presently see) is a huge magnificently decorated and furnished room.

We start with a CLOSE SHOT of a pair of near-knee-length plain woollen pants, lying on an ivory inlaid table. CAMERA TRACKS BACK to show the Khasi looking down at them wonderingly. Beside him, his daughter Jelhi. In front of the table, smiling excitedly, Bungdit Din.

Sidney James posing on the adjacent Pinewood set of Chitty Chitty Bang Bang, *with (left) Barbara Evans and (right) Wanda Ventham during the making of* Carry On . . .Up the Khyber.

Khasi: You speak truly? The Devil actually wore this garment beneath his skirts?

Bungdit: I swear it, Highness! Did I not remove it with my own hands?

The Khasi permits himself a little smile of triumph.

Khasi: You did well, Bungdit Din.

Bungdit: (Modestly) It was not difficult, Highness. It was only held up by elastic.

Khasi: Fool, I mean you did well to discover it. For many many years, we have been led to believe that the Devils wore nothing below their skirts and have feared them according. But now...(Chuckles nastily)

Jelhi: I do not understand, O my father. What is this thing?

Khasi: It is a form of breechclout, Light of my Darkness, which the British call a pair of drawers.

Jelhi: A pair of drawers? But there is only one of them.

Khasi: Who can understand the absurd language of the British? They refer to this one thing as a pair, yet call something which is obviously a pair, a bosom.

Jelhi: But, even so, why should we fear men who wear nothing below their skirts?

Khasi: My child, you have not made war. But think how frightening it would be to have such a man charging towards you, his skirts flying high, flashing his bayonet...!

And he shudders at the picture he has conjured up.

Bungdit: It is true. But who could be afraid of men who wear such a ridiculous thing as this?

Khasi: Precisely. When our people learn of this, they will rise up and drive the British out of Kalabar.

Bungdit: (Holding up drawers) This will be our talisman! With the help of this we will win!

Khasi: Would that we had more like this. Seven more.

Bungdit: Why seven more?

Khasi: There is a wise saying I learnt at Oxford. With eight drawers you cannot lose.

(Top and bottom) The Khasi of Kalabar (Kenneth Williams) 'draws' on his experience when explaining the tradition of the 'devils in skirts'.

The plot so far: With wind of the news that the Khasi (Kenneth Williams) holds an offending and potentially damaging pair of underpants from the British, the governor Sir Sidney Ruff-Diamond (Sidney James) and two of his officers, Captain Keene (Roy Castle) and Sergeant-Major MacNutt (Terry Scott), journey to the Indian palace. En route the British party have some problems with an elephant boy and the eccentric Fakir (Cardew Robinson).

SCENE 19: EXTERIOR. PALACE ENTRANCE. DAY.

Section of high wall and ornate entrance gates. There is the familiar English-type house nameplate: BIDE-A-WEE. CAMERA PANS DOWN "STREET" to pick up approach of elephant and Howdah.

The Howdah has curtains but is open at the sides so that we can see Sidney, in full ambassadorial get-up (including the plumed hat), Keene, and MacNutt sitting in it.

The elephant stops at a drinking trough set against wall and puts its trunk in. The Elephant driver gets down from the Howdah, as Sidney draws aside front curtains and calls impatiently.

Sidney: What's going on? Why have we stopped. We're not there yet!

And the end of trunk curls up into shot and gives him a damn good hosing, right in the face.

Keene: Good gad! I say, sir, are you all right?

Sidney: That damned elephant boy! (shouting down) I'll have your licence for this!

MacNutt: You! Get this elephant moving, do you hear?

Sidney: Never mind! We'll walk the rest of the way.

He tries to wring out his dripping plumes.

SCENE 20: INTERIOR. AUDIENCE ROOM, KHASI'S PALACE. DAY.

An absolutely magnificent room. The Khasi sits at one end, with Jelhi beside him. Draped artistically around are a number of his "wives", looking beautiful in their saris.

Bungdit Din hurries in and bows to the Khasi.

Bungdit: Highness, the Governor is on his way.

Khasi: (Smiling) Ah, I thought it would not be long before he came.

He signals to the women.

Khasi: Return to your quarters, O warmers of my feet.

As they get up and start filing out...he turns to JELHI.

Khasi: Not you, Light of my Darkness. I would like you to witness the discomfiture of the British pigs.

Jelhi: Yes, Father.

One of the Women, a particularly lush piece, has lingered. Khasi turns to her.

Khasi: What is it?

Woman: Will I see you tonight, Master? It has been many moons since...

Khasi: Yes. Yes, perhaps I will be in need of a little relaxation after this. Go, and make ready the ludo board.

Woman: (Obviously disappointed) Yes, Master.

Khasi: (To Jehli) Poor things. They have to have a little fun now and again, you know.

SCENE 21: EXTERIOR. THE PALACE ENTRANCE. DAY.

As Sidney, Keene and MacNutt approach. Squatting against a wall close to the entrance, is an Indian Fakhir. He is sitting on a bed of nails, head well down, contemplating his navel. Beside him, a large snake basket and music pipe.

Sidney comes to a stop near him.

Sidney: Wait a minute, let's see what we can find out from this Fakir. They have strange powers, you know.

He goes to the Fakir, prods him with his foot, and speaks in Indian to the effect. . .

Sidney: You! Fakir! Wake up!

The Fakhir looks up.

Fakir: (In English) Ooh, don't do that! Not when I'm contemplating my navel. Could have done me an injury, that could.

Sidney: (Surprised) You speak English!

Fakir: Of course I speak English. I'm an erasure.

Sidney: You mean Eurasian.

Fakir: No, erasure. My father was an Indian rubber planter. (Mad cackle of laughter)

Sidney: Oh, a half breed.

Fakir: Oh yes, they don't half breed.

Sidney: Listen to me, Fakir, and listen well. I wish to know what things are going to happen. Have you a crystal ball?

Fakir: No, thank you.

Sidney: For seeing things in?

Fakir: No, I gave that up. I couldn't see any future in it. (Laughs) But I can do it with the cards. Hang on a minute... (He reaches over and rummages in the basket) Cards...cards...got 'em here somewhere...

Snake's head comes out and he pushes it back down.

Fakir: No, not you, Mabel! She's so anxious, you know. (He exclaims, withdraws one hand quickly and sucks at a finger) Ooh, see that? She bit me! That's all the fangs I get! (Mad laugh) All the fangs I get...good? No, never mind.

Sidney: The cards, Fakir! I'm in a hurry.

Fakir: Yes, right...ah! Got 'em. (Brings pack of cards out) Here I have – ordinary pack of playing cards (They are circular) Nothing up my loincloth. Watch carefully. I throws them on the ground. So! (He does so. Examines them) Now what do they tell us? Let's see... Oh dear. Oh dear dear! Oh dear dear dear. That's terrible!

Sidney: What's terrible? What do they say?

Fakir: They say – much trouble coming! Guns banging! Soldiers dying! Death! Destruction! Havoc! Carnage! (Hand out) Ten rupees!

Sidney throws some money down.

Sidney: Oh, come on. I've heard enough from this miserable Fakir.

And he leads the others off through the entrance gates. Fakir gathers up the coins, with an exclamation of satisfaction, then pulls what looks like a pig's ear from his loincloth, puts the coins in, and laughs.

Fakir (Cardew Robinson) does a turn for Sir Sidney (Sidney James), Captain Keene (Roy Castle) and Sgt Major McKnutt (Terry Scott) in a historic missing scene.

Fakir: Who says you can't make a purse out of a sow's ear? (And tucks it away again) Right. Back to the contemplation. Where was I? Oh yes, the navel!

He tries to settle down on his bed of nails again and wriggles uncomfortably.

Fakir: I don't know what it is, but I just can't get comfortable on this thing today.

He gets off and examines it.

Fakir: Well no wonder! There's a nail missing!

The plot so far: With the Indian rebellion beginning to boil, the British party Captain Keene (Roy Castle), MacNutt (Terry Scott), Widdle (Charles Hawtrey) and missionary Belcher (Peter Butterworth) don tribesmen disguises and attempt to gain entrance to the Khasi's palace. Before being mistaken for the Burpa leaders and shown a good time in the harem, the men stumble across the manic Fakir (Cardew Robinson).

SCENE 53: EXTERIOR. MEETING PLACE. DAY.

MID-SHOT, as Keene comes around the corner of the building into the area in front. He look for the others, sees the three bearded Burpas squatting against wall, crosses to them, squats and starts talking...

Keene: Well, I've been all round and there's no other way in. So we'll have to trick our way in. Are you listening?

He becomes aware that they are regarding him rather strangely. He tries to peer through their whiskers, then reaches up and tentatively pulls at one of the beards. The Burpa exclaims in pain. Keene scrambles to his feet and backs away, apologetically.

Keene: I say, terribly sorry. Thought you were someone else...

He looks round for his party. At which point we hear a familiar cackling laugh. He looks in that direction. LONG SHOT as Belcher, MacNutt and Widdle are standing with their backs to him, watching something with interest.

They are watching the Fakir, standing at one end of a bed of hot coals.

Fakir: Now watch this trick carefully! Red hot coals – bare feet! Bare feet – red hot coals! Right! On the magic word Alioompah, I shall walk across the coals. Here we go then. Ali...what was the word?

Belcher: Oompah!

Fakir: Oh yes. Alioompah!

And starts walking across the coals, laughing insanely all the while.

MacNutt: What's so funny?

Fakir: It tickles.

Still cackling madly, he reaches end, and immediately starts hobbling.

Fakir: Ooh, these stones are hard.

He reaches his basket, sits down beside it and pulls of his joke plastic bare feet. He examines the soles critically.

Fakir: They could do with a re-tread!

And, chuckling, throws them into the basket. Belcher, MacNutt and Widdle gather round.

Fakir: And for my next trick...!

Belcher: Just a minute. Let me show you one.

Fakir: Eh? Are you a fakir?

Belcher: In my country I was such a big faker they wanted to make me Prime Minister!

He produces three playing cards

Belcher: Now watch carefully! Three cards! One lady! One lady! Three cards!

Throws cards down.

Belcher: Find the lady!

Fakir: Got it! That one!

Belcher: Ten rupees on it?

Fakir: Twenty!

Puts money down. Belcher turns the card over and as he does so palms the money. The card is the Lady.

Fakir: Got it! Wait a minute – where's my twenty rupees?

Belcher: Gone! That's the trick!

Fakir: Eh? Prime Minster? You should have been Chancellor of the Exchequer! All right, I'll show you one!

He starts rummaging in his snake basket.

An ordinary piece of rope. Where is it? Get out of the way, Mabel!

Exclaims and sucks at a finger again.

Ordinary piece of rope...must be in here

somewhere...ah!

Pulls out tail end of a large dummy snake.

Oh no, sorry Mabel.

Drops it back in, rummages again.

Ordinary piece of rope...aah, here we are!

Pulls out coil of thick rope.

Rope! Ordinary rope! Open at both ends.

Throws it down onto ground.

Now watch carefully. When I say the magic words the rope will rise into the air. No kidding! Straight up! Right! Here we go... (Utters some gibberish)

The rope just lies there. He gives it a prod with his foot.

Go on! Get up! What's the matter?

More gibberish. Keene comes up and beckons the others away. As they go out of picture...

Come on, rope! Its me, Frowsi. You've known me since you were a little piece of string! Come on now...!

He picks one end up, trying to start it on its way. As soon as he releases it, it falls to the ground again.

Ah get knotted! (Laugh) Hear that? Rope, get knotted!

Cackles insanely, looks round, stops laughing.

Where's everybody gone? (To rope)
You've let me down again! Now come on! Up! Up!

And as he continues coaxing the rope...

Keene and the others, by the entrance doors of the building.

Keene: There's no other way, chaps. We're going to have to try and force our way in!

MacNutt: (Tries the doors) We'll never force these doors, sir.

Keene: I know. That's where Mr Belcher comes in.

Belcher: You mean, this is where I go out!

Keene grabs him and holds him.

Keene: Mr Belcher, all you have to do is knock, ask to see the Khasi, and, as soon as the door opens we'll rush them.

We hear a scream of maniacal laughter and an excited shout from the Fakir.

Fakir: (Off) Got it!

Belcher: Ooh, frightened the life out of me!

They turn to look across at the Fakir.

LONG SHOT from their POINT OF VIEW, about twelve feet of the rope sticking straight up into the air and the Fakir clinging to it.

CLOSE SHOT Fakir clinging to the rope.

Fakir: How's that? Thought it was impossible, didn't you? (Laughs madly, then...) Wait a minute, how do I get down again? Help! Help!! Get me down!!

CLOSE SHOT Belcher. He raises his eyes to the heavens.

Belcher: Oh for heaven's sake, get him down, will you.

We hear a crash and a yell from the Fakir.

CLOSE SHOT Fakir, on the ground, all entangled in the fallen rope.

CLOSE SHOT Belcher, as he reacts.

Belcher: Blimey, it worked (Up to heavens again) That's all for the moment, thanks.

Chapter Four

A Weak-End Away!

The very ethos of saucy seaside postcards was a capturing of the freewheeling, carefree week or fortnight away from work, the city and mundane responsibilities. It was a world of kiss-me-quick hats, honeymoon couples, large ladies, fat chaps paddling in the sea and looking for their little Willie, and buxom blondes turning the head of every married man on the beach. In short, it was the blueprint for *Carry On* innuendo and there was little surprise when the series took a sideways glance at the British holiday. The very first *Carry On* trip came with the sixth film – *Carry On Cruising*. The first in colour and the last scripted by Norman Hudis, the film was based on an original idea by *Carry On* actor Eric Barker, who suggested a coach trip – an ideal notion for a *Carry On* comedy. The mode of transport was changed to an ocean liner and, hey presto, Sidney James was cast as Captain of the *SS Happy Wanderer*.

The notion of a coach trip…at least in the form of a day-trip to the films' spiritual home of Brighton, came in the 1971 classic *Carry On At Your Convenience*. The climatic orgy of pleasure on the Palace Pier saw the Donald McGill postcard come to life, with booze, birds, candy floss, helter-skelters, dodgem cars and manic rifle-range shooting dragging the ultimate collection of Brits out on the razzle – Sidney James, Kenneth Williams, Bernard Bresslaw, Charles Hawtrey et al. Perhaps the most celebrated *Carry On* holiday came at the very end of the 1960s when Barbara Windsor took part in that legendary exercise scene and lost her bra – and innocence – for all time. The film was, of course, *Carry On Camping* and while Kenneth Williams and Charles Hawtrey more than lived up to the title, lusty Sidney James and Bernard Bresslaw were all out for some bird-watching under canvas. The film has come to epitomise the cheeky, fun-packed pleasure that is *Carry On* and another saucy holiday was a natural choice for a following film. In 1972, *Carry On Abroad* took a satirical look at the British on the continental package holiday, with a half-finished hotel, incoherent staff, plenty of bed-hopping and copious amounts of drinking and cricket in a foreign field that would forever be Pinewood Studios car park!

The rich terrain of camping sites was revisited with the caravanning comedy *Carry On Behind* in 1975. Windsor Davies and Jack Douglas were the married men off on

A shocked Sadie Tomkins (Barbara Windsor) in Carry On Abroad *(1972).*

Bert Conway (Jimmy Logan) discovers that two and two don't appear to add up in Carry On Abroad *(1972).*

a fishing trip and hoping to land a couple of fresh dolly birds – Sherrie Hewson and Carol Hawkins – while archaeologist Kenneth Williams minced about the roman artefacts with international glamour puss, Elke Sommer in tow. However, perhaps the finest example of the series saluting the glories of the British holiday came a couple of years earlier, with the 25th film, *Carry On Girls*. Brighton may be pretending to be Furcombe-on-Sea, Sidney James may be looking a little tired and the jokes may be all from Talbot Rothwell's bottom draw, but the relentless parade of beauty queens, old queens and regal scenes marked a coming of age of *Carry On's* most important and enduring elements. Barbara Windsor, Angela Grant, Margaret Nolan and Valerie Leon provide the glamour, Bernard Bresslaw, Kenneth Connor and Peter Butterworth lust for England and Joan Sims is the ultimate hard-nosed, hard-done-by and hard-luck harridan.

There was certainly something magical about the *Carry Ons* on holiday. Whether in a tent, in a crumbling hotel or on the pebbled beach of England's premiere seaside resort, the gang could let their hair down and enjoy the pleasures of sex, beer and fish'n'chips...yes, it was an inviting place to be.

Carry On Camping 1969

Scriptwriter: Talbot Rothwell
Producer: Peter Rogers
Director: Gerald Thomas
Production started 7 October 1968

Sid Boggle (Sidney James) and Bernie Lugg (Bernard Bresslaw) decide to take their girlfriends (Joan Sims and Dilys Laye) on a camping holiday with a difference – they're planning a trip away to a nudist camp. On arrival, they discover they've been misled by the wily campsite owner Josh Fiddler (Peter Butterworth) and that everyone is fully clothed! If Sid and Bernie think they've got problems, wait until they meet Peter Potter (Terry Scott) and his nagging wife with a laugh like a horse backfiring (Betty Marsden); or Dr Kenneth Soper (Kenneth Williams) and his lusting Matron Miss Haggerd (Hattie Jacques), trying to stop their nubile finishing-school girls (led by Barbara Windsor) from being finished off.

The plot so far: A major strand for *Camping* was to be the blossoming of love for two of the characters Sally (Trisha Noble) and coach driver for the girls of the Finishing School, Jim Tanner (Julian Holloway). If the scenes proved popular, Trisha Noble was to become a new leading lady in the *Carry On* series. But the Australian singer and model was late for shooting on several occasions and had her role severely cut back. Here though are her missing scenes, as throughout the film and during several meetings, hate turns to love between young and not-so-innocent finishing-school girl Sally and the randy coach driver with a soft-heart, Jim.

SCENE 61: INTERIOR. HOSTEL CORRIDOR. NIGHT.

As Jim reaches the door numbered 17, look around to see if the coast is clear, and tentatively knocks at it.

Jim: Sally? Miss...? It's me, Jim Tanner. I'd like to explain. Sally? Can I?

Soper comes out of his next door room (16) in time to hear these last entreaties.

Soper: Tanner! What are you doing?

Jim jumps and turns guiltily.

Jim: Oh! I was just... I wanted to...

Soper: I'm quite sure you did. I know that these girls attend my school to be finished off but there are limits.

SCENE 88: EXTERIOR. THE HOSTEL. DAY.

The coach is outside and JimTanner is standing anxiously by the door of it, greeting some of the Girls as they come out and helping them up the steps. He keeps one anxious eye on the entrance to the Hostel, on the lookout for Sally.

Sally comes out, wearing a skirt. Jim goes to meet her shyly.

Jim: Oh good morning, can I help you?

He goes to take her case.

Sally: (Coldly) I can manage thank you.

Jim: No please, I insist.

He grabs clumsily at the bag, pulls at it and it flies open, spilling its contents onto the ground.

Sally gives an exclamation of annoyance.

Jim: Oh, I'm most terribly sorry...

In a fuss he kneels down and starts packing the things back in. Sally kneels down and tries to help, face like thunder. As Jim stuffs stuff back in...

Jim: I wanted to explain about last night...

Sally: You don't have to explain anything to me!

Jim: I mean, how Barbara's night-dress happened to come off like that...

Sally: I would rather not know, thank you.

Jim: All right. Only I didn't want you to think I made a habit of that sort of thing...

And he slams the lid of the case shut and snaps the catches.

Sally: I should hope not.

Stands up and goes quickly into the coach. But unfortunately Jim has packed the hem of her skirt into the case and it rips the skirt off, leaving her in a cute pair of panties. With a shriek of fury, she tears into the coach. Jim looks in dismay at the Girls looking out of the coach windows laughing at him.

Getting to grips with the part! Kenneth Williams during a break in production of Carry On Camping *(1969).*

SCENE 129: INTERIOR. LADIES ABLUTIONS. DAY.

Miss Haggerd and Joan smile triumphantly.

Haggerd: Well done! That'll teach him whoever it was!

Turns towards entrance and lets out a startled shriek.

SCENE 130: REVERSE SHOT:

A rather large and fierce-looking Ram has walked in through the open doorway.

The GIRLS start screaming.

SCENE 131: EXTERIOR. PARADISE. DAY.

Jim, just coming out of the coach, hears the screams and starts running towards the Ablutions Hut.

The Ladies' entrance, as Girls comes tearing out, shrieking, in all stages of undress, Joan amongst them. Miss Haggerd is one of the last and, as she comes out calling for "Doctor Soper" Jim runs up and catches hold of her.

Jim: What is it? What's happened?

Haggerd: In there! A mad goat! And poor Sally's trapped in a shower stall!

And runs on yelling for "Doctor Soper!"

Jim: Sally!

Fiddler runs up to Jim.

Fiddler: What's all the fuss?

Jim: She says there's a mad goat in there!

Fiddler: (Chuckles) Oh, don't mind 'er. That'll be my old Pansy. She's 'armless.

Jim: Really?

Fiddler: Ar, wouldn't hurt a fly wouldn't Pansy.

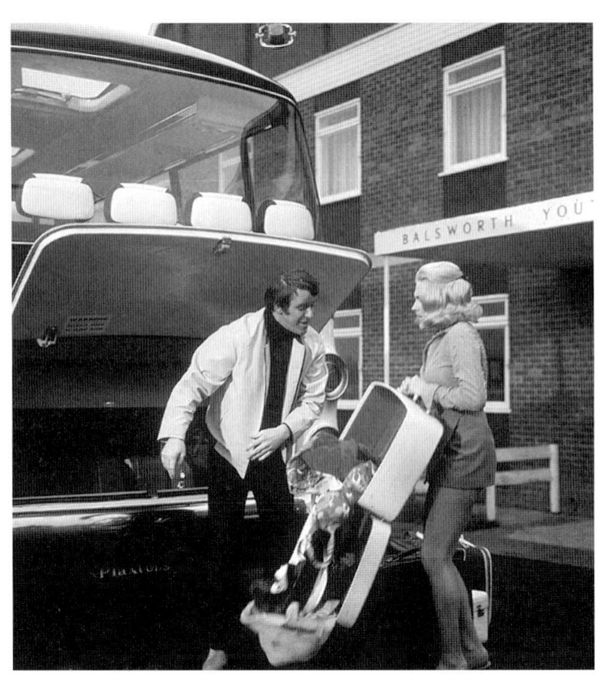

Jim Tanner (Julian Holloway) and Sally (Trisha Noble) struggle with a typical comedy suitcase…

Jim relieved, suddenly looks dead cunning.

Jim: Er, Mr Fiddler. I'd appreciate it if you kept that to yourself. About Pansy being harmless. Okay?

Fiddler: Can't see any reason why I should do that..

Jim produces a pound note.

Jim: You're not looking very hard.

Fiddler sees the note.

Fiddler: Oh.

Gives Jim a wink and pockets the note. Jim gives him a smile and runs over to the group of Campers gathered anxiously around facing the entrance to the Ladies' Ablutions.

Jim: (Dead serious) Keep calm everyone please! This needs careful handling! There's a girl trapped in there with a dangerous old ram!

Joan and Anthea in the group.

Joan: Where's Sid?

Jim: I'm going to try and get her out!

He turns and looks round for suitable weapons. There is an old kitchen chair against the hut and several bits of stick lying around.

He gets the chair and selects a suitable stick, then turns and faces the entrance, squares his shoulders, and enters like a lion tamer going into the lion's den.

SCENE 132: INTERIOR. LADIES' ABLUTIONS. DAY.

Sally is in one of the shower stalls, looking with frightened eyes at the ram standing in the room.

Jim enters and looks across at Sally appreciatively, forgetting his hero role momentarily.

Then suddenly remembering his role.

Jim: Don't worry. I'll get you out!

Sally: Be careful!

JIM faces the ram, using the chair and stick in approved animal trainer fashion. The Ram, just stands there, looking at him. Jim speaks sotto to the Ram.

Jim: It's all right, Pansy, I'm not going to hurt you.

And actually winks at the Ram.

The Ram just staring stolidly back.

Jim: All right, I'll hold him off while you get out!

... in the second of their scenes deleted from the final print of Carry On Camping *(1969).*

Sally: I can't! I haven't any clothes on!

Jim: Oh! Just a minute...

He sees bathrobe hanging and goes for it.

SCENE 133: EXTERIOR. ABLUTIONS. DAY.

To see the group of Campers watching tensely.

EXTERIOR. PARADISE. DAY.

Fiddler, still standing some distance from the hut, chuckling. He looks around and reacts.

As from his point of view to see a goat browsing in the field.

Fiddler: Oh there you are, Pansy. Oh dear, that must be old Garge's ram in there.

And he looks apprehensively towards the hut.

SCENE 134: INTERIOR. LADIES' ABLUTIONS. DAY.

Jim, back to Sally's shower stall, as she struggles into the wrap, holding off the ram.

Jim: Right! I'll see you to the door! Keep behind me!

Sally comes out, gets behind him, and he circles round until the door is behind her.

Jim: Right, get out now!

Sally: Aren't you coming?

Jim: No, I'm going to try and catch him. Far too dangerous to be left loose! Go on!

Sally darts out. (Probably better if there was no actual door. Just an opening with a partition set inside to avoid people being able to see in from outside.)

As soon as she has gone, Jim relaxes and gives the Ram a smile.

Jim: Thanks, Pansy.

The Ram, just staring back at him.

Jim: Now don't get nervous. I'm just going to make it look good.

And gives it another wink. He starts bashing the floor and walls with the stick, uttering hoarse cries, interspersed with...

Jim: No, you don't! Get back, you brute! Aaah! Etc.

SCENE 135: EXTERIOR. LADIES' ABLUTIONS. DAY.

To show Sally and the group of Campers, now joined by

Jim (Julian Holloway) proves his feelings for Sally (Trisha Noble) by fending off a seemingly placid ram . . .

an anxious Fiddler, watching tensely as the noises go on inside.

SCENE 136: INTERIOR. LADIES' ABLUTIONS. DAY.

Jim stops his dramatics and relaxes and smiles at the Ram.

Jim: That should be enough. All right, Pansy, we can go now.

He starts towards it, with the intention of getting hold of the broken end of rope hanging from its collar.

The Ram makes an aggressive movement, and paws at the ground.

JIM Comes to a stop. He looks a bit worried.

Jim: It's all right, I told you. I'm not going to hurt you, Pansy. But it's time...

Then looks downright apprehensive and starts backing up.

Jim: Now wait a minute! Don't...!

And turns frantically as we hear the rush of pounding hooves.

SCENE 137: EXTERIOR. LADIES' ABLUTIONS. DAY.

As we hear an anguished yell from JIM and a moment later he comes flying through the side wall of the hut.

SCENE 142: EXTERIOR. PARADISE CAMP. DAY.

Coach (or Minibus) as Sally runs up to it, looks around to see that she is unobserved, and quickly goes inside.

SCENE 143: INTERIOR. COACH. DAY.

Jim, with sticking plasters on his face, lying down on the make-up bed. He looks up as Sally comes in and struggles up.

Jim: Oh...it's you.

Sally: How are you?

Jim: Oh, all right. Haven't tried sitting down yet.

Sally: I wanted to thank you. You were wonderful this morning.

Jim: Oh no, it was nothing.

Sally: No, really, it was tremendously brave of you!

Jim: No please...I didn't...

Struggles with his conscience and then blurts it all out.

Jim: As a matter of fact, when I went in there I thought it was a tame goat. Pansy. So I cheated, you see.

Sally: It doesn't matter. You still saved me.

And, as he looks up incredulously, she impulsively gives him a kiss. Jim can hardly believe it. But before he can take any advantage of the opening, we hear Miss Haggerd's voice outside.

Haggerd: (Off) Right, into the coach, girls!

And she leads the Girls in, giving Jim and Sally a suspicious look.

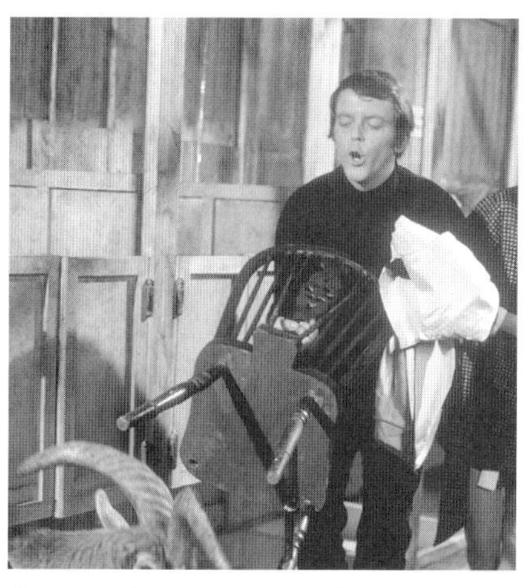

. . . and then discovering it is anything 'butt', in this missing scene from Carry On Camping *(1969).*

Haggerd: We're almost ready to leave, Mr Tanner!

SCENE 174: EXTERIOR. PARADISE. DAY.

Soper and Haggerd

Soper: Quickly! We must go after them, matron!

And he and Matron run off.

Jim, Bernie and Sid, looking stunned.

Sid: Did you see? They've got the girls?

Jim: All of them?

Sid: Every blinking one!

And Sally comes into shot beside Jim.

Sally: Not quite everyone.

Jim turns and sees her. They smile at each other and, as Jim slides his arm around her waist.....

Carry On Abroad 1972

Scriptwriter: Talbot Rothwell
Producer: Peter Rogers
Director: Gerald Thomas
Production started: 17 April 1972

A group of package holiday makers, led by incompetent tour operator rep Stuart Farquhar (Kenneth Williams) and his flirty assistant Moira (Gail Granger), arrive at the Mediterranean island of Elsbels, only to find their new hotel is so new it hasn't been finished yet. The hotel's manager Pepe (Peter Butterworth) and his explosive wife Floella (Hattie Jacques) attempt to look after their misfit visitors, including: cowardly husband Stanley Blunt (Kenneth Connor) and his frigid wife Evelyn (June Whitfield); girls who just want to have fun if only they could find a bit, Lily (Sally Geeson) and Marge (Carol Hawkins); boozing mummy's boy Mr Tuttle (Charles Hawtry), bickering pals Nicholas and Robin (David Kernan and John Clive), a group of Monks with some very odd habits, particularly Brothers Bernard and Martin (Bernard Bresslaw, Derek Francis); randy Scotsman Bert Conway (Jimmy Logan) trying his luck with husband-eater Sadie Tomkins (Barbara Windsor); and publican Vic Flange (Sidney James) who wants to pull more than pints if only his untrusting wife Cora (Joan Sims) wasn't around. Relationships start as rickety as the hotel's foundations, but as the holiday makers find themselves in all sorts of scrapes, including a night in jail, friendship and love win through. And the hotel falls down!

The plot so far: A group of misfit holiday makers have arrived at the offices of Wundatours Limited to board the coach that will take them to the airport where they will fly off to the holiday of their dreams – or rather nightmares. The following scene takes place on the aircraft, but was never actually filmed. Director Gerald Thomas seemed more than happy not going to the expense of building an airplane set and instead used general library film footage of an airplane in flight and then landing, to imply the trippers had made it to their destination.

Kenneth Williams and Barbara Windsor share a joke during the making of Carry On Abroad *(1972).*

SCENE 19: INTERIOR. THE AIRCRAFT. DAY.

All the Brothers of the Order are seated in a block down one side, and the "CIVILIANS" are in pairs down the other, with the exception of Sadie, who has a window-seat to herself.

Vic and Cora are in a seat up front. Cora sits rigid and tense, her eyes tight closed, her hands gripping the armrests.

Cora: Oh, I can't bear it! It's awful! I'm going to be sick!

Vic: Blimey, we haven't even left the ground yet!

Cora: Let me off! I want to get off!

Vic: Well you can't. Not now. Wait till we get up to ten thousand!

There is a sudden surge of power from the engines and Cora wails in concert with them and grips even harder.

SCENE 20: EXTERIOR. THE AIRPORT. DAY.

We see the aircraft take off and start climbing.

SCENE 21: INTERIOR. THE AIRCRAFT. DAY.

We see the "UNFASTEN BELTS" sign flash on.

Vic undoes his and turns to Cora, who still sits absolutely petrified.

Vic: It's all right, luv. Relax. We're up.

Cora: (Opens her eyes) Really? Oh, that wasn't at all bad.

Vic: Didn't I tell you? When you've flown as often as I have you don't even notice it.

Cora looks excitedly out of the window beside her.

Cora: Oh Vic, look! All the little villages down there.

Vic smiles and leans across her to look down.

SCENE 22: EXTERIOR. AERIAL SHOT. DAY.

As from the aircraft, looking down at the countryside. It starts to "bank" steeply as the aircraft turns.

Cora: (Over) Ooer, what's happening?

Vic: (Over) It's all right, we're only turning.

SCENE 23: INTERIOR. THE AIRCRAFT. DAY.

RESUME Vic and Cora. She is relaxed and smiling, but he is starting to look a bit queasy as his had "banks" with the scene below.

Vic: Nothing to worry about...it's just...just...

Shakes his head, grasps at his stomach, tears his eyes away form the window, pulls out a handkerchief, and struggles out of his seat.

Vic: Scuse me!

And tears down the gangway towards the Loo sign at the rear.

STUART and MOIRA are sitting together at the rear of the plane. He is busy with his papers, looking as worried as ever.

Stuart: I do hope this hotel is going to be all right. It's a new one, you know, and we're the first ones in there.

Moira: I'm sure it will, Mr Farquhar. And there has to be a first time for everything, you know.

The sexy implication of this is lost on Stuart.

Stuart: Maybe, but I don't like breaking fresh ground. It's always better if other people have tried it before you.

Moira: Oh good. Now I know we're going to get along well together.

Stuart reacts to this in some surprise....

Brother Martin and Brother Bernard. Martin, in the window seat, is the leader of the party. Bernard in the gangway seat is a rather hefty, awkward young man who is acutely aware of Marge and Lili, who are seated across the gangway from him. He keeps stealing shy but admiring looks at them as Martin pores over a textbook.

Martin: (Referring to book) I say, that's rather interesting, Brother Bernard.

Bernard: That's just what I was thinking.

He beams round at Martin and realises he is referring to something else.

Bernard: Oh, I beg your pardon, Brother Martin. What is?

Martin: There are directions here for finding the tomb of the founder of our order.

Bernard: (Unenthusiastic) Oh that's nice.

Martin: Yes indeed. "It is believed to be in the centre of the island, five miles north of the port of Elsbels, Santa Cecilia..."

He goes off into a mumble. At this moment, Marge's handbag slips off her lap onto the gangway floor, and BERNARD quickly bends to retrieve it for her.

Marge: Oh, thanks very much.

Bernard: It's a pleasure.

He is still smiling shyly across at Marge, when Martin speaks excitedly again.

Barbara Windsor, Kenneth Williams and Gail Grainger taking a happy stroll during a break from filming Carry On Abroad *(1972).*

Martin: You know, if we follow them, I think we might get somewhere!

Bernard looks back at him, shocked.

Bernard: Oh, do you think we should?

Martin: It's what we came for, isn't it?

Bernard: Is it? I thought we were going to look for our founder's tomb.

Martin: That's what I'm talking about!

Bernard: I'm sorry. I was thinking about something else...

Martin: (Sadly) Sometimes I feel your heart is not entirely in our mission, Brother Bernard.

And, as Bernard shrivels under the rebuke...

Stanley & Evelyn: She is in the window seat and he sits miserably slumped beside her.

Evelyn: I must say, I don't think much of the class of people they get on these holidays.

Stanley: Oh, they're not too bad, dear...

Evelyn: (Sighs) That's your great failing, Stanley. You've not got any taste at all. Anything will do as far as your concerned.

Stanley: Yes, I've been well aware of that since the day I married you, dear.

It is said quite mildly, and she completely misses the point.

Evelyn: Well, we'll just have to try and make the best of it, I suppose.

Stanley: That's what I said at the time.

Evelyn: Perhaps it will be better when we get to the hotel. You did make our requirements quite clear?

Stanley: Requirements?

Evelyn: About the rooms! They understand we must have separate ones?

Stanley: Oh yes, dear. I made quite certain of that!

At this moment the Hostess appears beside them with a tray of cups and saucers.

Hostess: Tea, sir?

Stanley: Oh, just for my wife, thanks.

The Hostess leans well over to pull out her little table, set cup and saucer on it and pour tea. Stanley's eyes bulge appreciatively at her plump charms. His eyes go to her bottom. He can't resist it. His hand sneaks around behind her and a moment later she straightens with a squawk and turns to glare at the person behind her across the gangway, which happens to be an inoffensive-looking Brother. As he looks at the Hostess with a benign smile, Evelyn glares across at him.

Evelyn: You should be ashamed of yourself!

As the Brother looks surprised and Stanley smiles to himself.....

Honeymooners at the rear, locked in each other's arms, nose to nose. The Groom reaches out, presses the button which puts the seats into a reclining position, then pulls a travelling rug right over their heads for more privacy.

Vic comes out of the Loo, looking slightly better. He comes level with the Honeymooners and comes to a stop watching the rug going through some amazing contortions. He tries to follow it with his eyes, shakes his head as nausea overcomes him again and bolts back to the Loo.

Bert and Tuttle, who has the window seat. Bert, bored, looks round as Tuttle gets out a magazine and opens it up. Then sits up, wide-eyed as he sees that it is a girlie mag, full of gorgeous nudes. He looks at Tuttle in surprise, then down at the double-page centre spread of a nude.

Bert: Very nice too!

Tuttle: I beg your pardon?

Bert: The bird.

Tuttle: Oh yes. She's a client of mine, you know.

Bert: Client? What business are you in then?

Tuttle: Oh, I'm a solicitor.

Bert: I'd 'ave thought she could've done her own soliciting.

Tuttle: Oh dear me no. Too tricky a case. She's suing the editor for perforation.

Bert: Perforation? You sure you don't mean penetration?

Tuttle: I mean perforation. They put a staple right through her navel. See?

As he indicates her navel at the centre of the crease of the double-spread.

Bert: Oh in the picture. Yes, I see now. Very tricky.

The HOSTESS appears with the tea tray.

Hostess: Will you take tea, sir?

Bert: Tea? You must be joking, darling. Bring me a large scotch.

Joan Sims as Cora Flange.

Sidney James as Vic Flange.

Tuttle: What a splendid idea. I'll have the same.

Vic emerges from the Loo, carefully shields his eyes from the travelling rug as he passes the Honeymooners, and goes back to his seat. Cora is drinking her tea quite happily.

Cora: Oh, feeling better now, dear?

Vic: What do you mean? There's nothing wrong with me!

Cora: I though you were feeling ill.

Vic: Ill? Me? Don't be daft! Never felt better!

The Hostees appears with a tray of sickly-looking teacakes.

Hostess: A cake, madam?

Cora: Oh yes please.

The Hostess bends over to let her make her pick, putting the tray right under poor Vic's nose.

Cora: Oh, you should have one of these, Vic. Full of the most gorgeous cream!

It is too much for Vic. He moans, puts his hanky to his mouth, and makes a bolt for it again.

Hostess: Oh, is your husband feeling ill?

Cora: Oh no. He's a very experienced air traveller, you know.

Vic passes the Honeymooners again. He comes to a stop, fascinated by further extraordinary movement. Reacts as he sees two pairs of feet appear out of the top of the rug, and tears into the Loo.

Robin and Nicholas sitting behind the Brothers' Party, across the gangway from the Honeymooners. Robin is watching them with disgust, Nicholas with interest.

Robin: Talk about kinky!

Nicholas: You know, I've never been out with a girl.

Robin: Oh, I have. Once

Nicholas: Go on? What was it like?

Robin: Oh all right, I suppose. But not a patch on the real thing.

Tuttle and Bert as the Hostess serves them with glasses, water, and a couple of miniatures of whisky. Bert reaches for the water as Tuttle lifts his glass.

Tuttle: Cheers.

And downs the lot in one go. Bert looks at him in surprise.

Tuttle: Very nice. I'll have some of that.

Bert: You want to go easy on that stuff, cocker. It's strong, you know. You want to put water with it.

Tuttle: Oh, I will next time. (Calling) Miss! Miss?

Sadie, in the seat in front of them, gets up to get something from the rack and gives Bert a good eyeful of her figure. As she sits down again...

Bert: Scuse me a minute.

He gets up and goes and slides into the vacant seat

Stuart Farquhar (Kenneth Williams) and Bert Conway (Jimmy Logan) prepare for their weekend away to Els Bels.

Eustace Tuttle (Charles Hawtrey) gets down to some serious sun worshipping as Lily (Sally Geeson) and Stanley Blunt (Kenneth Connor) look on.

beside Sadie, full of confidence. Sadie looks at him coolly.

Sadie: Oh, it's you again.

Bert: (Ingratiatingly) Just wanted to say sorry for spilling your suitcase, Miss...er?

Sadie: Tomkins. And it's Mrs.

Bert: (Taken aback) Oh. Where's Mister then?

Sadie: If you must know, I've just lost him.

Bert: That was a bit careless, wasn't it?

Sadie: He died.

Bert: (Cheering up) Really? Oh, that's too bad. An attractive young woman like you. I'm really sorry to hear that.

And to show how sorry he is, he slides an arm around her shoulders and pats her knee. Sadie is none too pleased.

Bert: How did it happen, darlin? Your husband, I mean?

Sadie: Oh. (Turning cunning) Well, if I tell you, will you promise to keep it to yourself?

Bert: Course, darlin, course.

Sadie: (Matter-of-factly) I killed him.

Bert: Oh well, that's...you what?

Sadie: I killed him.

Bert: (Not wanting to believe it) Go on...

Sadie: (Nods) Oh, it was an accident really. See, there was this rat poison, and it sort of got into his coffee somehow. Four teaspoonfuls. He always took four in his coffee.

Bert: (Removes his arm) You don't say.

Sadie: (Nods) But perhaps it was all for the best. I never really liked him. He was always trying to...well, touch me, if you know what I mean. And I can't bear being touched.

Bert quickly removes his hand.

Bert: Yes, I know exactly how you feel. (Getting up) Well...it's been nice having this little chat...

And makes his escape. Sadie stifles a laugh.

Bert slides into the seat beside Tuttle.

Bert: Blimey, where's that drink?

And sees that there are now a dozen more miniatures on the table.

Bert: What the...?

Tuttle: I thought it would save time.

Carry On Behind 1975

Scriptwriter: Dave Freeman
Producer: Peter Rogers
Director: Gerald Thomas
Production started: 10 March 1975

Arthur Upmore (Bernard Bresslaw) and Major Leep (Kenneth Connor) out for some bird-watching in Carry On Behind *(1975).*

Anna Vooshka (Elke Sommer) is a Russian archaeologist who has come to England to help Professor Roland Crump and his team of students with their excavations. Their digging takes them to a campsite during the height of the holiday season. The site employs penny-pinching handyman Henry Barnes (Peter Butterworth) and among the visitors are: frustrated husband and wife Arthur and Linda Upmore (Bernard Bresslaw and Patsy Rowlands) and Arthur's cantankerous mother-in-law, Daphne Barnes (Joan Sims) – who turns out to be Henry's long-lost wife – fishing friends, randy Fred Ramsden (Windsor Davies) and Ernie Brag (Jack Douglas); young couple with a great big dog that runs havoc with its bone; Joe and Norma Baxter (Ian Lavendar and Adrienne Posta); and the dirty-old man campsite owner Major Leep (Kenneth Connor). As the digging gets deeper so do Anna Vooshka's feelings for Roland Crump. Water springs erupt across the site and great holes appear in the ground taking caravans and campers into them. But love conquers all – the two Professors start to dig each other together and the Barnes are reunited.

The plot so far: Daphne Barnes (Joan Sims) has brought two precious possessions with her on holiday with her daughter and son-in-law – a cactus plant and her beloved Mynah bird. The bird – which has a habit of squawking out rude messages – has escaped after the Baxter's dog collided with the cage. The owner of the site, Major Leep (Kenneth Connor) – unaware of the dog's disappearance – is leading the search for the Mynah bird along with Daphne Barnes and the Upmores (Bernard Bresslaw and Patsy Rowlands.) Barnes (Peter Butterworth) meanwhile – unaware of the bird's disappearance – has struck a deal with the Baxters (Ian Lavendar and Adrienne Posta) and is now searching for their great Dane.

SCENE 104: EXTERIOR. EDGE OF WOODS. DAY.

Standing in a group are the Major, Arthur, Daphne and Linda. The Major is just finishing an apology to Daphne.

Major: In that case, I apologise

The Major and Daphne obviously like the look of each other.

Daphne: Oh that's quite all right, Major.

Major: And don't worry about the Mynah bird. I'll find him for you. I know every inch of these woods.

Raising his stick in farewell he strides off into the woods.

Daphne: He seems awfully nice.

Arthur: Yes, well he didn't clout your backside with a walking stick.

Arthur glares after the departing Major and rubs his backside.

SCENE 105: EXTERIOR. WOOD. DAY.

Barnes is walking through the woods carrying a piece of string. He whistles.

Barnes: Come on boy.

The Major comes into shot.

Major: You're looking for him as well are you?

Barnes: That's right.

Major: Well now, he should be round here

International star Elke Sommer prepares for 'action', as Anna Vooshka in Carry On Behind *(1975).*

somewhere. Unless of course he's gone up a tree.

Barnes: Gone up a tree?

Major: Yes, they're damned curious things you know.

The Major takes a hip flask from his pocket. Unscrews the cap and takes a quick swig. Barnes grins.

Major: Yes it was seen around here. Then it shouted "show us your knickers" and flew up a tree.

He takes another swig.

Barnes: I should lay off it a bit if I was you, sir.

Major: What!? What are you talking about?

Barnes: Well if you see dogs flying up trees...

Major: Dogs?

Barnes: You're telling me a great big dog shouted "show us your knickers" and flew up a tree.

The Major gives him a look of concern.

Major: Barnes! Have you been drinking?

Barnes wipes a grubby sleeve across his mouth.

Barnes: No Major, but I wouldn't mind a drop.

And he reaches out a tentative hand for the hip flask. The Major withdraws it hastily and puts it back in his pocket without screwing the cap on. They glare at each other, and then the Major reacts as he feels whisky from the open flask in his pocket.

He gingerly pulls the flask out sideways from his pocket and reacts in horror.

Major: (Screwing on cap) Damn you Barnes, now look what you've done.

Barnes: Well don't waste it...wring out your pockets.

Screenwriter: Talbot Rothwell

Carry On Girls 1973

Producer: Peter Rogers
Director: Gerald Thomas
Production started: 16 April 1973

Pulling the birds! Sidney James in a publicity stunt for Carry On Girls *(1973).*

Fircombe (pronounced 'Fir-coom') is a seaside resort in desperate need of visitors and events to attract them. The tired old local council is happy with the broken-down amusement arcades and a dodgy what-the-butler-saw machine. But new boy Sidney Fiddler (Sidney James) thinks he cracked it. A Beauty contest is what's called for to put Fircombe back on the map. Staunch feminist Augusta Prodworthy (June Whitfield) is against such an idea and, when it gets voted on in her absence, she vows to disrupt the event with every tool in her Women's Lib armoury. Among the contestants are Miss Easy Rider, Hope Springs (Barbara Windsor) and Miss Dairy Queen, Dawn Brakes (Margaret Nolan). Connie Philpotts (Joan Sims) runs the hotel at which the 'ladies' are staying. Sid's public relations pal Peter Potter (Bernard Bresslaw) is on hand to help with press 'uncoverage', and the whole mess is overseen by local Mayor Frederick Bumble (Kenneth Connor) with a capital Bum.

The plot so far: A committee of Fircombe council has gathered to discuss ways of improving the area's reputation to boost visitor numbers to the area. The meeting is chaired by the Mayor (Kenneth Connor) and among the members are local businessman Sidney Fiddler (Sidney James), Women's Libber Augusta Prodworthy (June Whitfield), and former mayor and now with one-foot-in-the-grave Alderman Pratt (Arnold Ridley). The meeting is underway and already tempers are flaring.

SCENE 3 (CONTD.): INTERIOR. COMMITTEE ROOM. DAY.

Fiddler: Oh blimey! Look, why don't we face facts? We're not attracting any visitors to the dump because there's nothing for them to bleedin' well do!

Augusta: We have nature's amenities. No one can deny that we have one of the most impressive beaches on the coast!

Fiddler: It's impressive all right. There's more tar on it than we have on the flippin' roads!

Augusta: It's hardly our fault if the passing shipping befouls our beaches.

Fiddler: No, and it's not our fault that all the dogs in the town do the same, but it happens!

Augusta: (Acidly) Of course we are all well aware that Mr Fiddler would like to see more people in that so-called Amusement Arcade of his, playing on those dreadful machines.

Fiddler: You're dead right! You know how much "What the Butler Saw" took last season? One pound sixty! That works out at about tuppence a grope.

Bumble: Yes yes yes, but I feel we are rather straying from the point here...

Fiddler: But it is the point. That's about the only indoor amusement there is. Apart from snogging under the bandstand.

Bumble: I think that Councillor Fiddler may have a point there. Particularly when one

Kenneth Connor, Marianne Stone and June Whitfield in a much-edited scene from Carry On Girls *(1973).*

considers our rather high seasonal rainfall figure.

Augusta: Really, Lord Mayor? Personally I think it's quite an average one.

Fiddler: If you think nine inches an average one, you've been spoilt!

Bumble: Yes yes, but as I was saying, there may be a case for providing more attractions, but I do feel it is important to preserve the dignity of the town.

With which Alderman Pratt comes to life.

Pratt: Bowls!

After the initial shock...

Bumble: I beg your pardon, Alderman?

Pratt: A Bowls Competition, that's what we want. It's all the rage these days.

Bumble: An excellent suggestion, Alderman. Excellent. If it weren't for the fact that we had no greens.

Pratt: What's that you say?

Bumble: We haven't any greens

But Pratt has already nodded off again.

Bumble: Oh dear. I fear Alderman Pratt is really getting past it. Has anyone else any bright suggestions we could consider?

Fiddler: Yes, I have.

Fiddler pauses for dramatic effect, then lets them have it.

Fiddler: Miss Fircombe!

They are puzzled and shocked by the pronunciation

Bumble: I beg your pardon?

Fiddler: Miss Fircombe! A Beauty Queen that's what we want. All the best resorts have 'em.

Augusta: I realise of course that Councillor Fiddler is a newcomer to the town, but I should point out that it is usually pronounced "Fircoom".

Fiddler: Not by most of our visitors, I can assure you! (Dirty laugh)

Sidney Fiddler (Sidney James) puts his point across as Alderman Pratt (Arnold Ridley) sleeps through the council proceedings.

Bumble: A Beauty Contest? Yes, that's a possibility, I suppose.

Augusta: What! Are you seriously proposing that we should have women parading around Fircombe half naked?

Fiddler: Oh! Why don't you fancy it?

Augusta: I think it's a disgusting idea, and I for one will have no part in it!

Fiddler: Pity. You'd look good in a bikini.

Augusta starts to pack up her papers.

Augusta: I think we've wasted quite enough time here today. I propose that you close the meeting, Your Worship.

Bumble: Oh, one moment please, Mrs Prodworthy. I do feel the proposal merits some discussion. I mean, if there's a way in which it could be handled with due propriety...

Augusta: Mr Mayor, you are well aware of my views on women's rights and there can never be anything proper in young women being shown off like cattle for the sexual gratification of a lot of drooling men!

Fiddler: Oh come on! I've never been turned on by cows in my life!

Bumble: Yes...well, if anyone else has any views to offer on a Beauty Contest?

And old Pratt comes to life again.

Pratt: We might be able to lay some of 'em!

Bumble: What?

Pratt: Bowling greens.

Fiddler: Oh blimey!

Pratt: It's not difficult. Just means getting hold of some sods...

Bumble: Yes yes, Alderman Pratt, but we are discussing Beauty Queens now!

Pratt: No good. You need sods...from Cumberland preferably...

And drops off again.

Bumble: Oh dear, he really will have to go.

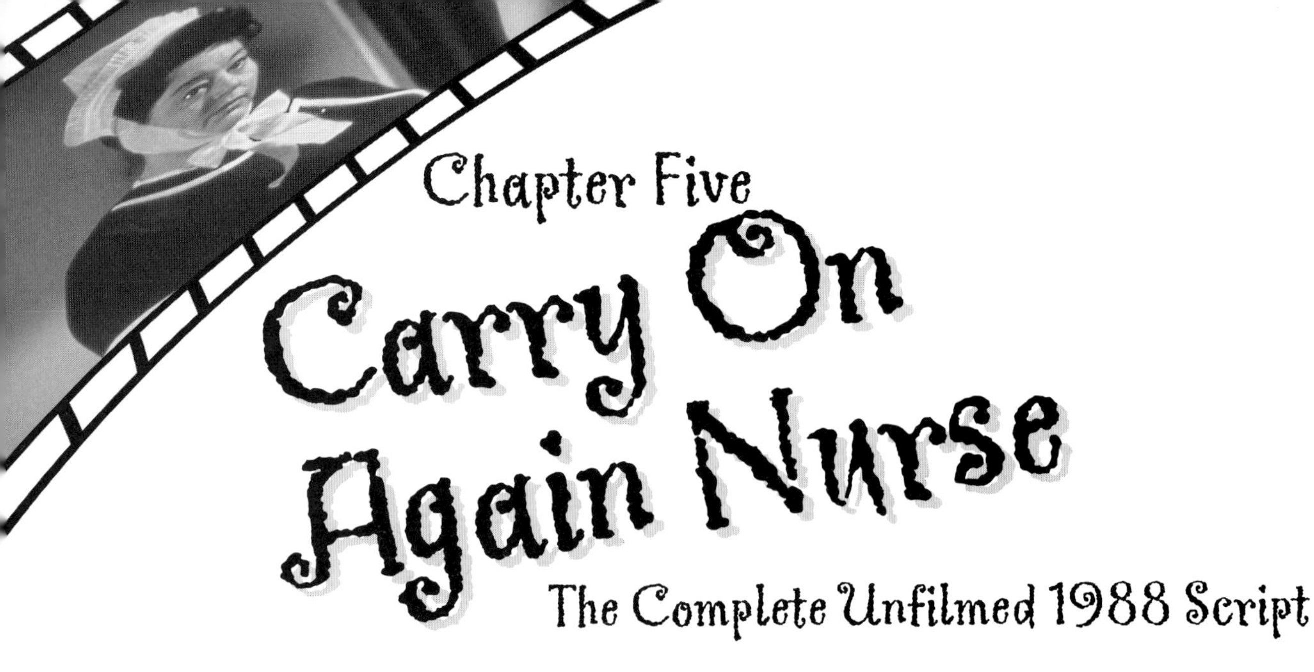

Chapter Five
Carry On Again Nurse
The Complete Unfilmed 1988 Script

Introduction by scriptwriter Norman Hudis

This is a story of a few Last Things.

The Last Thing I expected all those well-told years ago, was to be asked to take a crack at writing a comedy which became *Carry On Sergeant*.

The Last Thing I expected was for that inexpensive movie to be an historic hit, and that I'd write five more to spawn a series totalling more than thirty productions.

The Last Thing I expected when the phone rang at my Los Angeles home (just around the corner from O.J. Simpson), years and years and years later, was Peter Rogers to ask me to come back to England for a few weeks to write *Carry On Again Nurse*.

The details of the history of the first two Last Things are so well-worn by now, that they should have elbow-patches. Some reflections on the third, however, now that the script is being accorded the permanence of the printed page, may not come amiss.

On arrival, dizzy with jet-lag, I didn't even first go to the flat I'd rented in London. Straight from Heathrow, Peter and Gerald Thomas had me driven to 'The Bull' at Gerrards Cross for a hilarious reunion lunch, rendered the more raucous because I was hysterical with fatigue.

It was uncannily like old times in that, within 30 minutes, we'd agreed, as quickly as we did for all my *Carry Ons*, the premise of the script-to-be: a beloved old London hospital, threatened with closure by NHS cuts, is saved, mostly by the unconquerable combined British forces of sentiment and slapstick.

(Ahead of its time, that theme: only now, as this is penned, years later, are such NHS crises everyday issues.)

I scarcely needed to be told that the cast was, at its core, to be composed of the stalwarts, that unshakeable company of superb artists, born to Carry On. At that time, of course, they were – almost – all still available...

So, with familiar joy and gusto, I wrote again of Kenneth Williams as a surgeon; Joan Sims as the Sister recently become Matron (with the same name as she had as a student nurse in *Carry On Nurse*): Charles Hawtrey as the patient self-deluded that he is a brilliant author,

Dr Kilmore (Jim Dale) in a subtle reaction shot on first setting eyes on Nurse Sandra May (Barbara Windsor) in Carry On Doctor *(1968).*

unpublished because sabotaged by envious best-selling writers; Kenneth Connor as the larcenous Hospital Porter; and so on – including the abundantly adorable and near-legendary Hattie Jacques, to whom I gave the very final and deserved close-up – after her death (see script).

It was an unashamedly sentimental touch, but when were the *Carry Ons* (mine at any rate) ever anything else in their trademark "serious" scenes? Instinctively, I tried to prove, at least once in each script, that we had something to do with real existence, in which tears of laughter can be replaced, in an instant, by a lump in the throat. Life is a ruthless editor and can switch from one to the other, as we did, arbitrarily, in the space of a single cut from one mood to the contrasting next.

In this connection, especially interesting in the terms of this volume, there seems to be a straight firm line of consistency between two situations, one in the original *Nurse*, the other in *Again*. Though both contained their share of laughs, the sequences were firmly based in the realities of the tougher side of marriage. Gerry and Peter called them my "Mum and Dad" scenes.

In *Nurse*, the incapacitated Bill Owen (broken leg) is visited by wife Irene Handl, a lady so lugubrious, despite her doomed determination to be upbeat, as to psychologically put back his recovery by a month. But the love is still there.

In *Again*, a recently-divorced man, in hospital (curiously, also with a broken leg), receives a token visit from his ex. The bickering which led to their split, resumes, even in these circumstances. But the love is still there. I can't name the actors for these roles, for the dour and obvious reason that this film never got anywhere near the casting stage. If it had, this book would never have been dreamed of.

So what scuppered *Carry On Again Nurse*?

When the script was done, Gerry, who liked being read to, was the sole audience of the one reading-by-writer it ever received. All doubts were resolved. I found that I liked it almost as much as he, characteristically beaming, did.

When Peter, who did not like being read to, turned the last page, he called me to say "Well done. If this one isn't made it won't be your fault." Peter, of whom I have spoken at some length elsewhere (see his biography, by Ross and Bright), is essentially a reserved man, so these few words were the equivalent of a knighthood and are, to this distant day, still much valued.

Why, then, did *Carry On Again Nurse* not get filmed?

Too expensive, said those with the power to veto: at £1,500,000 estimated budget, too expensive for a film so essentially British. "Parochial", I believe, was the term employed. Compared with the budget of *Sergeant* and other early ones, and even taking inflation into account – yes, I suppose it might have been un peu pricey.

However (and there's nothing like fighting a lost battle, decades later...), the "essentially British" *Carry On Nurse* cleaned up, among other seemingly unlikely places, in New York, Chicago, and Los Angeles, where it ran for an unprecedented full year at one theatre.

Well, well. Were the money-men right? Perhaps. We'll never know now. But I am relieved for my contemporary colleagues that the same yardstick was not negatively applied to *Four Weddings and a Funeral*, *The Full Monty*, *The Long Good Friday* and other Brit flicks which somehow and very profitably overcame their parochialism when marooned on foreign shores.

Do not read these comments amiss. I have long since lost any taste I ever had for sour grapes. And who is exempt from error, especially under the glare of hindsight? Close-to-home-example: you are now reading the words of he who doubted that anyone would pay to see the umpteenth remake of *Titanic*.

As this book meticulously records, *Carry On Again Nurse* was not the only script or scene, in this elusive genre, never to reach the screen. In America, sometimes with my collaboration and/or advice, several attempts were made to transplant a British miracle in foreign soil. When I first went over there, CBS and Four Star, NBC and Bob Hope bid for me to create a hospital sitcom in *Carry On* style. I went with CBS/Four Star. The show was called *Oh Nurse!* (now there was a surprise.)

Later, David Lawrence sought my input on a syndication sitcom series called *T.H.E. Hospital*. MGM filmed a pilot (not mine) at a cost of $1,500,000. I don't doubt there have been many other US TV hospital-comedy projects inspired by the phenomenal pictures

Left to right: Peter Gilmore, Anita Harris and Jim Dale relax outside Maidenhead Town Hall on location for the exterior hospital sequences for Carry On Doctor *(1968).*
Above: Barbara Windsor in publicity pose as Susan Ball for Carry On Matron *(1972).*

from Pinewood. None has made it to an American series.

Why not? A good friend, the late writer Milton Gelman, offered this succinct reasoning: "Any comedy there may be in an American hospital is silenced when you get the bill." How bullseye-right and how much honest but misconceived effort might have been saved if this had been perceived earlier!

To elaborate: a medical comedy in *Carry On* vein rests on absolute basics: a social system of health-care which is not entirely privatised, and possesses the crucial custom of the Army-like camaraderie of the open ward as opposed to the rugged and introspective isolation of the private room. End of the *Carry On* medical-comedy outlook, as applied to America. It just doesn't take.

Example: I wrote for *Marcus Welby MD* for three seasons. To give it a new look we turned the milieu into a Family Practice. This was not liked: viewers voted with their remotes. Despite clear explanation that Welby had not joined the staff of a charity-style County Clinic, working under "socialised medicine", ratings dropped. They rose when he became a "regular doctor" again.

Well, anyway, and summarily dropping sociological debate: arising from Gelman's very acceptable analysis, I find I have to report on two more Last Things:

The fourth: I never expected rejections, in England and America, both to be based on money-values. In the one case, what we prepared was funny – until they did a budget. In the other – funny until they "got the bill."

An even more ironic tag? Certainly.

Much has been made of whether or not the *Carry On* actors were ever offered percentages of box-office profits. Of this, I know not. But, after six years under straight contract to Peter Rogers, and many years in America, he sweetened his offer to me, to write *Carry On Again Nurse*, over and above the writing-fee, with 5% of his profits.

Though the world of entertainment is shot through with loony inconsistencies, to which I should be accustomed by now, the fifth Last Thing I never expected was to be offered, with perfect Film Biz Logic, a percentage of a film that was never made...

Carry On Again Nurse 1988

Screenwriter: Norman Hudis
Producer: Peter Rogers

FADE IN:

TITLES

FADE OUT:

FADE IN:

EXTERIOR. LAW COURTS. DAY.

Establishing. Narrow down to sign:
ADMIRALTY, PROBATE AND DIVORCE
Narrow again to:
DIVORCE
Bill Unwin, walking sedately out of the building. He's young-ish, conventionally dressed, and in total emotional control. Suddenly, however, he screams:

Bill: I'm free!

In the incongruous celebration, he attempts an entrechat. We PAN with him and stay there. He descends and THUMPS down out of frame. We join him, sprawled helpless on the ground.

Bill: Ah ow oo my leg oo ow ah oh my leg etc., ad lib.

Sound of ambulance off screen.

EXTERIOR. MERCY STREET HOSPITAL. DAY.

Huge, sprawling, old: identified.

EXTERIOR. PUB. DAY.

Opposite hospital. Sign reads :
THE DOCTOR'S DILEMMA

INTERIOR. PUB. DAY.

Harry Drummond, 60-ish, wiry and a skiver, is conspiratorially in a cosy corner with Dan, roughly the same type. Harry wears the hospital porter's outfit. Harry gulps – but not beer. Staring at Dan, he's in shock.

Harry: Close dahn Mercy Street 'Ospital? Combine us with Monkton Avenue Medical Centre – that new glass and concrete monstrosity?

Dan: Close down your voice, will ya? I'm telling' you 'ighly-sensitive Regional 'Ospital Board policy-making stuff.

Harry: You're sure?

Dan: 'Ow long've I worked at the Regional 'Ospital Board?

Harry: Since the first cholera plague, I reckon.

Dan: 'Ave I ever been wrong?

Harry: No, Dan, you ain't. Nothing' you've ever told me 'as been unreliable about the Regional 'Ospital Board and the devious masturbations of its buroocracy.

Dan: Even when I told you they was investigatin' the local hincidence of that tropical disease yaws, remember?

Harry: No I don't. What's yaws?

Dan: I'll 'ave another pint, thanks.

Harry signals appropriately to Barman. Dan beckons Harry even closer. Wide-eyed, Harry gives him even more attention.

Dan: There is a ray of 'ope 'owever.

Harry: Thank Gawd.

Dan: The Regional Board *may* decide to close down the Monkton Avenue place. Instead of yours.

Harry: Don't sound likely. It's brand new and cost a fortune... yours.

Dan's new pint arrives. He raises his glass.

Dan: Your very good National 'Ealth.

INTERIOR. ACCIDENT AND EMERGENCY. DAY.

Bill lifted on to table with gorgeous Emergency Nurse in attendance.
Houseman, Charles Murray, briskly appears. Clean-cut, rather stuffy, likeable, he's a wholesome and essentially innocent youngster.

Charles: How did this happen?

Left to right: Sidney James, Joan Sims, producer Peter Rogers, director Gerald Thomas, Barbara Windsor, Charles Hawtrey, Kenneth Williams, Hattie Jacques and Jim Dale pose outside the Mansion House at Pinewood Studios during the making of Carry On Again Doctor *(1969).*

Bill: Well I'd just got divorced.

Charles: (Already starting prelim. exam.) I see...

Bill: Yes, that's right. I strained it celebrating...

Big reaction from Charles who gets entirely the wrong idea.

Bill: ... in the street.

Charles: You – did it in the street?!

Bill: Couldn't wait. Right outside the Divorce Court.

Charles: In broad daylight?

Bill: Well there isn't yet such a backlog of cases they divorce you in the middle of the night.

Charles: Who were you with?

Bill: No-one, doctor. I did it on my own.

Charles: On your own... in the street...?! (flabbergasted) Honestly – how anyone can toss off a remark like that... Hmm. Looks like this leg'll be out of action for a while.

Bill: (Eyeing Nurse) But everything else is working normally.

Charles tries not to look more disgusted than he already is and, anyway, is still overwhelmed by what he has just misinterpreted.

Charles: Did it in the street, well, I don't know... No shop doorway's safe these days, eh Nurse?

Nurse: I hope not, Doctor...

Grunting disapprovingly, Charles continues the exam...

EXTERIOR. PUB. DAY.

Harry walks slowly out of pub, preoccupied with his own thoughts. He crosses the road. A scream of brakes. Harry heart-clutchingly halts, a Rolls Royce within inches of him. It bears a DOCTOR label on windscreen. Harry yells:

Harry: What's-a-matter – ain't you got an 'orn?

Consultant Surgeon Sir Roderick Haddon looks out of car.

Sir R: Don't be ridiculous, Drummond – looking at you?

He drives on. Harry gulps, realising who he's yelled at, resumes across street.

EXTERIOR. MERCY STREET HOSPITAL. DAY.

Harry comes to entrance of hospital.

INTERIOR. ENTRANCE HALL. DAY.

INTERIOR. PORTER'S OFFICE. DAY.

Here sits Assistant Porter Ted Marley. Younger than Harry but not a moment less rascally. Harry sits, sags. Ted rises, moves to door. Shaking his head, Harry kicks it shut.

Ted: But 'Arry – it's my turn for a pint at the Emma.

Harry shakes his head again. Ted tenses.

Ted: Trouble?

(Harry nods)

They've – found us out?

(Harry shakes his head)

But – they could?

(Harry waggles one hand, meaning 'they could')

You don't mean – Sir Roderick?

Harry: At least we've been spared that – so far – what I've always 'ad nightmares about – Sir Roderick some 'ow creepin' up on us while we're like, you know, relievin' pressure on 'Orspital storage space.

Ted: You mean knockin' off stuff right and left from the Stores and floggin' it to Foxy the Fence in Finsbury.

Harry: Well, yes, if you must put it like that...

Ted: What I do put to you is this: if we 'aven't been found out – what makes you think we might be, all of a sudden?

Harry: Listen...

INTERIOR. SIR RODERICK'S ROOM. DAY.

Sir Roderick and Secretary in his room at the hospital. Secretary with notebook.

Sir R: That the lot?

Secretary: Yes, Sir Roderick.

Sir R: Good. I'll do my rounds. Don't forget to book me a table for lunch.

Secretary: I've done that, Sir Roderick.

Sir R: Good.

He goes out of the room. Secretary tidies his desk.

INTERIOR. PORTER'S OFFICE. DAY.

Panic – a staring, trembling and now informed Ted is shaking Harry by the lapels.

Ted: (hoarsely) We're knackered! Don't just stand there waiting to be measured for handcuffs. Can't you think of something?

Harry: Tell you what. I'll turn Queen's evidence – you go to gaol – I'll visit you with grapes.

Ted: You can't hide a file in a bunch of grapes. You... You don't mean that! 'Arry! Where's your Dunkirk spirit? You're always tellin' me about them days!

Harry: Dunkirk was different. All we 'ad to do there was get 'alf-a-million men orf a narrer beach while bein' bombed to Boulogne an' back.

Ted: You're right... 'Ere, we gotta put back into the 'Orspital Stores, two dozen beds, four thousand rolls of bum-paper and five gross of sheets.

Harry: Don't panic.

Ted: All right.

His knees give way. To save himself, he stretches out a hand, topples a tea-tray and contents. Harry helps him up.

Harry: Methodical. One item at a time. First, I'll scare up some sheets.

Ted: That should be easy. You look sheet-scared.

INTERIOR. WARD CORRIDOR. DAY.

The Ward is identified as MEN'S SURGICAL, WARD 4F. Entering, Sir Roderick is now seen to be elegant and urbane. A brilliant surgeon and a merciless teacher, he frequently becomes abstracted and is liable to plunge into the middle of a topic without telling his hearer what it is first. His attendant flock of Housemen includes Randolph Firkin, who is not called Randy for nothing, and Jim Vernon. Nurse Margot Walton, capable and attractive, waits to greet Sir Roderick and Company at the entrance from the Main Corridor.

Sir R: Good morning, whoever you are.

Margot: Nurse Walton, sir.

Sir R: Why aren't you a Sister? Am I to do my rounds without the usual Sister in quivering attendance? Where is the woman?

Margot: Having her car fixed, Sir Roderick. She won't be long.

Sir R: Women shouldn't drive, and her length is immaterial.

Margot begins to lead them towards the Ward doors.

INTERIOR. WARD. DAY.

Dave Beaton, early 20s, Cockney, physically unprepossesssing, with an intense, careful way of speaking, is in the second bed. Very worried, he's conferring with Cohen in first bed.

Cohen give Dave some spicy magazines.

Cohen: Try these magazines. Can't take them back to the wife, can I?

Dave: Well she brought 'em in for you.

Cohen: That's true. Do you think she's trying to tell me something?

Dave: Yeah – she's telling you to let your spare room to a Merchant Seaman... (Flicking through mags) I don't even know if these'll help – the way I feel... Oh Lor'. Here he comes.

He hides magazines under mattress. One falls to floor unnoticed.

Cohen: Why give yourself such aggravation over a simple symptom? Just ask him about it – straight out.

Jack Douglas makes his first, flamboyant appearance in the series with a gag role in Carry On Matron *(1972).*

Dave: Not about this. I can't. He's too posh.

Cohen: Posh-shmosh. By a doctor you're just a technical problem – like in any other trade. You could be a trouser-waist needs letting out – or a mini with your exhaust hanging down.

Dave: That's easy to say.

Cohen: So say it? Tell him: "Sir Roderick, I'm worried. This morning, the day after my op, I didn't wake up feeling sexy." Finish.

Dave: I just can't say that to him – just like that.

Cohen: Why not, Dave? You don't have to be circumspect.

Dave: Blimey, at my time of life, I hope not. It wouldn't half hurt.

Enter Sir R and Company. Margot hands Sir R Cohen's chart.

Sir R: Comfortable, Mr. Cohen?

Cohen: (Shrug) Thank you, making a living.

Sir R: You may go home today.

Cohen: Thank you very much, Sir Roderick. Any time I can sew anything for you...

Sir R nods politely, moves on to Dave who gulps, worried and indecisive. Sir R checks his chart, hands it to a nervous Jim who drops it, evidently on Sir R's foot.

Jim: I'm terribly sorry, sir!

Sir R: Not at all, Dr Vernon. I have another foot.

Jim: I'm all thumbs.

Sir R: A rare condition. Perhaps, as in the case of "The Elephant Man", a vibrant drama will be written about you – "The Thumbs of Navarone". But, alas! Such glories lurk in the future. For now, may we consider our gall-bladder patient, Mr Beaton?

Jim: Oh yes sir, yes of course...

Sir R: You may retrieve his chart, Dr Vernon. I shall remain upright. Otherwise, my voices tell me, we are doomed to terminal cranial collision.

Jim bends, Randy steps aside. This brings him into contact with Margot. Both whisper, in different moods:

Randy: Sorry about last night.

Margot: I wasn't with you last night.

Randy: That's what I'm sorry about. So – tonight...?

Margot: For the last time, no. Move away from me. You're melting my starch.

She moves away from him, but this only brings her up against another Houseman who doesn't yield. Trapped – these Housemen! (says her expression) She looks Heavenward.

Cohen suddenly scribbles a quick note. Dave looks at him.

Dave: What you writing?

Cohen: Thinking about your trouble reminds me: to buy some Vienna sausages and pickled cucumber on the way home.

Jim stands up in confusion and doesn't notice he's holding the spicy magazine and not the chart. He hands the magazine to Sir Roderick.

Jim: That should tell us something about his condition sir.

Sir R: He's lucky to have a condition at all reading these.

Sir Roderick hands magazine back to Jim – who is utterly bewildered as to where it has come from. He hands it to Margot, and picks up chart this time.

Sir R: Well what do you think?

Jim completes frowning study of Dave's chart, announces, as if it's an inspired diagnosis.

Jim: I'd say, sir, he's doing as well as can be expected.

Sir R: I'd say more. (To Dave)
I'm quite pleased with you.

Dave: Er – I'm not, Sir Roderick.

Sir R: Indeed? Listen closely, all of you.

Dave: Er, I'd rather tell you private-like.

Sir Roderick waves the others away. Cohen, getting out of bed to dress, makes encouraging "Go-on-tell-him" signs to Dave.

TWO SHOT. SIR RODERICK AND DAVE.
Dave stumbles into:

Dave: Does this operation have, you know, like side-effects?

Sir R: They're always possible – but there's no sign of one with you, Mr Beaton. Your chart...

Dave: Er what I'm worried about they don't, like, measure...

Sir R: And what side-effect might that be?

Dave: Er it's more of a front-effect really...

Dave glances down to his midriff. Sir Roderick doesn't get it.

Sir R: You're really pricking my curiosity. Go on.

Dave: Well, you know, it's – how's-your-father...

Sir R: In fine fettle, thank you, considering he's 93 and thinks he's a hamburger. But what's my father got to do with...?

Dave: (Sweat) Let me put it another way. Every day, before this, I've woken up knowing what I am.

Sir R: A plumber, yes.

Dave: No, no. A man, a man, a man.

Sir R: I see. You like to wake up convinced you're a man... (Dave nods, relieved)... the capital of Jordan?

Dave: (Desperate) You know the old, old story?

Sir R: No. Tell me the old, old story.

Dave: Somebody asked Mao-TseTung: "Do you have elections in China?" And old Mao says, "Course we do – same as in England – evely morning." (Sir Roderick looks blank) Weell, doctor, this morning...

Dave gloomily points to himself again, shaking his head. Sir Roderick still working on the joke.

Sir R: Every morning... Elec... (dawn) Oh! That! You're complaining of mututinal detumescence?

Dave: Does that mean I feel like a windsock when there's no wind?

Sir R: (Nod) But don't worry. Your operation had nothing to do with it. One can't expect to be aroused each and every dawn, as regularly as egg for breakfast, by a tickling sensation under the chin.

Dave: You're sure?

Sir R: (Fingering chin) Alas, yes.

Dave: So I'm all right!

Sir R: Doing splendidly. And I'm sure you'll keep it up.

Sir Roderick moves on.

Cohen: There – that wasn't too hard, was it? (Beat) Not that you were complaining of that...

Sister (Jacki Piper) breaks some good news to happy father Mr Tidey (Kenneth Connor) in Carry On Matron *(1972).*

Close shot Sir Roderick
Moving on. A brief raspy chuckle.

Sir R: Voting every morning. Frightfully funny quip... Awfully clever, these Chinese...

RESUME SCENE
At next bed. Patient: Dennis Harper. He's unremarkable except for an egg-cosy, worn with considerable insouciance, on his nose. It is held in place by elastic sewn in either side and extending round the back of his head. Housemen and Margot grouped at the end of his bed, awaiting Sir Roderick, cannot help staring at Dennis and are having a tough time trying to contain their disoriented hysteria. Sir Roderick steps in, poker-faced, studies the proffered chart.

Sir R: Mr Harper.
Dennis: Sir Roderick.
Sir R: You're absolutely normal.
Dennis: Thank you.
Sir R: And I apologise for the giggling inanity of these infantile and unworthy representatives of the healing art. If they don't realise, and respect, that your nasal attire is probably part of some obscure religious celebration...
Randy: Like Sniffmas...
Cohen: (Getting dressed) Or Yom Hooter.
Dennis: Oh it's nothing like that.
Sir R: Then I am bound to enquire, Mr Harper, as plainly as I can: why are you wearing an egg-nose on your cosy?
Dennis: I try not to make a fuss of it, Sir Roderick – but I just have a very cold nose. Sometimes I wear this at home. My wife bought it for me because even with the central heating here...
Sir R: Why didn't you tell us?
Dennis: No medical point, Sir Roderick. It's harmless and hereditary. And don't worry: I'm not going to say cold noses run in my family.
Sir R: (Humourless) Why not? It's a perfectly acceptable lay term for genetic probosco antarctica.

Sir Roderick leads the group on to Bob Marchant, a beaming, healthy-looking young fellow.

Sir R: You were not with us yesterday, Dr Firkin. So Mr Marchant is new to you. Examine and diagnose. You have five minutes.

Randy's face falls.

INTERCUTS of Sir Roderick, Margot, Jim, Dennis the Egg-Cosy Man and others, during the following, until scene-end.

Randy: Open your pyjama-jacket please.

Bob complies. Randy stethoscopes him, turns back his eyelids, chucks him under the chin. Leans in very close to him, ostensibly to look in one ear, but uses the proximity, in the TWOSHOT, to whisper:

Randy: You got me stumped, Mr Marchant. Tell us?
Bob: Up yours, Doc. Find out.
Randy: Oh come on. Help me a little. Do you smoke after intercourse?
Bob: Don't know. Never looked.
Randy: Your father alive?
Bob: No.
Randy: Ah. What'd he die of?
Bob: Nothing serious.

Randy reacts.

INTERIOR. CORRIDOR – OUTSIDE ANTE-NATAL CLINIC (IDENTIFIED). DAY.

Two very pregnant women, seated plumply and comfortably, very content, and knitting. Their hair in curlers.

Pregnant woman 1: Triplets, eh? 'Ow marvellous!
Pregnant woman 2: Yerss – and the doctor says they're not very common.
Pregnant woman 1: I should say not.
Pregnant woman 2: Yerss, 'e says you get twins once every eighty times, and you only get triplets once every six thousand four 'undred times.
Pregnant woman 1: Blimey! When do you get time to go shopping?

INT. ACCIDENT AND EMERGENCY DAY

Irishwoman being treated for black eye by a Doctor other than Charles, and explaining...

Physician heal thyself! Charles Hawtrey as psychiatrist Dr F.A. Goode in Carry On Matron (1972).

Irishwoman: She asks me, where do you live? Balls Pond Road, sez I. Where? Says she. Balls Pond Road, I sez. What Pond? Sez she. Balls, sez I. Up you, sez she – and that's how the fight started...

Charles completing whatever his work is on Bill, saying:

Charles: There. That's as much as I can do here to prepare you for surgery.

Bill: What a pity. I'd like to stay here longer.

He's still eyeing Emergency Nurse as he's wheeled away. Charles is again embarrassed.

Charles: Some people, really. I don't know why you put up with this constant flirtation.

Emergency Nurse: (Kindly) No, Doctor. I don't think you do...

Charles simply doesn't understand. Next Casualty is brought in.

INTERIOR. WARD. DAY.

Cohen, dressed, ready to leave.

Dave: Thanks for making me ask Sir Roderick. I'd've gone mad by now.

Cohen: Mad-shmad – so long as you don't go out of your mind. Goodbye, everybody!

Ad lib goodbyes to him from all and he turns to leave. Two Patients say their goodbyes to Cohen and return to their preoccupations at once. They're in adjoining beds. 1st is reading a popular newspaper. The other, looking haggard, sips orange juice.

1st Ward Patient: Fascinating – what they're writing here about bondage.

2nd Ward Patient: Never mind writing. Why don't they do something about it? I've been bound for two days.

INTERIOR. OPERATING THEATRE. DAY.

An Indian Woman, halo'd by the huge overhead light, looks down on Bill.

Bill: (V.O.) Hello Nurse...

Anaesthetist: It's Doctor, actually...

Bill: You're going to do me?

Anaesthetist: I'm the Anaesthetist.

Bill: Wow. You can put away the bye-bye juice.

Anaesthetist: Sorry?

Bill: I'm knocked out just looking at you. When can we have dinner?

Anaesthetist: At dinner-time. Separately. (injects) Count backwards from one hundred.

Bill: I've forgotten how... (gazing at her)

Anaesthetist: Then spell something...

Bill: I-L-O-V-E-Y-O-...

He's out.

INTERIOR. PORTER'S OFFICE. DAY.

Harry and Ted, gloomily sipping tea.

Harry: What 'aunts me is that Sir Roderick. I'm positive 'e's sussed us all along. Been watchin' us – with eyes like an 'awk. I tell you, mate, I'm getting paratroop about 'im...

Ted: What 'aunts me is the 'Erculinoleum task of puttin' back all the stuff we've nicked. Oh if only we could stop the 'ole thing 'appenin' in the first place...

Harry: ... then there wouldn't be the first proper stock-takin' this dump's 'ad in an 'undered and nine years. But you're dreamin', chum. Buroocracy rolls on regardless. No-one can stop it.

Ted: You're right there. It takes a special breed to tackle the burro, the burra, what-you-said. I mean, you don't find a cross between Attila the 'Un and Boadicea poncin' along the corridors of Mercy Street 'Ospital every day of the week now...

Tea-cup frozen in mid-air, his voice dies away, swamped by hope.

Ted: ... do you...?

Harry halts tea-drinking too, equally awed. He turns, shakily, to Ted, asking, tremulously:

Harry: 'Er?

Ted: (Gulp) I can't mean – 'er, can I?

They stare at each other, voices a-shake.

Harry: 'Oo else?

Ted: She could do something. No-one else.

Harry: (Deflated) What's the use? She don't even know what the Regional 'Ospital

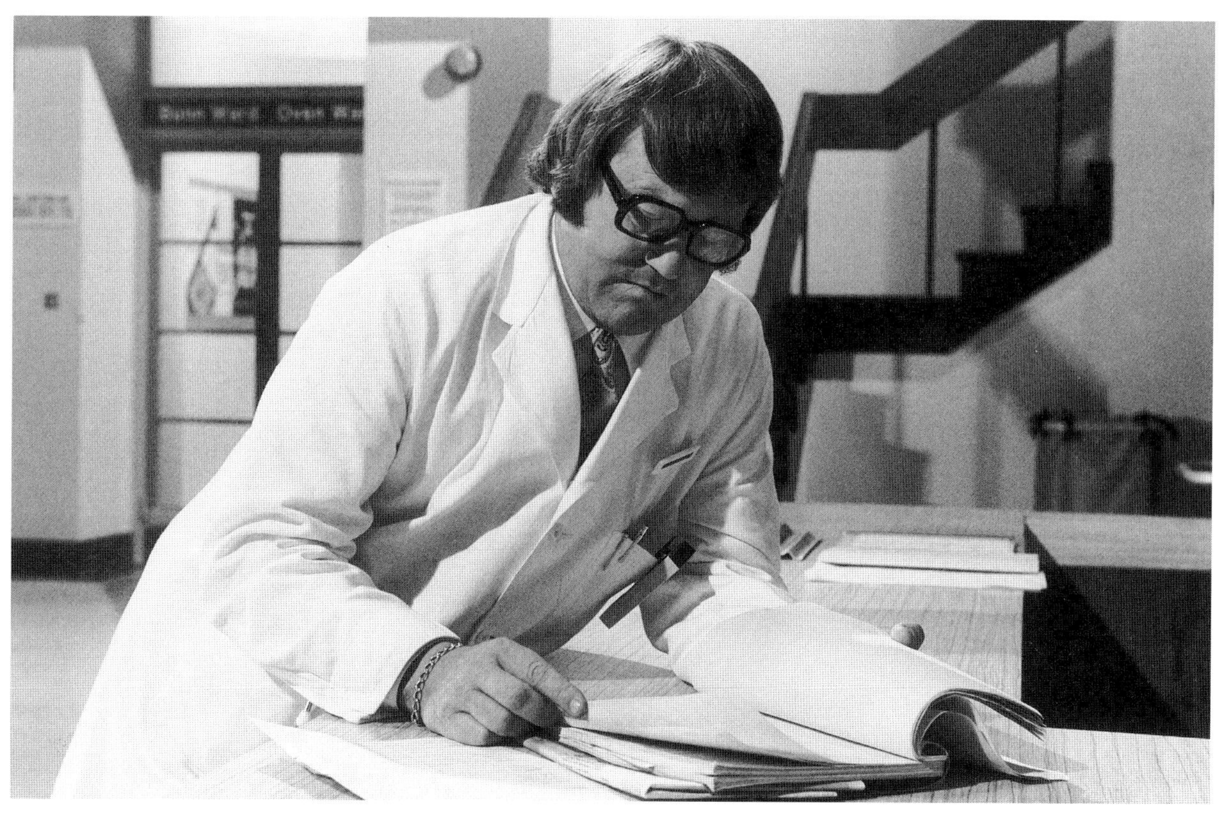

Terry Scott consults the Matron script to check the next hilarious lines for his randy character Dr Prodd.

Board's up to... (Slowly) But she could.

Ted: 'Ow?

Harry: Someone could tell 'er.

Ted: 'Oo?

Harry: You.

Ted: Me? Tell 'er? I get goose-pimples when she's still two floors away. Me? Not me. You tell 'er.

OFFICE-DOOR NAMEPLATE. MATRON'S OFFICE

MATRON BULLIVANT SNR

INT. MATRON'S OFFICE DAY

No new-fangled 'Senior Nursing Officer' nonsense. She is Matron and that's that. Seated, majestic and forbidding, at her desk, this veteran Matron, like Sir Roderick, is so absorbed by and good at her calling that she too is abstracted when it comes to other matters. Occasionally, she also makes the wrong connection or starting-point in thought and conversation. She is also inclined, almost without knowing it, to hum the opening of her favourite song every so often – "Ah Sweet Mystery of Life". Harry stands in fair fright before her desk, the surface of which is far from untidy, but it does bear photos etc. – the accumulated memories of a lifetime's nursing. Her first word ranges sweepingly upward over an octave or two...

Matron: We-e-e-e-ell? What is it, Mr Drummond?

Harry: Confidential information, Matron. (Gulps, plunges) There's a fifty-fifty chance Mercy Street 'Ospital will be closed down.

Matron: (Steely) And?

Harry: And merged with the new 'ospital in Monkton Avenue.

Matron: Source?

Harry: Yes I think it's a dead liberty too.

Matron: Where did you hear this rumour?

Harry: 'Taint a rumour. I got it from the lavatory-cleaner at the Regional Board.

Matron: Then this is from the horse's mouth. Hmmm... You mentioned – a fifty-fifty chance?

Harry: Yes, Matron. My hinformant tells me it could go the other way: they might close the new place and merge it with us.

Matron rises, muses shrewdly, pacing, head down, hands behind her back.

Matron: To close us would be merely historically unimaginative. But to shut the new place is plain financial lunacy – a flagrant waste of taxpayers' money. (Figures, halts) We might be all right.

Harry: Could be. That's buroocracy all over.

Matron: But we can't rely on it.

She suddenly whirls to him, her eyes boring into his soul. The shock makes him retreat a pace or two.

Matron: You're close to retirement, Mr Drummond. What difference does it make to you, if we close?

Harry: (Ready with his con) It 'orrifies me to think of a place, like this goin' through stock-takin' an' inventory like it's nothin' more'n a – a bankrupt po-factory.

Matron: (Misty-eyed) Beautifully put. 'Bankrupt po-factory'. That has – exactly the right ring to it.

Harry: 'Orrifies me... (With perfect truth)... more'n I can ever possibly tell you. (Soulful) I – aven't achieved much in my life, Matron. This is my last chance to defend what I most care about: tradition. And this temple of 'Ippo-crates... (He pronounces it just like that: in three syllables) ... is tradition to me. I've always thought – if Queen VIctoria 'ad been an 'ospital – she'd've looked like Mercy Street.

Matron: Another beautiful use of words, Mr Drummond. And talking of venerable piles...

Harry: No. No. I can't let my personal problems interfere with progress.

Matron: ... this one goes back further than the Widow of Windsor. There has been medical activity, however primitive, on this site, since the Middle Ages. Why, the apothecaries of Mercy Street were the biggest bleeders of their time.

Harry: An' another thing. Where it finally counts, we're literally streets ahead of Monkton Avenue: when one of our patients 'as 'ad it, we're much nearer the cemetery.

Matron is briefly lost in a swift sigh and reverie. Apparently the reference means something to her...

Matron: (Half to herself) Cemetery... (Hums) "Ah Sweet Mystery of Life..."

She pulls herself together, gets back to business, approaches Harry.

Matron: Now. Two big points.

His eyes flick, impressed, to her comfortable bosom.

Matron: First: I must assume that efficiency will be a factor in the decision of the Regional Board. So I shall bear down on my Nurses more heavily than ever before.

Harry: Poor little loves.

Matron: Second: (Instant paranoia) they may already have planted spies here – and at that Monkton Avenue Ear Nose and Throat Disco. To compare our efficiency with theirs. They call them moles, you know...

Harry: (Lost) Moles... Yerss...

Matron: In the spy-business. Moles – they burrow into your business.

Harry: Any mole sticks his nose in my business, I'll kick 'is tail in for 'im.

Matron grinds on, narrow-eyed, relishing battle and strategy.

Matron: If they know that we know that their security has been breached as 'twere, they'd close us, out of sheer spite. That's a buroocracy all over. So: not a word to anyone else. (Pauses, puzzled) Did I say buroocracy?

Harry: You mean bureaucracy.

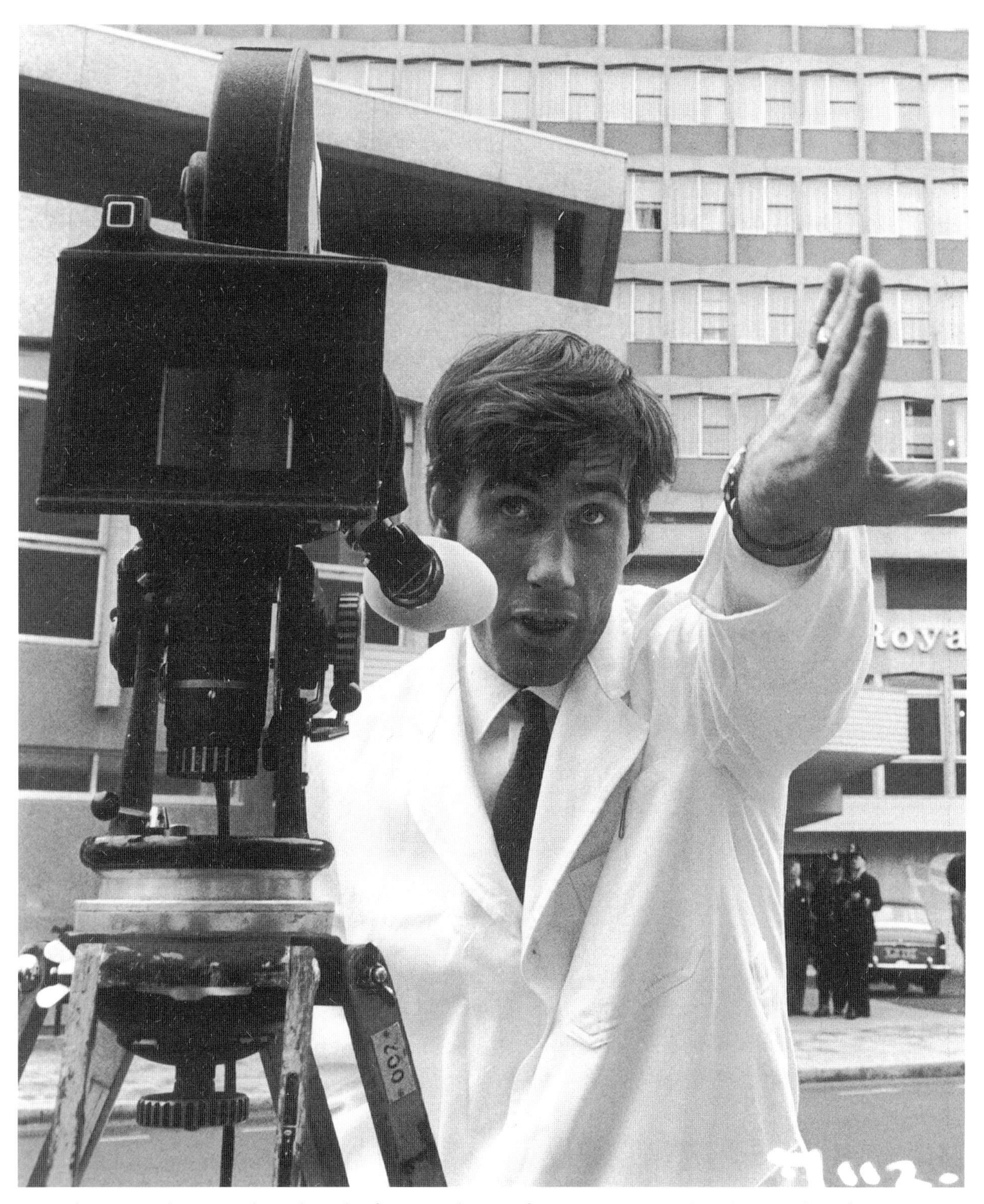

Jim Dale acting as 'director' as the media gather for a press showing of Carry On Doctor *(1968) in central London.*

Matron: But <u>you</u> say buroocracy.
Harry: I know. But it sounds wrong when <u>you</u> say it.
Matron: (Creeping to door: whispering) You mustn't be seen leaving here. There may be a spy in the corridor.
Harry: Or a beaver (Gets it right) Mole...?

Motioning him behind her and the door, Matron suddenly hurls the latter open. He is, of course, with a low groan, instantly felled.

INTERIOR. MATRON'S CORRIDOR. DAY.

Sir Roderick is about to knock. Matron is chilly and suspicious. He's bubbling, almost giggling.

Sir R: I can't stop.
Matron: Then I won't ask you in.
Sir R: It'll be just as good on your threshold.
Matron: What will?!
Sir R: Something I haven't done to you in thirty years.

She bridles in extreme indignation and puzzlement, but, before she can talk back:

Sir R: Tell you a joke. Why has it been so long?
Matron: Because, with due respect, Sir Roderick, you have all the sense of humour of a Siberian elk.
Sir R: Granted, but <u>this</u> anecdote tickled even <u>my</u> almost-atrophied fancy. I have to tell <u>some</u>one, even if it's only <u>you</u>. (Gushes) There's this Korean, you see. Someone asked him, do you use eggs for breakfast in your country and he says of course we do, every Christmas, just like Mr Cohen!

Beaming happily, he waits, fruitlessly, for her to dissolve into laughter. She merely looks blankly at him for a moment, then:

Matron: Make that, <u>less</u> than a Siberian elk?

She shuts the door.

INTERIOR. CONSULTING ROOM. DAY.

Mrs Briggs sits contentedly, even dreamily, opposite Doctor who consults document.

Doctor: Ah yes, Mrs Briggs... I saw you last week – yes – you told me your husband hadn't been – uh- very active.
Mrs Briggs: That's right – and you gave me them tablets.
Doctor: To put in his cocoa at night.
Mrs Briggs: Right. Well he was away until yesterday so I put the whole lot in last night.
Doctor: My God! What happened? How did he do?
Mrs Briggs: <u>Very</u> well, thank you. Seven times last night – three times again this morning – just before he died...

EXTERIOR. MERCY STREET HOSPITAL. DAY.

A parking-space marker: SISTER H. CHESTERTON. In comes her car, fast.

INTERIOR. SISTER'S CAR. DAY.

Sister's in uniform. Not wearing safety-belt. A quick look in the swung-around rear-mirror, a quick pat at her hair and she opens the door to exit car. Finds herself looking at the legs of a Policeman – his parked motor-cycle in background

EXTERIOR. HOSPITAL PARKING AREA. DAY.

Sister begins ingratiating herself at once.

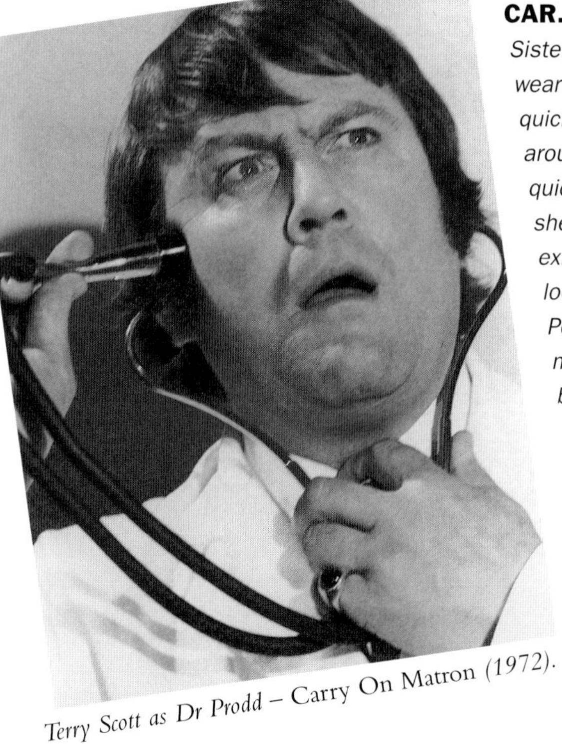

Terry Scott as Dr Prodd – Carry On Matron (1972).

Policeman: May I see your driving-licence, madame?
Sister: (Sweetest) I'm not a madame, I'm a Sister. (Hands licence to him) What can I possibly have done...?
Policeman: Driven too fast and not worn a seat-belt.
Sister: Still, no harm done eh?
Policeman: Could have been. It's for your own protection. I mean, if you'd had to stop suddenly, you've got nothing to cushion you.
Sister: (Breathing deeply) You reckon...?

INTERIOR. MAIN CORRIDOR. DAY.

Sister hurries along to intersection with Ward Corridor. She's a down-to-earth townie, terrific at her work, doesn't pettily harrass her Nurses. But there's a practical and no-nonsense air about her which transcends her informality. She manages both to get things done properly and promptly – and to be very well-liked as well.

A young Black Vendor pushes his cartful of confectionery, stationery, etc., on way to another Ward, i.e. in opposite direction from Sister. A rather vague visitor (woman) walks towards him. The following takes place as Sister passes.

Vendor: Hi, Sister Chesterton! Still not eating sweets?
Sister: That diet's gone for a burton, Jack. Buy some later. In a hurry now.
Vague Visitor: Have you got any Black Magic?
Vendor: You've got to be kidding, love.

INTERIOR. WARD CORRIDOR. DAY.

Sister meets Margot.

Sister: The blessed car took longer than I thought. I think they gave it a hysterectomy. And I got a ticket.
Margot: What for?
Sister: Speeding. Only (She looks rather triumphant about it) Anyone new?

INTERIOR. WARD. DAY.

Bill, in what was Cohen's bed, appreciating Sister who's writing something on his chart. His leg is in traction, but his spirits are good. Sister handles his flirtatiousness automatically and pleasantly.

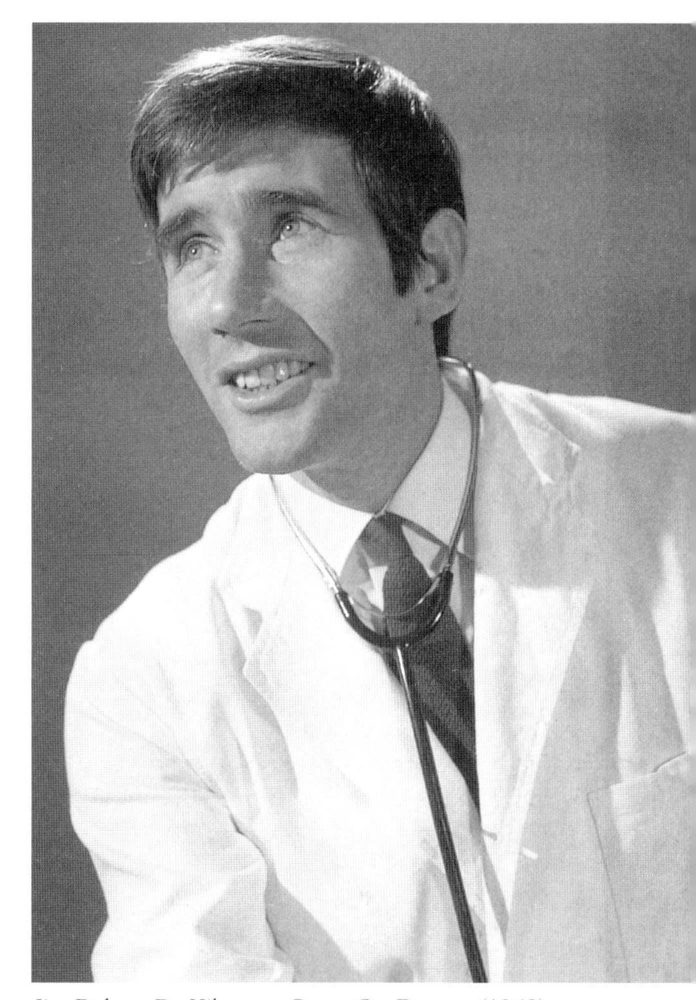

Jim Dale as Dr Kilmore – Carry On Doctor *(1968)*

Sister: You do have a nasty break.
Bill: From where I'm sitting, it's a lucky one.
Sister: Sorry?
Bill: Meeting you.
Sister: Now-now.
Bill: Now, tonight, tomorrow. Any time you like.
Sister: Settle down, Mr Unwin.
Bill: No thanks. I've just said goodbye to all that.
Sister: Sorry?
Bill: Why do you keep apologising?
Sister: (Sweetest) Because in your state you can't do everything for yourself.

INTERIOR. MAIN CORRIDOR. DAY.

Two Nurses hurrying along. First one is a dear – somewhat plain, however, flat-chested. Second is wildly glamorous and pneumatic.

1st Nurse: I couldn't believe my eyes. I did his bed-bath and this patient's got the word "Swan" tattooed on his you-know-what.

2nd Nurse: Funny – when I did him it said "Saskatchewan".

Two Elderly Doctors walking in the opposite direction. Nice old lads, stethoscopes swinging, rumpled, untidy old-timers.

1st Elderly Dr: 'Strawdinary symptom you do have, old boy, I must say. Every time you sneeze, you say?

2nd Elderly Dr: Yes, old man. The most amazing sexual reaction, every time I sneeze.

1st Elderly Dr: What are you taking for it?

2nd Elderly Dr: (doing so) Snuff.

The Two Nurses seen above, still walking – now past Two Old Patients, rheumy old boys, in wheelchairs, waiting to be pushed somewhere. Second Nurse drops something, bends to retrieve it. Both old devils look eagerly.

1st Old Patient: 'Erbert?

2nd Old Patient: 'Allo...

1st Old Patient: Remember that stuff they put in our tea in the Army to take our minds orf the old grumble?

2nd Old Patient: Yerss... why?

1st Old Patient: I think mine's beginnin' to wear orf...

INTERIOR. SLUICE. DAY.

Sister joins Margot who's sorting glassware.

Sister: Mr Unwin doesn't waste much time, does he?

Margot: He's just been divorced.

Sister: I should've guessed. Another Freedom Fighter. Every time I run across one of them I wish someone'd invent Anti-Pinch Panties. Designed to give an electric shock through three layers of tweed. But with my luck there'd be a short-circuit and I'd blow me skirt off.

Penelope: (Voice over) Excuse me...

They turn. Penelope is revealed, in ward corridor. She is ravishing, marvellously groomed: languid air, finishing-school accent, husky voice.

Penelope: Is it sort of all right to sort of visit Mr Beaton?

Sister: Yes of course.

Penelope: Where sort of is he?

Sister: Well actually he isn't sort of anywhere: he's exactly in the first bed on your right/left.

Penelope: Thanks terribly sort of.

She drifts off screen towards the ward.

Sister: Blimey – I bet she wears gloves to eat fish-and-sort-of-chips.

INTERIOR. WARD. DAY.

Penelope enters. Every Patient (except Dave) is transfixed. Bill almost topples his traction. Penelope only has eyes for Dave however, and there's no 'sort of' limpness about her now. She hurls herself at him, all languidness gone.

Penelope: God how I've missed you!

Dave: Hello Penelope, love... (Extends arms) Everything's OK. Just avoid this area here. It's a bit sore.

Penelope: Oh I will I will Dave darling. If I hurt you – I'd kill myself.

She kisses and embraces him, contorted appropriately to avoid contact with his op-scar. He responds with expertise and relish. The smooching is ecstatically prolonged. Their hands roam.

CLOSE UPS of all other Patients, in reaction.

RESUME SCENE

Kiss and grope continuing as Charles enters, goes to Bill, intent on him, not seeing the lovers.

Charles: Treating you all right are they, Mr Unwin? Just wondered how you're getting along.

Bill: As well as most, I think – but obviously not as well as some...

He indicated Penelope and Dave, still at it...

Charles is briefly but clearly embarrassed by such lack of inhibition. And more so when Margot enters "casually" as he turns to leave. They bump lightly. His

3rd from left: Proud 'nurse' Cyril Carter (Kenneth Cope) poses with the real student nurses of Wexham Park Hospital, Slough, during filming of the exterior scenes for Carry On Matron *(1972).*

conversation with her is awkward:

Charles: Sorry. My fault.

Margot: That's all right. Did you see Mr Unwin through Casualty?

Charles: Yes. Why?

Margot: I hear you did a nice job. Saved 'em some time in Surgery.

Charles: Oh I don't know... Margot... (as she moves on into Ward) When – are you off-duty?

Margot: Usual time. Why?

Charles: It's a long shift. Must be tiring.

Margot: Not really.

Charles: No? Well... (resolve, such as it was, dies)... that's good...

He nods and makes an untidy exit. Margot looks after him. She unnecessarily straightens a flower at a bedside. Clearly she only came in to give Charles a chance.

INTERIOR. WARD CORRIDOR. DAY.

Sister: How far did the ball of fire get this time – two blushes and a blurt?

Margot: Almost asked me out.

Sister: This isn't 1903. Why don't <u>you</u> ask <u>him</u>?

Margot: Look, I'm as liberated as the next woman...

Sister: But she seems to be having more fun.

Margot: Somehow, I don't want it to happen that way with Charles.

Sister: I know what you mean. A woman can dump her bra, drive a tank, become Prime Minister. But every so often she does need... (Sigh)... a touch of the Barbara Cartlands...

Margot: Sir Roderick'd love to hear you say that. He's been frothing at the mouth ever since women started wearing trousers.

INTERIOR. OPERATING THEATRE. DAY.

Unconscious Surgical Patient is wheeled in amidst Eight Medical Students and Surgical Team (including the Indian Woman Anaesthetist) complete except for Sir Roderick. He makes a theatrical entrance. All medical personnel are hatted, masked, gowned, of course. In this scene, in CLOSE UPS, the eyes have it – eloquently.

Sir R: Good morning. All ready for the Battle of Gutland?

Students(respectful mumbles)

Sir R: Your first sight of surgery. One way or the other, it's always memorable for the medical student. Let's see how you get on. You all know what this operation is. A simple matter. First, naturally enough – incision.

None of the op is seen, but, at each stage, Sir Roderick makes the appropriate and very deliberate move down out of screen. Even before the incision is completed, 1st Student, huge and muscular, faints without a sound.

Sir R: Oh dear. Such a superb scrum-half too. Clamps!

Sir Roderick and Assistants get to work with these off screen as:

Sir R: Firmly in place there. Got to open the thing wide, now.

2nd Student turns away, sweating, hand over mask over mouth – and vanishes.

Sir R: I said wide, damn it. I have to see what I'm doing. You wouldn't open the doors of a Fire Station half an inch in an emergency would you? Well then! Wide! Flesh is strong. It can take plenty of pulling apart. Apart – wide – so's I can get in there. That's better. Clamp it. Take a good strong hold of the edges where I cut...

3rd Student tries to preserve the dignity of walking away, but only takes two uncertain backward steps and crumples in a swoon. Sir Roderick pokes merrily around o.s.

Sir R: Good healthy stuff there and no mistake. I'd give him all mine and a thousand pounds in part-exchange. Amazing! Nature's supreme miracle, isn't it? The pictures in the books are all very well, I always say – but – actually to see it, the whole pounding human machinery, pulsing and gurgling away like a butcher's shop doing the rumba...

4th Student: Grooooo!

Sir R: ... absolutely fantastic. Look at that, will you? What a lovely liver – kidneys – absolutely gorgeous lower bowel...

5th Student spins round completely, glassy-eyed and staring, before dropping to the floor.

Sir R: ... and there's the little devil we're after – coyly hiding – there!

He makes a drive for it outside

6th Student: Oh my God...

He staggers back. Intent solely on watching op with unblinking eyes, 7th student steps aside to let him pass out, than steps back in, fascinated, not wanting to miss a thing on the table off screen.

Sir R: Absolutely nothing dangerous – but a bit frayed round the edges so – grip – SNIP – and out with you!

8th Student: (clutching throat) Mother...

He covers his eyes with the other hand and totters away out of the light-area. A Thump is heard off screen as he collapses.

Sir R: (To 7th Student) Textbook stuff, eh? (7th Student nods) You the only one left, what? (To the appropriate Assistant) Finish and close. (to 7th Student) Just like a bad year at the Grand National. Good for you, my boy.

7th Student: Sir Roderick – I am not, and have never been, a boy.

Sir R: (Almost brokenly) Only one left – and it's a gel? What is the world coming to?

7th Student: Its senses, perhaps, Sir Roderick?

Sir R: You're impertinent (continuing cold-eyed) Come closer and watch the end of the procedure.

CLOSE UP 7th Student

Her hand pulls mask down. She is coolly attractive, gleams with intelligence and self-confidence. She's in:

INTERIOR. SCRUB ROOM. DAY.

Surgical team is leaving. Sir Roderick barely pauses by 7th Student on his way out, to rap at her:

Sir R: I still think you're impertinent. But I also consider it possible you'll be a good surgeon.

He marches out, stiff-backed. Anaesthetist smiles and winks, encouragingly, at the radiant 7th Student.

INTERIOR. MAIN CORRIDOR. DAY.

Jolly Fat Mum ambles placidly, followed and flanked by Nine Children.

Woman Dr: (Approaching) I hear you're pregnant again.

Fat Mum: Yes ducks – but this one was planned.

INTERIOR. CONSULTING ROOM. DAY.

Three cubicles. In the first, Randy is tapping someone's chest when an indignant Merchant Seaman – all rolltop sweater, balaclava and muscle – bustles in.

Merchant Seaman: 'Ere, you. What's this about my wife being eight months pregnant, then? Impossible. I've been away for over a year.

Randy: It's what we all a grudge pregnancy.

Merchant Seaman: What the 'ell's a grudge pregnancy?

Randy: Somone's had it in for you.

Second cubicle. Charles is looking amazed, over what an Old Rip has just asked him.

Charles: You're 93 years of age – and you want me to – (Gulp) – give you something to lower your sexual urge?

Old Rip: Yus, mate. What bloody good is it to me up 'ere? (Taps his head)

Third cubicle. Doctor is seated there, his back to us, writing. Person with long nose, a Cyrano, waits on chair. Nurse approaches.

Nurse: The plastic surgeon will see you now.

Person goes in to cubicle.

Shave a leg! Barbara Windsor helps Kenneth Cope find his feminine side during the making of Carry On Matron *(1972).*

Carry On Again Nurse

Doctor: What can I do for you?

He turns around. He has exactly the same unfortunate nose.

EXTERIOR. NURSES' HOME ENTRANCE. NIGHT.

Randy walks Nurse Lottie Lowry to front door. She opens it. Home Sister is seen at table within. For her benefit:

Randy: (Loudly) There we are. Eleven o'clock on the dot.

He gives Lottie a chaste kiss on the cheek.

Lottie: (Whisper) See you in five minutes.

Randy: (Loudly) Goodnight, Nurse Lowry. So glad you enjoyed the concert of sacred music.

Lottie goes inside. Home Sister shuts and locks the door. Randy runs round the corner into:

EXTERIOR. NARROW ALLEY. NIGHT.

This separates the Nurses' Home from the Hospital Stores.

ZIP TO:

Other end: doorway into Stores building. Dim-lit, marked:
MERCY STREET HOSPITAL
STORES DELIVERIES

Harry, cold and tense, waits in doorway, reacts to sound of Randy's running footsteps offscreen. Peers out carefully.

Harry's POV: At other end, on Nurses' Home side of alley, Randy arrives and halts by a faint-lit window.

Stores End: Harry reacts to lorry sound offscreen nips around the corner waving his arms at Ted who's backing lorry, looking out of it. Ted halts lorry. They whisper:

Harry: We'll 'ave to wait a couple of minutes. One o' them perishin' 'Ousemen's waitin' to be let in the window of the Virgins' Retreat.

Ted: Bet it's Dr Firkin. 'E gets more bangs than a shutter in a gale.

Harry: Got the beds?

Ted: (Nod) 'Ad to pay more'n we got when we nicked 'em though.

Harry: That fence is a bloody crook.

Ted: Nah – it's the bloody inflation.

Nurses' Home End: Randy waiting, shivering. The window is opened by Lottie. He moves to enter. She stops him. Urgent whispers.

Lottie: It's all off. My room-mate didn't go away. She's asleep in the other bed.

Randy: (Moving to enter) Well we'll have to be quiet.

Lottie: (Restraining him) Don't be silly. You know I always hoot and gurgle.

Randy: Do I! It's like sleeping with an owl in a bathtub. But don't worry. I'll gag you. We'll manage somehow.

Lottie: No. I'm sorry.

Randy: I should hope so. Why can't you choose me reliable room-mates?

Lottie: Don't blame me.

Randy: Well I didn't choose her. There must be

Charles Hawtrey and Kenneth Williams became 'blood brothers' and take a sacred oath in Carry On Matron *(1972).*

	other accommodation in there.
Lottie:	Dr Firkin: I will not be crammed into a broom-cupboard with a mop-handle up my nightie and your great feet stuck in a bucket.
Randy:	I knew it. you have absolutely no sense of romance.
Lottie:	And you have all the self-control of a sex-mad stoat.

Stores end: Harry cautiously peeps round the corner.
Harry's POV: Along the alley to the unheard but clearly acrimonious end of the affair. Lottie finally slams the window shut. Gesticulating in exasperation, Randy stalks away.
Stores end: Harry withdraws his head, and directs the lorry round the corner, backwards. Lorry halts, its back near Deliveries-door.

Harry and Ted open lorry. Ted begins lugging out one of several hospital-beds. Harry opens Deliveries-door. Key is on a gaoler-size ring with a briefly-seen tag: MASTER KEYS, MERCY STREET HOSPITAL.

ANOTHER ANGLE

WIth Deliveries-door open, Harry and Ted manhandle the first bed out of the lorry. It's heavy and awkward. There is a bit of to-you from-me and don't-drop-it manoeuvring and whispering. In the ungainly process, one end of the bed breaks a window in the lorry. They get the bed to the door-space. It's too big. They try the bed all ends up, with more sweat and manoeuvring. No good. With the bed held unsteadily and strainingly between them:

Harry:	Of course. Shoulda remembered. These things are always delivered in bits. We'll 'ave to take 'em to pieces.
Ted:	I don't have the right tool.

Harry gives him a look which changes to one of horror as they hear footsteps offscreen.

Ted:	'Oo's that?
Harry:	(Obsessed) Sir Roderick! I know it! 'E's got us! We've 'ad it! We're...!

Their tension doesn't relax much as they realise it's only Randy walking by this end of the alley: hands thrust into pockets, shoulders hunched, preoccupied with frustration and therefore incurious about their doings.

Randy:	(Wanly) Hello, Harry...
Harry:	(Stiff, wary) Evenin' Dr Firkin...
Ted:	Evenin'...
Harry:	(Re bed) Er – we can't get it in...
Randy:	I know how you feel...

He sighs hugely and walks on.

INTERIOR. WARD. NIGHT.

CLOSE UP Bill. Also sighing, feeling the same way – wide-awake and wistful. Night Nurse, Anna Francis, approaches, making:
TWOSHOT – DOMINATED BY BILL'S BANDAGED LEG IN TRACTION.

Anna:	Can't you sleep?

Bill: New Zealand just ran out of sheep.
Anna: Maybe I can help you.
Bill: Easily. Kiss me goodnight.
Anna: I meant give you a pill.
Bill: Had one. I don't want to become addicted – except to you.
Anna: Try to sleep.
Bill: Kiss me.
Anna: It's against the rules.
Bill: What can they do – tear off your name-tag and break your thermometer?
Anna: I have to set a good example to the Junior Nurse.
Bill: Do that. Then I can kiss her too... Damn. Now I've spoiled it.
Anna: There was nothing to spoil.
Bill: I always go too far. Say or do something that shows I don't understand women at all.
Anna: No-one does. Not even women.
Bill: You only say that to make me feel good.
Anna: Kind of.
Bill: No need. I feel good just looking at you.
Anna: Then let's leave it at that, shall we?

He sighs again – but nods, ruefully. She smiles, not unsympathetic as she turns away.

INTERIOR. CONSULTING ROOM. DAY.

A Postman is being seen by a Doctor, who's filling out an examination form.

Doctor: I see... How long have you had the diarrhoea?
Postman: Can't say exactly, Doctor.
Doctor: Why not?
Postman: Didn't know I'd got it until I took my bicycle-clips off.

INTERIOR. PHONE-BOX. HOSPITAL. DAY.

CLOSE UP Patsy Furness on phone, door open. The youngest Nurse we've yet seen. Student, eager, idealistic, achingly pretty and fresh.

Patsy: (On phone) Mr Furness please. This is his daughter, Patsy. Yes. Dad? Patsy! Well, this is it! I'm assigned to Ward experience. Men's Surgical. 4F! Just think, Dad – in a little while, I'll be saving life!
Jim: (offscreen) Or living it.

She looks in his direction.

Patsy: Pardon?
Jim: I'm young Dr Vernon. The sort they do TV series about.
Patsy: You fancy yourself. (On phone) Not you, Dad. Got to go now. 'Bye.

She hangs up. Without offence, smiling Jim won't let her out of phone-box.

Patsy: Now look...
Jim: (Gazing at her) I can't think of anything I'd like to do more – for a start.
Patsy: I've heard about Housemen.
Jim: It's all true – so you can relax and enjoy it.
Patsy: Let me pass.
Jim: You have. 98%
Patsy: Why not a hundred?
Jim: You didn't give me your name.
Patsy: (Despite herself) Furness.
Jim: Bet you don't need much stoking. Joking aside...
Patsy: Just stand aside, doctor...
Jim: I liked you – from the moment I saw you.
Patsy: When was that?
Jim: Just now.
Patsy: I'll be late...
Jim: (Standing aside) I wouldn't want to hold you up. (At once) Yes I would. In both arms.
Patsy: You go too far.
Jim: As far as I can.
Patsy: I don't know why I'm still talking to you.
Jim: Neither do I. But it's a good sign. See you?
Patsy: Que sera?
Jim: Who's she?

She grimaces, leaves. He looks after her, pleased with progress – especially when she looks back instinctively, becomes confused, turns away, trips slightly, hurries on. He grins.

Clumsy Bertie Muffett (Richard O'Callaghan) and Sally Martin (Jacki Piper) get romantic in this hospital sequence from Carry On Loving *(1970).*

INTERIOR. MAIN CORRIDOR. DAY.

CLOSE UP Margot. Taut and anxious. She almost runs along towards Ward Corridor entrance. As she leaves frame, Two Patients, deep in hypochondria, approach, keep walking.

1st Patient: Oo, try not to be seen by 'im.

2nd Patient: Why not? If 'e don't know what's wrong, 'e can refer me to another doctor.

1st Patient: The only doctor 'e ever refers anyone to is the Coroner.

INTERIOR. WARD CORRIDOR. DAY.

Margot runs into view, and almost into Sister.

Sister: 'Ullo. What you practising for, girl – the Bedpan Olympics?

Margot: Matron's on her way.

Sister: A bit early today. So what?

Margot: This round is different. She's on a total rampage.

Sister: Can't be. Go on with you! Dear old Bullivant's a tough bird, but I wouldn't call her Florence Vulture.

Matron: (Offscreen) Wouldn't you, Sister Chesterton?

ANOTHER ANGLE – MATRON'S ARRIVED

Shattered, Sister giggles nervously.

Sister: Why Matron, what a pleasant surprise, you're early...

Matron: The early vulture catches the snake-in-the-grass...?

Sister: (Wordless giggles, glassy-eyed)

Matron: If it's not too much trouble, Sister, I'd appreciate your extending me the privilege of an awed look at the perfection of this Ward...?

Sister hastens to take Matron in. Praying, Margot follows.

INTERIOR. WARD. DAY.

Entering, Matron marches to first bed. Sister hands Bill's chart to her. She scans it

Matron: You're new, Mr Unwin.

Bill: Actually a bit shopworn, but in working order.

Matron: (Sniff) You have obviously encouraged back-chat, Sister. This is bad for Nurse – Patient relationships. It undermines efficiency – our watchword. Such – gentlemen – can be dealt with. Observe. (To Bill) Have you any complaints about the Nurses?

Bill: No. They're both beautiful.

Matron: That's not what I'm thinking about.

Bill: I can't think of anything else.

Matron: Are you getting everything you need?

Bill: But not a thing I want.

Matron: Mr Unwin: I have been in Nursing for thirty years. There isn't an innuendo of that kind which I don't fully understand. You can't slip one past me!

Bill: Then I'd better stop tossing them off.

Matron: If you please.

Bill: I expect I only do it because I'm feeling dicky.

Matron: Quite.

Bill: But I'll pull out in time. I don't want to go down in your estimation.

Matron nods, primly forgiving. Margot and Sister try not to gape at her – especially when, as they move on to Dave:

Matron: You see? All you have to do is take him firmly in hand. In no time, he isn't so cocky.

Sister nods, swallowing hard, hands Dave's chart to her, but Matron freezes in outrage.

Matron: There's fluff under that man!

Margot flies out.

Matron: Such negligence, Sister!

She fumingly studies Dave's chart. Sister quails. Margot flies back in, with broom, deals with fluff. Matron looks up from chart.

Matron: Any complaints?

Dave: I wouldn't have the gall.

As Matron nods, unsmiling, returning the chart to Sister, Margot starts leaving, broom in one hand, fluff between finger and thumb of the other. Matron rivets her with:

Matron: Why did you wield the broom, Nurse?

Margot: I, um, er.

Matron: (To Sister) Where's your Student Nurse, on Ward experience?

Sister: (Absently) Prob'ly committed suicide b'now.

Margot: (Hastily) We're on turnover, Matron.

Bill: (Relentless) Lovely...

Margot: The new one hasn't reported yet.

Matron moves to Dennis' bed. He wears the egg-cosy. She is poleaxed. But controls. Slowly receives his chart.

Matron: Mr – Harper?

Dennis: Something wrong?

Matron: Such skylarking is really not...

Sister: Excuse me, Matron. It's not skylarking. It's just that the convector heater hasn't arrived yet.

Dennis: For my cold nose.

Sister: Northpoleitis or something, Sir Roderick called it.

Matron: Never heard of it. (Thoughtfully) Sir Roderick, eh...?

Sister: (Near exasperation) Well perhaps it's

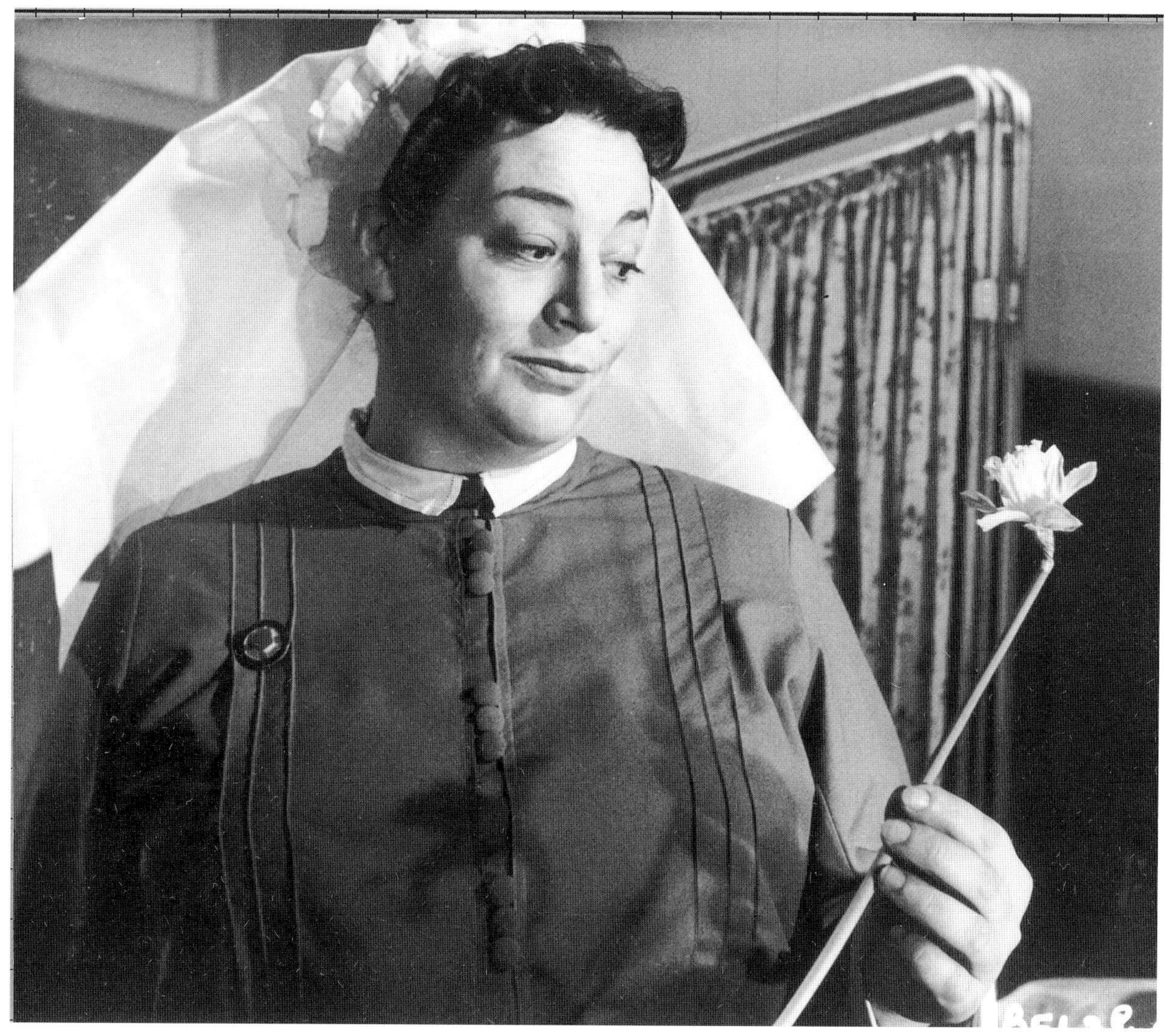

The most famous Carry On medical moment of them all - Hattie Jacques as Matron in Carry On Nurse (1959) holds the daffodil supposedly used to take a patient's temperture!

better known as Conk Glace or Schnozzle's Disease. I don't know. Anyway, he wrote up a little convector heater and we'll place it in the vicinity of Mr Harper's nose when it arrives.

Matron: Sir Roderick, eh? (Eyes narrowed) Did he, by any chance, also prescribe Korean eggs?

Sister: Pardon??!!

Matron: (Mysteriously) No matter... Later...

She moves on. Sister and Margot look wide-eyed at each other, then hurry after her. All arrive by Bob's bed. As Matron receives chart, Delivery Boy sidles in.

Delivery Boy: 'Scuse me, missus.

He delivers fruit-basket to Bob, who tips him. Delivery Boy gets the atmosphere. Shivers.

Delivery Boy: Chilly in 'ere. Somebody just die?

Matron freezes him with a look. He shrugs and departs.

Matron: (Re fruit) These edibles will, of course, be thoroughly washed, Sister. To eliminate any possibility of infection.

Bob: OK with me. The last thing I want on top of appendicitis is Passion Fruit Blight. Let's see the card though?

He plucks it from the basket. As he reads it and Matron studies his chart, Margot takes the basket out.

Matron: Do delivery-persons habitually wander unchecked in and out of your Ward, Sister?

Sister: Only when Nurse Walton and I are both in here, Matron, going through this sh – eer delight.

Bob: (re card) Thought so. From all at the old RB.

Close up Matron

Still perusing chart, just making polite chat.

Matron: How nice. What's RB, Mr Marchant?

Bob: (o.s.) Regional Board.

Matron looks up slowly.

INTERIOR. WARD CORRIDOR. DAY.

Patsy arrives, approaches Margot who's just taking basket into kitchen.

Patsy: Excuse me. I'm Student Nurse Patsy Furness. Here for experience.

Margot: Thank God you've arrived. We need you urgently.

Patsy: (Thrilled) To save life?

Margot: To wash fruit.

Margot hands Patsy the basket, indicates sink in Kitchen and hurries back into Ward. Patsy reacts bewildered, wanders uncertainly into Kitchen.

We see a Doctor and a Very Old Man pass slowly along Main Corridor at end of this corridor.

Doctor: But you've got to understand. You're 87 and you plan to marry a girl of twenty. It could be fatal.

Very Old Man: She dies... (Shrug) I'll find another.

INTERIOR. WARD. DAY.

Sister and Margot are (quite unnecessarily) tidying Bob's bed, watched closely by Matron.

Bob: I'm all right, really, Matron. Perfectly comfortable.

Matron: Oh no you're not, young man. You're just too easy-going to complain.

Her hints are now the HEAVIEST, so that they get through to Bob, "the spy" she believes him to be.

Matron: I don't want you going home – or ANYWHERE ELSE – say, to your OFFICE of that Regional Board of yours ha-ha – complaining about our standard of CARE and EFFICIENCY.

Bob: (Mystified) Everything's fine, really...

Matron: (Crashing on) You certainly can't say it's crowded here. We could comfortably accommodate another TWO HUNDRED BEDS in the event of ANOTHER FACILITY experiencing overflow or... (HEAVY) – CLOSURE! !

Sister and Margot finish, look somewhat puffed.

Matron: There, Mr Marchant. That better?

Bob: There was nothing wrong, really...

Matron: Oh tush – maybe not by the standards of OTHER PLACES with LESS TRADITION. You're too tolerant. But I'm not.

She smashes headlong into a coy and atrocious pun.

Matron: I certainly don't want anyone from any REGIONAL BOARD being BORED when he's in my REGION – eh – what – o-ha – ha-hohee etc.,?

She goes into immoderate laughter which, because of her actual tension, rapidly becomes helplessly raucous. Sister, Margot and others – especially nose-cosied Dennis – react to her bizarre outburst.

INTERIOR. KITCHEN. DAY.

Washing a banana, with the peel still on, Patsy looks up in puzzlement, not to say alarm, at Matron's uncontrollerable fit offscreen. Lost Visitor, on the edge of anger, looks in from Ward Corridor.

Lost Visitor: Excuse me, I'm trying to find... Why are you washing that banana?

Patsy: I've just started my nursing career.

Lost Visitor: Good luck. I hope you soon work your way up to watermelons.

With a "Cor-I-don't-know" look, Lost Visitor retreats.

INTERIOR. WARD. DAY.

Matron turns away from Bob's bed. Her continued fevered cackling converts without pause into a shriek of sheer terror. She is facing:
A young Girl in an outrageously daring costume more suited to night time.

Girl: Am I right for Dave?
Matron: Dave?
Girl: Mr Beaton.
Matron: Oh, Mr Beaton. Why, yes. I don't think he minds...
Girl: (Seeing Dave) Oh, there he is!
Matron: ... anything.

The Girl hurls herself at Dave. It's a re-run of him and Penelope.

Matron: You permit this kind of thing in your Ward, Sister?
Sister: How do you suggest I separate 'em, Matron – with the fire-hose?

INTERIOR. WARD CORRIDOR. DAY.

Matron and Sister emerge.

Matron: Keep a special eye on Mr Marchant, Sister. There are wheels within wheels. Moles within moles, perhaps... But – I've said enough.
Sister: Not for me you haven't, Matron. I don't know what you're...
Matron: Suffice it to say I naturally want him to report nothing but good of us to his – office-colleagues.
Sister: (Utterly baffled) Office...?
Matron: Yes, office, Sister. Never forget, as Queen Victoria so graciously said – this is a hospital, not a po-factory.

Matron pokes her head into the Kitchen, past Margot, transfixed on the threshold of the Ward. Margot and Sister exchange a glance, mutually mouthing, in mystification: "Po-factory...?" Matron turns from Kitchen-perusal.

Matron: A private word with you Sister, if you please.

Margot opens Sister's Office door. Matron sails in, humming "Ah Sweet Mystery of Life...". Sister goes in too, closing door. Margot shakes her head.

INTERIOR. SISTER'S OFFICE. DAY.

Matron sits, eagle-eyes the office, straightens a pencil. Sister swallows comment.

Matron: Though displeased with your Ward today, Sister, I still have respect for your intuition. Therefore I want your opinion on an important matter.
Sister: Thank you, Matron.
Matron: I speak in absolute confidence.
Sister: Of course.
Matron: What do you think of this? A Japanese gentleman asks an Israeli, "Do you have omelettes each day?", and he replies, "Only when they're Korean."

Sister is expressionless and disoriented in the extreme. Matron nods grimly.

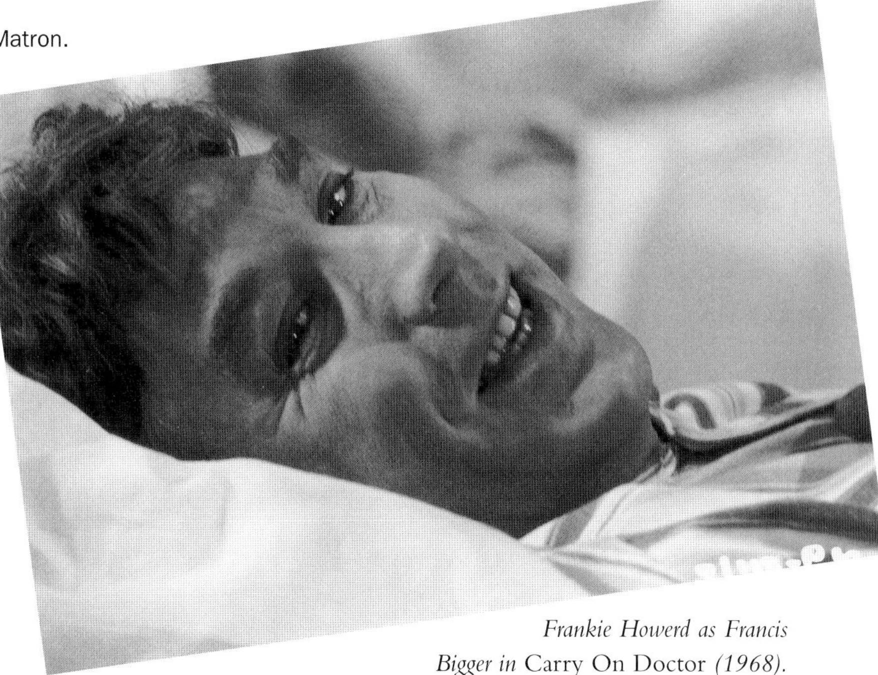

Frankie Howerd as Francis Bigger in Carry On Doctor *(1968).*

Matron: Not funny, eh?

Sister: Er, ah, well, no?

Matron: I thought not. That confirms it. (Rises) Someone in – authority – in this hospital – is under a very great strain. You realise now why I asked you about Korean eggs and Sir...?

She breaks off.

Sister: Er um well you I yes?

Matron: Again – I may have said too much. At any rate – thank you. And, remember Mr Marchant.

Matron taps her nose confidentially.

Sister: Don't you mean... (taps her nose)...Mr Harper with the cosy?

Matron: No. And – I think you may well understand why.

Sister: A wild guess but – because he's not from the old RB?

Matron: Enough said.

She leaves. Sister's shaky gape after her is monumental.

INTERIOR. WARD CORRIDOR. DAY.

Matron sails away. Margot emerges from Kitchen as Sister comes out of her office. Both look after Matron.

Margot: What do you make of it?

Sister: (Tremulous) You tell me. She's raving – about moles, wheels and eggs – and wants us to impress the local Regional Board of – British Railways.

INTERIOR. CONSULTING ROOM. DAY.

We start in CLOSE on a weighty document headed:
MERCY STREET HOSPITAL
FULL MEDICAL EXAMINATION REPORT
We TRACK from it along an ECG sheet which extends the length of a conference-table. For sharp eyes in the audience, the ECG line records the heart-beat of a perfectly healthy adult. We halt at the end of the table where Fusspot is seated. He (or she) is the picture of health, and gazing unblinkingly at:

Sir R: There's absolutely nothing wrong with you. Except hypochondria. You just like talking to doctors.

Fusspot: That's absolute nonsense. I demand a ninth opinion.

INTERIOR. AN EMPTY WARD. DAY.

Ladders, paint-pots, etc. – evidence that re-decoration is in progress. But no-one around. Enter Harry, stealthily. Then Matron, likewise.

Matron: We must be quick, Drummond. The painters will soon be back from lunch. I – I know who the mole is!

Harry: The spy, from the Regional 'Ospital Board?

Matron: A Mr Marchant. Men's Surgical. 4F. No doubt a high-ranking officer. Very much an upper mole.

Harry: That's how I feel about the Regional Board too – up 'em all.

Matron: I don't quite understand that. But I have the distinct feeling I'd agree with it if I did. Now. I want you to pump Mr Marchant.

Harry: I can't do that. I don't even have a First Aid Certificate.

Matron: Contrive to be with him. Find out, subtly...

Harry: Subtly, yerss...

Matron: What kind of a report he's going to make on us to the Regional Board.

Harry: Oh ah yes. Leave it to me, Matron. (looks around) Funny innit! They might close us down any minute – yet they're re-decoratin '...

Matron: It isn't funny at all, Drummond. It's...

Together: ... buroocracy...

EXTERIOR. NARROW ALLEY STORES-ENTRANCE. NIGHT.

This time all is going well – so far. Ted and Harry are efficiently carrying bales of bedsheets out of the lorry and into the Stores. The bales are not entirely unwieldy, but fairly hefty and heavy.
Harry suddenly stops, fearful.

Harry: I 'ear it! Sir Roderick's Rolls!

Ted: No you don't, an' belt up.

Ted shoves him impatiently into Stores.

Ted: Can't you give over about Sir Roderick? You've got a right recession about 'im...

EXTERIOR. NURSES' HOME. NIGHT.

Margot gets out of taxi, pays off.
Charles walks "casually" by her, turns even more "casually" .

Charles: Oh hello, Margot.
Margot: Hello.
Charles: Just happened to be passing.
His "fancy-us-meeting" act is painful to observe.
Margot: Yes... Been out for the evening?
Charles: Worked late. I like Casualty.
Margot: So did I, when I did a spell there.
Charles: We have something in common. (She nods, encouraging) There, er, you never really know what's going to happen next.
Margot: Just like in life generally.
Silence.
Margot: Except – sometimes you do. With a deadly certainty.
Charles: What do you mean?
Margot: I mean I know I'm freezing, I know I'm going inside, and I know you're going home.
Charles: Er, quite.
Margot: Goodnight, then.
Charles: Goodnight. I – just happened to be passing.
He leaves. She bares her teeth and extends clutching hands after him in wishful strangling.

INTERIOR. STORES. NIGHT.

It's implicitly vast, but only the area we're concerned with is lit. Bales of bed-sheets are on the floor. A tall stepladder bears Harry at its flat peak, level with some empty shelves up there. Ted enters via door from alley, bearing the final bale.
He shuts the door as quietly as can with one foot. The weight of the bale he's carrying makes him overbalance while he's thus on one foot. Dropping the bale, he falls against the ladder. It rocks. Ted stumbles and sprawls.
Harry: Careful, you great nurge.

Medical low-jinks on the high seas as ship's doctor, Arthur Binn (Kenneth Connor) takes liberties with Flo (Dilys Laye) in Carry On Cruising *(1962).*

The ladder settles. Ted picks himself and the bale up, strainingly, stretches to hand the bale up to Harry. They can't make contact. Harry, bending and leaning, almost falls off the ladder trying to do so. They can't see each other because the bale's in the way between them.
Ted: Got it?
Harry: No way. Start again.
Ted puts the bale down, places an empty crate, hops up on its lid, sweatingly bends down and picks the bale up – and up – and up – like an Olympic weight-lifter – until Harry, bending down from ladder-top, can almost reach it. At the last second, before he's got a hold on it, the crate's lid splinters and Ted falls into the crate. The bale lands on top and cuts him off from the outside world. Harry puts his arms akimbo, shakes his head.

EXTERIOR. NARROW ALLEY. NIGHT.

Miserably, Charles begins to walk through, towards lorry-end.

INTERIOR. STORES. NIGHT.

Harry is off the ladder, manhandling the bale off the crate. It falls from his hands and knocks the ladder over. Harry bends into the crate to help Ted out, as Ted groggily rises. Heads collide. Harry dizzily stumbles one foot into the steps of the toppled ladder, instantly entangled.

Ted clambers unaided out of the crate, looks at it.

Ted: We'll 'ave to replace that 'nall.

Harry tries to extricate his foot from the ladder-steps.

Harry: I'd like to replace you.

Ted: Don't be like that. (Harry reels, foot-trapped) Got yer foot caught? Let me 'elp.

Ted lifts one end of the ladder which slides up Harry's trapped leg and strikes him in the crotch.

Harry: Drop it, drop it!

Apologetically, Ted does so. The ladder hits Harry's other foot. Contrite, Ted hurries forward to assist – but falls over the ladder-steps himself, and disappears down out of frame.

EXTERIOR. NARROW ALLEY STORES-ENTRANCE. END NIGHT.

It's a re-run of Randy's preoccupied walk-through. The sufferer now is Charles – grim and frowning in frustration, nearing the parked lorry.

INTERIOR. STORES. NIGHT.

Very delicately, and in residual crotch-trouble, Harry stands upright again atop the restored ladder, gestures appropriately for:

Harry: 'Url 'em up. I'll catch 'em.

Ted: (Very doubtful) I'd rather get another crate, 'Arry. I don't think 'urling...

Harry: Don't stand on no more crates. They're as thin as paper. 'Url them sheets up or we'll be 'ere all night playing Patience on a flamin' monument.

Ted shrugs, flexes his muscles, spits on his hands, picks up a bale, swings it for momentum, and 'urls it up. It hits Harry in the legs. It bursts open and Ted disappears as the sheets rain on him. Harry falls headfirst into the lidless crate, his legs kicking. The ladder falls. At its mid-point, it smashes a six-stack of Waiting Room chairs. At its end, it demolishes a shelf-full of medical glassware.

EXTERIOR. NARROW ALLEY. STORES-ENTRANCE. END NIGHT.

Charles walks by – oblivious to the lorry and the sounds of destruction from behind the closed door to the Stores.

INTERIOR. CONSULTING ROOM. DAY.

Mr Springett is the picture of respectability. If this wasn't indoors, he'd be wearing the bowler hat he holds primly on his lap. Jim is taking notes and is very sympathetic and tactful indeed.

Jim: So, Mr Springett – just to confirm – and I do apologise – this must be very painful for you – both your first and second wives died from eating poisonous mushrooms?

Springett: (emotions under control – marvellous) Yes, Doctor. That's correct.

Jim: And now your third wife...?

Springett: Also – passed on – yes.

Jim: From what, Mr Springett?

Springett: Fractured skull.

Jim: How did she get that?

Springett: SHE WOULDN'T EAT THE MUSHROOMS!!

INTERIOR. WARD. DAY.

The small convector heater in place, near Dennis, glowing comfortingly. Dennis is happily reading, wrinkling his unclad nose to freedom. Enter Ballet Girl, flinging off raincoat, revealing herself in practice-costume. Her movements are more graceful than any of the others, but she's like them in the important respect: she too is crazy about...

Ballet Girl: Dave, Dave, oh Dave, Dave...!

Dave, ever-ready, embraces her. Next bed: Bill tries not to look envious. Further on, reacting to Dave and the Ballet Girl.

Bob: He's a plumber, you know.

Dennis: Really.

Bob: Specially good with ballcocks.
Dennis: I was hoping you wouldn't say that...
Bob: Someone had to. It's behind us now.
Dennis: I'm glad it's out of your cistern.

Enter Harry with wheelchair.

Harry: Ready, Mr Marchant?
Bob: Oh yeh. My final tests. But I can walk.
Harry: Oh dear me and bless you no sir, Mr Marchant. Rules, you know. Tradition and rules, sir. The two things what make an 'orspital great, as 'as been written in many a report to many a Board, Regional and otherwise, ho-ha-yes-oh-dear, since time immoral.

Dressing-gowned, Bob gets into the wheelchair.

INTERIOR. MAIN CORRIDOR. DAY.

Harry pushing Bob in wheelchair – and being "subtle".

Harry: I'm ever so fascinated by what our fine patients do, Mr Marchant. You're at the, uh, Regional Board, I 'ear?
Bob: Right. I'm an Investigator.
Harry: Of – anything special?
Bob: Pilfering.
Harry: (Halting) GULP !!
Bob: Don't want to boast, and I hope I'm not vindictive, but I've put people away for a total of 357 years in prison.

Harry leans against the wall, looking ghastly.

ANOTHER ANGLE

Matron on the march, in opposite direction. She reacts and hurries to – the dressing-gowned Bob pushing Harry who's now slumped in the wheelchair.

Matron: Why, whatever's the matter with Drummond?
Bob: I don't rightly know. I was just telling him about my work and he – 'come over queer...'
Matron: Your work... (Suddenly ultra-taut)... at the – Regional Board?
Bob: (Very puzzled) Er – yes...

Matron comes over queer and leans, palpitant, against the wall. Bob looks, bewildered, from one to the other.

Director Gerald Thomas and producer Peter Rogers on location in Maidenhead, Berkshire during the making of Carry On Doctor *in late 1967.*

INTERIOR. WARD. DAY.

Enter Sister, clipboard under arm, also carrying medicine. She supervises a Patient taking the medicine, looks casually past him and FREEZES. She stalks along the row of beds to an empty one. Empty, that is, except for Patsy, curled up asleep on top of the bedclothes. Sister hisses:

Sister: Nurse Furness. (Nothing. Shakes her) Nurse Furness.
Patsy: (Waking) I fell asleep...
Sister: Always report symptoms as clearly as that and you'll be hailed as a Nursing genius... I can see you fell asleep! Suppose Matron saw you?
Patsy: (A little pout-y) Well it's kind of her fault, if you'll excuse me: all this extra work – I'm

so tired – doing everything two and three times over to make sure it's just so...

Sister: Pull that bed apart and remake it.

Patsy: But it only needs straightening!

Sister: You'll need straightening, my girl, if you argue with me. Matron can tell if a bed's had a sparrer's fevver...

She corrects herself quickly and "smoothly".

Sister: I mean, of course, a pigeon's plume drop down on it, let along a deadweight Student Nurse crashing like a sack of spuds.

Patsy: (Seething) Yes, Sister.

ANOTHER ANGLE

Cecil Cholmondeley arrives, escorted by a weary Ted.

Cecil: Goody-ho-ho, here we are at last.

Cecil is very slightly built, has an earnest, owlish expression, is completely innocent, absolutely open and trusting, and very friendly.

Ted: Alright now then, are you, sir?

Cecil: Thanks to you. Without you, oh conscientious custodian, I doubt if I'd ever have found my way to this Ward.

Ted: Your kind words are reward enough to me – almost.

Ted extends him hand slightly.

Ted: They practically TIP me over into 'ysterical joy.

Cecil seizes and shakes his hand warmly.

Cecil: You're too kind.

Ted: Yerss – - I'm beginnin' to think I am...

Sister arrives in frame, consulting clipboard.

Sister: Ah you must be Mr Cholmondeley.

Cecil: No I mustn't. I'm Chumley.

Ted looks legubriously at his released and empty hand.

Ted: I knew a Bottomley once – pronounced Bumley.

Cecil: Did you?

Ted turns sad, tired eyes to Heaven.

Cecil: And, more important, did I fly-by-night forgetful me! Did I forget to thank you properly?

Cecil gives Ted a little money. Ted's attitude warms slightly.

Ted: I'll drink to your very good 'ealth, sir.

Cecil: Most appropriate. Goody-ho-ho!

Exit Ted, looking reminiscently at Dave and Ballet Girl. Cecil becomes aware of them too, as they smooch on.

Cecil: (To Sister) Isn't that nice? All the world loves a lover.

Sister: Then the entire solar system must be crazy about our Mr Beaton.

Cecil: Is he good at it?

Sister: Goody-ho-ho I should think. This way please.

She leads him to the bed Patsy has just laboriously remade. The Student's expression is naturally eloquent... Sister nods to her. Patsy turns back the bedclothes for Cecil as:

Sister: I see you're in for observation, Mr Cholmondeley.

Cecil: I've felt funny lately. Nothing too baddy-ho-ho but you can't be too careful.

Sister: Very true.

Cecil: I work at the Butch Cassidy Gymnasium.

TWO SHOT. BOB AND DENNIS

Dennis: What's he then – the Sundance Kid?

Bob: I was hoping you weren't gonna say that.

RESUME ANGLE on Cecil's bed.

Cecil: I service the men's equipment.

Sister: You're in the same line of business as me then, aren't you, really?

Cecil: Of course I may have strained myself doing it.

Sister: Can't say I've had the luck.

Cecil: But that's not what I really love doing. Would you like to know how I spend every spare minute?

Sister: I bet I'd never guess.

Cecil: With the fairies.

Sister: (To herself) I'd've lost... Screens, Nurse.

The wide-eyed listener to all this, Patsy shuts the beaming Cecil off from view. As they walk out of the Ward together, Sister restoring a couple of flowers to military precision en route, Patsy whispers:

Patsy: I say, Sister, is he, d'you think he's, you know, gay?

Sister: No. Just cheerful.

INTERIOR. MAIN CORRIDOR. DAY.

Vendor again approached by Vague Visitor.

Vague Visitor: My sister did enjoy the Black Magic.

Vendor: We aim to please, darling.

Vague Visitor: But I think, this time, she'd prefer a package without any soft centres. What've you got?

Vendor: They're hard to come by.

Vague Visitor: Do the best you can.

Vendor: Try my Chocolate Rock Balls. They're recommended by the doctor.

Vague Visitor: Which doctor?

Vendor: Yes love.

She buys. She goes. Good-humoured, Vendor shakes his head, smiles tolerantly. Stella crosses towards entrance to Ward Corridor. Young, well-groomed, sharp, very chic. She disappears into Ward Corridor.

INTERIOR. WARD. DAY.

Bill reading or doing crossword. He looks up. Is surprised (but masters it) to see the revealed Stella, arriving at his bedside. She is a little squeamish about the leg in traction, but masters it, in her turn. Scene starts quietly – but gets louder as they fall into dispute.

Bill: Hello, Stella.

Stella: Hello, Bill.

Bill: What brings you here?

Stella: Simple human concern.

Bill: (Wry) There speaks the same woman who, on twenty-seven separate occasions, openly wished me dead.

Stella: (Cool) I certainly did. But never once did I want to see you hurt. You could ask me to sit down.

Bill: Surely you can only stay a minute?

Stella: I never said so.

Bill: You don't have to. In four years of marriage, you could never stay more than a minute anywhere I had to be or wanted to be. Would you like to sit down?

Stella: I can only stay a minute.

But she sits. Glances at his leg, sidelong.

Stella: I heard how this happened. I couldn't believe it.

Bill: Me neither.

Carry On Matron *publicity shot with Barbara Windsor as Susan Ball.*

Stella: Why did you do it? You don't even like ballet dancing.

Bill: Never will. But now I have a lot more respect for the skill of those tightbums who do it.

Stella: Are there going to be any complications? I mean, they're not going to cut it off or anything?

Bill: Stella – stop trying so hard to cheer me up?

Stella: I believe in facing facts.

Bill: You believe in being pessimistic at all costs. The last time you saw the bright side of anything was the light outside an all-night undertakers. And it was you started this divorce-caper. I was ready to try again.

Stella: For the eighty-third time.

Bill: I'm an optimist.

Stella: You are not. You expect life to be a series of treats and presents – like a spoiled child. Which you are. Your mother…

Bill: Kindly leave my mother out of this.

Stella: That was always my hope. I prayed for it to all three major religions.

Bill: My mother only ever had my best interests at heart.

Stella: Your mother's deepest regret was that you wouldn't wear a dress after the age of fourteen.

By now they're screaming at each other, heedless of surroundings and other people.

Bill: That's criminal bloody libel and slander!

Stella: I don't care if it's forgery with a touch of arson – I don't mean it literally and you know what I mean. (Rises) The minute's obviously up. This is not helpful to either of us. Look at the way we're having a go at each other. Why the hell did I come here?

Bill: Because although you can't stand the sight of me, you do care!

Stella: Exactly – but don't ask me why!

Bill: Well don't think I don't appreciate it, you bitch!

Stella: I never thought you quite so selfish that you wouldn't, you foul-mouthed egomaniac!

SCENE

Everyone's frozen, fascinated, listening: Dave and Ballet Girl, hand-holding, and Cecil, head peeping out from the still-closed curtains round his bed, included – and all Three Nurses are "casually" around the door-space, well within earshot and busily doing nothing very much.

Bill: Are you going to marry again?

Stella: Why do you want to know?

Bill: Simple human concern – for the next poor bugger.

Stella: I don't know. Probably yes. What about you?

Bill: ME? Marry again? Never! I'm going to have a ball.

Stella: Half-measures – always half-measures…

She begins to stalk out, Nurses stepping aside hastily.

Bill: Look after yourself!

Stella: And the same to you!

She's out.

Cecil: (To all) Lovers' tiff.

He runs around his bed, opening the curtains, revealing he's wearing pyjamas as described.

Cecil: Do you like 'em? I can't sleep unless I'm covered with goblins.

INTERIOR PHONE BOX. DAY.

Patsy: (On phone) It's just terrible, Dad. We're run off our feet. Just my luck. Everybody says ward-work's never been so bad before. Nobody can understand why.

INTERIOR. WARD. DAY.

Patsy: (Voice over) Nothing we do is right for her. From the Sisters right down to us.

Matron, at Bob's bed, tapping her foot and checking watch. Margot with her. Sister rushes in, carrying papers.

Matron: Twenty-three seconds. Not good enough. Records should be to hand much quicker. Why? (HEAVY HINT) Because in THIS hospital – as I am sure Mr Marchant has noted – we begrudge any time not spent on direct, EFFICIENT NURSING – eh, Mr

Marchant? (Generously includes others) And everybody...?

INTERIOR. WARD CORRIDOR. DAY.

Patsy: (Voice over) She's never satisfied.

Matron, Sister, Margot and Patsy, all crouched, gazing at the floor and an invisible blemish thereon.

Matron: I don't care if the cleaners missed it. We must not. Clear this unhygenic spot at once.

Sister: (Hardly patient) Matron – I can barely see it.

Matron: It is my dearest wish, Sister, to be able to say the same...?

All rise. Sister indicates Patsy to get to work.

Patsy: (Voice over) And we're all so tired.

INTERIOR. LOUNGE. NURSES' HOME. DAY.

Several off-duty Nurses – selecting gramophone record, reading mags, writing letters, sewing buttons, playing draughts, studying etc., all normal activities – except that they've all fallen asleep in the course of them.

INTERIOR. SHOWERS. NURSES' HOME. DAY.

Nurses under several showerheads – and all asleep, in various poses, under the soothing, steaming cascades.

EXTERIOR. NURSES' HOME. NIGHT.

Randy in a fierce embrace-kiss. He finally unglues his lips from his date (Emergency Nurse). She still has her eyes closed as he continues holding her close. He's pleased with himself. Until she snores.

INTERIOR. WARD. CORRIDOR. DAY.

Workman taking convector-heater away.

Workman: Just going to work on Mr Harper's element.

Sister: Without anaesthetic?

Enter Cecil's Mum as Workman leaves. She's even more spry and fey than Cecil.

Cecil's Mum: I'm for Mr Cholmondeley.

Sister: That's Chumley.

Cecil's Mum: I never got used to that, and I was married to his father for what seemed like centuries, know what I mean, dear? Anyway, I'm for him – alright?

Joan Sims as Ellen Moore in Carry On Again Doctor *(1969).*

Sister: Certainly. Nobody here's against him.

Cecil's Mum: Goody-ho-ho!

INTERIOR. WARD. DAY.

Cecil writing industriously. His Mum arrives.

Cecil: Dearest Mum!

Cecil's Mum: Sweetest boy!

They kiss, as if taking a snack.

Cecil's Mum: Have they found it for you?

Cecil: I didn't know I'd lost it, luvviekins.

Cecil's Mum: What's wrong with you?

Cecil: They're still testing. Yesterday they stuck a tube up my nose, to get to my stomach.

Hattie Jacques as Matron in Carry On Again Doctor *(1969).*

Cecil's Mum: That seems a long way round.
Cecil: Yes, I think we had to change at Liverpool.
Cecil's Mum: I think you've just been over-doing it. There's only so many fairies you can handle a night.
Cecil: But, mama-poodles, that's the only time I have to write my stories.
Cecil's Mum: No it isn't – if you give up that gym.
Cecil: I don't know anyone called Jim.
Cecil's Mum: Leave that job at what's-it-called – Crotch Chastity's. Write full-time.
Cecil: How would we live?
Cecil's Mum: I'll go on the game.
Cecil: That doesn't quite sound right. Try again.
Cecil's Mum: I've got a game-plan?
Cecil: Better.
Cecil's Mum: The best. I'll take my old job back.
Cecil: In the NAAFI? But the war's been over for years.
Cecil's Mum: Is that why it's so quiet at night?
Cecil: What a lovely surprise for you!
Cecil's Mum: I've got one for you too.
Cecil: Goody-ho-ho!
Cecil's Mum: (Producing pyjamas) Brought you a clean pair of goblins.

INTERIOR. WARD. DAY.

Vera Harper visiting Dennis. As might be expected, she is a very nice lady indeed, practical and loving.

Vera: I've got a surprise for you.

She produces a knitted nose-cosy. Even the tie-around is knitted – no dreary plain elastic. The colour is yellow with a bright red heart, right on the conk-tip. Dennis is briefly taken aback but is clearly touched and recovers quickly. She hands him the new cosy and picks up the old one from his bedside locker.

Vera: I felt ashamed – you wearing this old thing outside the house. This – (She taps the bespoke nose-cosy) – well, this is the difference between a brown-paper bag and a leather briefcase.
Dennis: (Solemnly) You didn't finish the job properly, though.
Vera: (Horrified) What?
Dennis: Where are my initials?
Vera: Oh get away. Try it on.

Unhesitantly, he does so. Since this one covers the entire nose snugly, he looks even more ludicrous than before.

Dennis: Perfect fit.
Vera: If I don't know your size, who does?
Dennis: You're the best wife...
Vera: Oh don't be soppy.

Dennis: I want to be soppy, Vera...

He kisses her warmly. It turns into a nose-rub.

Dennis: You could make a fortune, exporting these things to the Eskimos.

Vera: You stay warm now. I've got to leave.

A further kiss and hand-squeeze – and she goes. Bill reflects.

Bill: You know something, Dennis? If that'd been me, I'd've not been able to stop myself saying very nice darling but they've provided a heater so I don't really need this. (Sighs) And I'm beginning to think that's what went wrong with my marriage...

He looks, enviously, in the direction taken by Vera.

INTERIOR. MAIN CORRIDOR. DAY.

Vera leaving, busy and bright-eyed, as Mrs Bob and Little Bob arrive and go into ward. The boy has two communicator-sets, with earphones, and is obviously proud of and excited by them. The following happens as mother and son go through.

Two Male Patients, in wheelchairs, are being trundled in opposite directions. Mutual astonishment.

1st Male Patient: 'Ullo, 'ullo – 'aven't seen you for years. What you done?

2nd Male Patient: Put me back out, mate.

1st Male Patient: Count your blessings. I done the opposite.

INTERIOR. WARD. DAY.

Mrs Bob and Little Bob with Bob who is obviously a happily married man and a good father. There are hugs and kisses during:

Mrs Bob: Lovely to see you looking so well.

Bob: I feel like a fraud. Shouldn't be long now, before I'm home.

Little Bob: I couldn't wait till then to try these.

Bob: You got 'em! The two-way superspace communicators!

Mrs Bob: Yes, he finally saved up enough pocket-money.

Bob: Well we've got to try 'em right away. Go on out into the grounds.

Leaving one set behind, and nodding eagerly, Little Bob hurries out.

INTERIOR. MAIN CORRIDOR. DAY.

Little Bob rushes through and away, past the following: Fat Mum and Kids walk. Vendor approaches from opposite direction. Kids rush forward offscreen. to surround him and his wares.

Kids: (All yelling at once) I want sweets – I want a lollipop – Give me that – stop shoving – I'll tell Mum on you – where's the chocolate? Why isn't there any ice cream? No crisps? Cor what a swiz! (etc., ad lib).

Fat Mum looks to be perfectly capable of sorting them out and is figuratively rolling her sleeves up as she steps forward – when a Social Worker, with clipboard, intercepts her, posh and gushing:

Social Worker: Excuse me. I'm doing a survey. Tell me. If you had your life over again – would you still have children?

Fat Mum: 'Course I would. (Grimly) But not this lot. (Continuing offscreen) 'Orace! Ermyntrude! All of you I

Social Worker looks after her, not quite knowing, pencil poised, what to write in her report...

INTERIOR. WARD. DAY.

Bob wears the earphones. Speaks into microphone.

Bob: Can you hear me?

He lifts up one earpiece.

Bob: (to Mrs Bob) Not a word.

Mrs Bob: Oh he'll be so disappointed. He's got a whole spaceman drama worked out.

Bob: I know where there'll be better reception.

He begins to get out of bed.

Mrs Bob: I'll come with you.

Bob: 'Fraid not, lovey.

INTERIOR. MAIN CORRIDOR. DAY.

CLOSE UP on door sign, "GENTLEMEN".

Pan to Bob, wearing earphones, carrying microphone, entering the Gentlemen's. Two people Freeze on seeing him do so – Matron, walking in from one end of the

corridor, and Harry, from the other. They exchange (past and through the bustling folk in the corridor, on all kinds of errands) a look of sheer terrified excitement. They hurry towards each other – and try to look like they are not doing so. When they meet, at the toilet door:

Matron: (Hissing) Blatant! A blatant mole! About to report urgently to the Regional Board! Flashing his electronic equipment in the toilet!

Harry: It's buroocracy gorn barmy...! I'll go in and...

Matron: Not alone you won't.

Harry: Eh??!!

Matron: I want to hear every sneaky word for myself.

Harry: (Hoarse) But – Matron! You can't go in there! It's – it's for gentlemen!

MATRON is at her most magnificently scornful for...

Matron: Rubbish! These days, there aren't any left. (Shoving him) Stand aside, Drummond! This – is for ENGLAND!

She has the luck of the extremely bold, it seems, because no-one hurrying by appears to notice her barging into the Gents. Gulping, Harry looks around fearfully – and follows her into:

INTERIOR. GENTS. DAY.

High window, top part open. PAN DOWN to the cubicle it is above. Bob is just entering, closing the door. He angles the communicator antenna (or whatever) towards the open window.

Matron and Harry creep in, see the one cubicle with its door closed, nod significantly and triumphantly to each other, enter the cubicle next to it, close the door too. Because these are sets with earphones, Matron and Harry can only hear what BOB says, not what he hears on the phones from his son in the grounds.

A beat – then, in low, thrilling, very military tone:

Bob: Are you receiving me, Command?

Matron and Harry react to the somber tone and phraseology.

EXTERIOR. HOSPITAL GROUNDS. DAY.

Little Bob: (On communicator, excited) Yes, Dad, yes! I mean – Roger, loud and clear. I'm orbiting Mars. Port rocket motor is smoking.

INTERIOR. GENTS'. DAY.

CROSS-CUT with Little Bob in grounds as necessary.

Bob: Suggest close down immediately. It is dangerous and inefficient.

Matron and Harry react, while:

Little Bob: (Unheard, of course, by Harry and Matron) How do I get back from Mars on one motor?

Bob: Use the other one.

Little Bob: What's the reading of its power?

Bob: It'll be all right. It's big enough to do the work of two.

Little Bob: Will shut down port motor as instructed.

Bob: Make it as soon as possible. Otherwise, there could be great loss of life.

Matron looks like she wants to charge through the wall and clobber Bob. Harry restrains her. They listen on, progressively more aghast, to their one-sided impression of the conversation.

Little Bob: Why is the motor smoking? Is the fuel dirty?

Bob: My reading is – excessive dirt all over the place.

Matron's eyes almost pop from her head at this insult.

Little Bob: Mayday! Mayday! I smell burning.

Bob: I'm not surprised. The smell alone is a warning-sign of great danger. Close down NOW – repeat NOW...! You are lucky to have another which can take care of the full workload of both – efficiently, safely and cleanly.

Little Bob: I can't risk a sudden shut-down. The gravity shock might destroy everything.

Bob: Then as soon as you can, REPEAT, close down as soon as you can. Over and out.

INTERIOR. MAIN CORRIDOR. DAY.

Bob emerges from Gents. A beat. Harry emerges from Gents. A beat as he looks up and down corridor. Mercifully, it's briefly empty. He taps on the door behind him. Matron emerges – with dignity. They walk away together.

Harry: What are we gonna do?

Matron: Drummond – it's a relief.

Harry: It usually is, commin' out of there...

Matron: A relief to know. Now I can bring the fight out into the open. Give me a few hours to think – to plan strategy. Then – I shall strike! As Churchill did not become Prime Minister to preside over the dissolution of the Empire, neither did I – nay! – become Matron here to see this mighty medical force surrender without a fight. Fight, I said, Drummond – and fight I mean, Drummond – for – make no mistake about it, Drummond – now, this is WAR!

Arthur (Derek Francis) looks askance with Mr Tidey (Kenneth Connor) in Carry On Matron *(1972).*

Breathing fiercely through her flared nostrils, her eyes shining with the exhilaration of combat, Matron strides ahead, humming "Ah, Sweet Mystery of Life" in rousing march-time. Overcome, Harry halts, gazing after her, inspired. Ted ambles into picture.

Ted: Where you bin?

Harry: Dunkirk!

Ted blinks, nonplussed.

INTERIOR. PUB. DAY.

Randy: The problem is: the Nurses are exhausted and we're not.

Jim: The situation is desperate. Romance is at a standstill. That Matron! What's got into her?

Randy: What hasn't? That's the point.

Jim: (Eyes narrowing) And the answer.

Randy: You mean...?

Jim: Someone's got to relieve her frustration.

Randy: You mean...?

Jim: Fall in love with her.

Randy: You mean...?

Jim: Pretend to, at any rate.

Randy: You mean... (hand over Jim's mouth)... if she's romanced, soothed, at peace, she'll ease up on the Nurses – and our Sexual Security System will be pulled back from the edge of ruin?

Jim: (Nod) Toss you.

Randy: I'm not that desperate.

Jim tosses coin.

Randy: Ah yes. Tails.

Jim: (Displaying coin, grinning) Start practising, my son: "But soft – what light on yonder Matron breaks...?"

Randy reacts to losing.

INTERIOR. SISTER'S OFFICE. DAY.

Papers and books are in neat but unsteady piles all over the room, desk, chairs etc. Shelves are empty, filing-cabinets' drawers are open and vacant too. Sister is in the midst of it, with an aching back and a harrassed expression. Suddenly, she sniffs.

Sister: Oh no.

She begins to hurry out. Piles of stuff, near her, tremble. She's forced to go slowly, tip-toe. A whistling sound begins and rises off-screen as she steps into:

INTERIOR. WARD CORRIDOR. DAY.

The medicine-cart is briefly but ominously seen as SISTER hurries across into:

INTERIOR. KITCHEN. DAY.

Catheters are smouldering on the stove, causing the odour. As Sister instinctively grabs for the container and realises it will be hot, stopping short, the whistling sound peaks. It's from the boiling kettle, also on stove. Its cap flies off. She ducks and it hits the ceiling lampshade which breaks. Sister grabs a teacloth, folds it rapidly, takes the catheters off the stove, dumps them in sink, turns tap on. More steam rises, added to that issuing from the kettle. She looks absolutely furious as she vigorously turns the kettle off.

INTERIOR. SLUICE. DAY.

Patsy, at the sluice, has almost completed preparations to operate it. But she realises:

Patsy: Oh. The catheters. Oh. The kettle. Oh. Sister.

Gulping, she turns the sluice on – without closing it properly. She's drenched in an instant and so is the floor. Gasping, she nevertheless hurries out.

INTERIOR. WARD CORRIDOR. DAY.

All three emerge at once: Sister from Kitchen, Margot, sniffing, from Ward, Patsy, soaked, from Sluice. Together they announce:

Patsy: I left...

Margot: I smelt...

Sister: I found... Quiet. (to Patsy) Speak.

Patsy: I was doing three things at once, Sister. I had to. It's such a pile-up of work...

Margot: I couldn't help her. The new rule about Ward-tidiness. I was hard at it. So busy...

Sister breathes deeply.

Sister: And I was reorganising my filing system. Matron's perishing orders. (to Patsy) Go and change. And don't fall over the medicine-cart.

Patsy: Yes Sister. No Sister.

Very carefully, Patsy moves the medicine-cart from her path. That's good as far as it goes – which is against the door of Sister's office. As soon as it touches...

INTERIOR. SISTER'S OFFICE. DAY.

... Every pile of laboriously-sorted material collapses. Chaos in four seconds. Sister, seen in Ward Corridor, with the equally upset Margot, fumes finally:

Sister: That does it. I'm just going to ask Matron – straight out – why in the name of the Crimean War she's' doing all this to us?

Striding forward to enter her office, she slips on the watery surface of the Ward Corridor floor.

INTERIOR. WARD. CORRIDOR. DAY.

MARGOT catches her – but they both tumble to the floor. In the process, the medicine-cart gets kicked and begins to roll towards the Main Corridor. Both slitheringly rise, in plain panic, to reach and halt it before it gets into Main Corridor to cause unimaginable mayhem. They succeed – by inches – and look, gasping and wan, at each other...

INTERIOR. CONSULTING ROOM (PSYCHIATRIC SECTION – MARKED "PRELIMINARY EXAMINATIONS"). DAY.

PAN DOWN from the identifying notice to a cubicle. Psychiatrist sits facing a Mr Jenkins who is seated quite normally, one leg crossed over the other. The only odd thing is that he wears a dog-collar with a leash trailing from it. The Psychiatrist is ostentatiously patient and understanding – but is soon worn down.

Psychiatrist: So you think you're a dog, Mr Jenkins?

Jenkins: Yes-yes.

He pants happily for emphasis, his tongue hanging out.

Psychiatrist: Well, just get up on the couch.

Jenkins: Can't. I'm not allowed.

Psychiatrist: That's interesting. Why not?

Jenkins: I once wet a couch.

Psychiatrist: How did that come about?

Jenkins: What a silly question. Because I couldn't get to the lamp-post in time, of course. (Scratches self, dog-style, under arm) Bloody fleas. I keep telling 'em to get me one of those special collars. (Straight on) Are you a real doctor?

Psychiatrist: What makes you think I'm not?

Jenkins: If you're really out to help people in distress, where's the keg of brandy round your neck?

Psychiatrist: (Smile is very tolerant) Wait a minute. I don't think I'm a dog.

Jenkins: That's only your opinion.

Psychiatrist: Which is what you're here for, Mr Jenk...

Jenkins: Get on with it then. I haven't heard an intelligent bark out of you yet.

Psychiatrist: I do need to ask a few...

Jenkins: But then, you're not interested in me – not interested in getting to know me.

Psychiatrist: Oh but I am.

Jenkins: Then why haven't you sniffed under my tail yet?

Psychiatrist's mouth opens – but what would he say to this anyway, if JENKINS didn't roll on with...?

Jenkins: In any case, I don't need you. You think I don't'know how I got to be like this?

Psychiatrist's professional smile is becoming somewhat fixed now as...

Psychiatrist: I'd be glad to hear your version, yes...

Jenkins: Well if you knew the first thing about psychiatry, you'd realise – it all started when I was a puppy...

Cyril Carter (Kenneth Cope) and her 'proud' father, Sid (Sidney James) 'case the joint' in Carry On Matron *(1972).*

Wedded Bliss when Matron (Hattie Jacques), finally marries her doctor, Sir Bernard Cutting (Kenneth Williams), at the end of Carry On Matron *(1972). Charles Hawtrey and Jacki Piper witness the happy event.*

Psychiatrist does his best not to hold his head in his hands...

INTERIOR. MATRON'S OFFICE. DAY.

Sister: Oh I see. The Regional Hospital Board. (Matron nods) Oh I do wish you'd felt able to tell me earlier.

Matron: I'm glad you asked me when you did. It's saved me from what would have been a most puzzling conversation with that man from the railways.

Sister: That still leaves the question: who is the mole?

Matron: Someone so outrageously unlikely...

Sister: (Inspired) Goody-ho-ho I That's who!

Matron: Is there no escape from the Chinese?

Sister: (Unhearing) Of course! I should have known! Such obvious eccentricity! All that rubbish about working for Butch Cassidy and keeping his balls properly inflated!

Matron: (Narrowed eyes) So – this Mr Ho-Ho really works for the Regional Board?

Sister: Mr Who-Who? He isn't... I mean... (Getting organised) I'm talking about a new patient. Supposedly in for tests. Mr Cholmondeley. Pronounced Chumley... An alleged lover of goblins...

INTERIOR. WARD. DAY.

Convector Heater Back in Place. Cecil in bed, happily scribbling. BOB dressed, ready to leave. Two Lovely Girls enter. But they're not for him. Guess who. They descend on Dave and mutually caress him.

TWO SHOT Dennis and Bob:

Bob: Now I've seen everything. Look at 'em. Not even the littlest bit jealous of each other. What's he got?

Dennis: Technique. Some ancient Oriental technique, closely guarded in the foothills of Southall. He probably does it under water and coos like a dove.

Bob: To get as many girls as him, I'd snort like a hippo and do it in a mudbath.

Dennis: Whatever – it's a big secret.

Bob: Size has nothing to do with it.

Dennis: Take comfort from that, Shorty.

Bob: Well, I'm off. Goodbye all.

Cecil: Pity. You'll miss my latest story: "Fairy Lightfoot At The United Nations". She turns the Russian delegate into a big cuddly bear.

Dennis: Like Paddington?

Cecil: Like Tschaikowsky. And the whole world waltzes to peace.

Bob: How many of your stories have been printed?

Cecil: None.

Dennis: I wonder why?

INTERIOR. SLUICE. DAY.

Patsy at her eternal washing of things. She wags a finger at the sluice.

Patsy: Now you behave yourself.

She turns it on. No flood. Her satisfaction at having intimidated it is expressed in a grim little nod – future Matron. She turns, sees something offscreen and rushes into:

INTERIOR. WARD CORRIDOR. DAY.

Patsy: Mr Marchant, Mr Marchant.

Bob: (Halting exit) Don't tell me they've decided to put my appendix back in again.

Patsy: I just want you to know – you're the first patient I've seen walk out of here alive.

Bob: I'm glad I didn't know about this Ward's record on the way in.

Patsy: Oh I wasn't here then. And I mean, you know, you're the first one I've actually helped to really genuinely nurse properly back fully to restored health again.

Bob: (Touched) Ovaltine when I really needed it. I'll never forget you.

Patsy: (luminous) Really...?

Anna, the Night Nurse, in civvies, strides purposefully past them. As Margot emerges from the Ward:

Margot: Don't you see enough of this place on night-duty?

Anna: Being Night Nurse here's all over. But something a touch more permanent may just have started. All right for me to visit the leg, Margot?

Margot: Of course.

Anna: Don't look so agog. I don't mind telling you what I'm going to tell him. I'm attracted to him.

Margot: La, how bold...

But, behind the lightness, as she looks after Anna, entering Ward, there is ruefulness and not a little envy...

INTERIOR. WARD. DAY.

TWO SHOT Bill and Anna.

Anna: (Seated) I'm never hypocritical or coy, I hope. Like telling you I'm here by chance. I can't bear that kind of "fancy-meeting-you" pretence from a woman. It went out with long drawers.

Bill: Dropped not a moment too soon.
Anna: Now don't be sexist, or I might change my mind. About you. I'm interested.
Bill: You weren't the other night.
Anna: I was later. When I wasn't with you.
Bill: Funny. That's my ex-wife all over. Potty about me when I was 5000 miles away for a minimum of seven weeks.
Anna: Perhaps you attract the same type over and over again.
Bill: I hope to God not.
Anna: (Bolt upright) Thanks very much!
Bill: There I go again. That one remark too many. Why do I always make that mistake?

Anna rises, properly huffed.

Anna: The mistake is mine.
Bill: No. Wait. See you tonight?
Anna: (headshake) I'm off night-duty. Standing by for transfer.
Bill: Where to?
Anna: What'd suit me perfectly is mortuary-duty.

She flounces out. Bill looks glumly after her, then to Dave.

Bill: Why didn't I break my <u>head</u>, and let some sense in?

INTERIOR. SOLARIUM. DAY.

Cecil, dressing-gowned, reading one of his stories - enthusiastically. His ever-changing expression reflects, in rapid succession, the moods of the tale: joy, tragedy, fear, tension etc.. Enter Matron in background. She "chats" briefly and unheard with a couple of Patients, then approaches Cecil. He talks at his usual heedless, bland, breakneck pace – and gets her into bewilderment almost at once.

Matron: I hope I'm not intruding on your writer's reverie.
Cecil: Not at all. I can turn my dear creative juices on and off like a faggot.
Matron: Don't you mean spigot?
Cecil: That reminds me – I must do that one day.
Matron: Must you? Uh, do what?
Cecil: Write that story about the jockey. It's all in my head, you know.
Matron: How fascinating. But I have a question in mine, and before I forget I...
Cecil: This jockey, Sam Stirrup, is hated by the Hee-Haw Horrors for refusing to ride a donkey in the Derby – pricks himself on his spurs and will sleep for a hundred and two years unless...
Matron: (Despite herself) Pricks himself with his 'spurs?
Cecil: (Nod) Kicking up his heels during flamenco dancing.
Matron: I knew I shouldn't have asked... (Can't help it) How can he come too?
Cecil: Only if his horse kisses him.
Matron: (Hypnotised) Why a hundred and two years?
Cecil: To make my story different from "Little Red Riding Hood".
Matron: You mean "Cinderella".
Cecil: Her too. Mum!

Enter CECIL's MUM. They again make a meal out of kissing each other.

Cecil's Mum: Dolly-boy doodle-darling!
Cecil: Mummy-diddle cuddles!

The pace, if anything, quickens – and Matron is bounced verbally and mentally from one to the other until she's dizzy.

Cecil: This is the Matron.
Matron: How d'you...?
Cecil: I was telling her the jockey story. The one I know they'll make into a film. Fairy Lightfoot in – "They're Off" I
Cecil's Mum: (To Matron) He's not right yet.
Matron: (Half to herself) I don't think he ever will be...
Cecil: She means I haven't got the story right yet.
Cecil's Mum: (Playfully slapping his wrist) Who's 'she' – the cat's mother? And why don't you introduce me?
Matron: That's all right. You're his mother.
Cecil's Mum: (Aggressively) I know that. (To Cecil) What's she think I am – daft?
Matron: Even if I thought so, dear Mrs

A cure for all ills – Valerie Leon in a stunning publicity pose for Carry On Matron *(1972).*

Cholmondeley, I wouldn't say so.

Cecil's Mum: (Amicably) Well that's different.

Matron: (To Cecil) You had a question? (confused, remembering) No. I had a question…

Cecil's Mum: I think she's daft. (To Matron) Present company excepted, of course.

Cecil: What was the question?

Matron: What question?

Cecil: I think I can guess. You want to know how the story ends?

Matron: That wasn't it…

Cecil's Mum: It's no trouble. He'll tell you just the same.

Cecil: (Playfully wagging finger) Who's 'he' – the pussy's papa? (To Matron, earnestly) I want to be honest about this one. No more happy endings just for commercialism. No. His horse does kiss Sam Stirrup – but it's too late. He's died in his sleep.

Matron: Have you ever had a story published?

Cecil: Not an anecdote.

Matron: I wonder why…?

Cecil: (Patient shrug) Envy.

Cecil's Mum: What was the question?

Matron: (Wearily) I was going to ask, Mr Cholmondeley, what you think of our solarium and, indeed, of the spirit and style of Mercy Street Hospital in general…? But…? I must not trespass any further on your visit…

She turns away – rather thankfully – and as they are rendered offscreen by her leaving, we hear:

Cecil's Mum: (Voice over) Letting me stand here all that time like a spare brick on a building site. Why didn't you introduce me…?

Near door, Matron is joined by an agog Sister.

Sister: Well?

Matron: (Decisively) Never. He's not the mole. Not even the Government would employ someone that potty.

INTERIOR. CONSULTING ROOM. DAY.

Sir Roderick is with Bucolic Old Gentleman, wearing club tie, holding walking-stick with silver-knob.

Sir R: I really don't see your problem, Colonel. You don't have diarrhoea or constipation. You may be retired but you're still a very "regular" soldier, eh, what, ha-ha?

Colonel: (Humourless) Damned regular, sir. Every morning at seven o'clock sharp.

Sir R: Well what's wrong with that?

Colonel: Don't get up till eight.

EXTERIOR. NURSES' HOME. DAY.

Patsy emerges. Jim waits. She's pleased.

Jim: Thought I'd walk you to work.

Patsy: Nice thought.

Jim: (As they walk) What about tonight?

Patsy: I expect to be just as tired as I was last night.

Jim: I don't know why you all put up with it.

Patsy: I've been thinking about that. (they halt, on her initiative) And for me it's because this hospital is the best. No nurse is here who doesn't want to be. It gives marvellous training and out of it come super nurses.

Jim: OK. But why all the old bull – just to please the old cow?

Patsy: Don't call her that.

Jim: Hey – you're serious.

Patsy: She scares the pants off me, but…

Jim: What does she charge per scare?

Patsy: Oh you!

Jim: Yes me, please.

INTERIOR. MAIN CORRIDOR. DAY.

Unhappy Patient, swathed in bandages and splints, being pushed in wheelchair by Orderly. He indicated to stop by Vendor.

Unhappy Patient: I've got to write to my mother-in-law.

Vendor: We all have to sometime, man.

Unhappy Patient: Just a postcard. Got one that says "Wish You Were Here"?

Vendor: Sure – and you can sign it – "Hoping this finds you as it leaves me…"

Matron (Hattie Jacques) with patient Mrs Tidey (Joan Sims) in Carry On Matron *(1972). In the unfilmed* Carry On Again, Nurse *it was intended that Joan Sims would take over the role as Matron.*

INTERIOR. CORRIDOR TO MATRON'S OFFICE. DAY.

A very reluctant Randy escorted by Jim. They halt at door to Matron's office.

Jim: Right. Go on in. Tell her you love her.

Randy: ('Airily') You don't have to wait.

Jim: I do. You lost – and I want to see you actually go into Matron.

Randy: You could have phrased that differently... I feel quite faint...

Jim: Rubbish. After all the girls you've wooed and won?

Randy: You're talking of sweet little hillocks, lightly trod. This is in the Everest class. Nothing in my experience has readied me for an assault on Mount Bullivant. Do you realise – if you make me go in there – I may never be seen again. DON'T DO THAT!!

For Jim has knocked on the door.

Matron: (Voice over) Come.

Jim opens door, standing aside out of Matron's view, shoves Randy in.

INTERIOR. MATRON'S OFFICE. DAY.

Randy unsteadily completes awkward shoved-on entrance. Matron looks up, puzzled, not thrilled, from paperwork.

Matron: Dr Firkin?
Randy: The same.
Matron: The same what?
Randy: Yes. Well. Er. I'm here, er, on a matter of some delicacy.
Matron: Then it might be as well to close the door.

Randy turns to do so, nodding and gulping. Too eager and too fast, he falls over a chair, grabs at a small table. It bears flowers. Inevitably, they are daffodils. The table and flowers fall with him. Aghast, he rises, bumping into Matron as she steps into him en route to close the door herself. They waltz briefly. She disentangles, closes door. Faces him. He has a bent daffodil in his hand.

Matron: Please, for both our sakes, sit down?

She makes a broad, generous gesture with her arm to indicate the chair he is to occupy. Anticipating the invitation, anxious to please, he has stepped forward in that direction. He therefore receives a mighty backhander under the chin which lifts him off his feet. He sprawls and slides over her desk-top, clearing it, disappearing down the other side, knocking her chair over. She waits. He rises groggily from behind her desk, clutching its edge. The daffodil, more bedraggled, is now in his hair.

CLOSE-UP Matron:

Matron: (Frowning) That strikes a chord of memory – only it wasn't in his hair...

RESUME SCENE

Randy re-positions her chair. Not without some trepidation, she goes round and sits. He sits too, where first indicated. She waits. He still has the daffodil in his hair.

Randy: I, er, there's, I want, he, yes – there's a very shy man who, he who... (Plunge) Well, he loves you.

Matron tends, as we have seen, to take some astonishing news calmly. This certainly does not cause her to go to soppy pieces. She just waits for elaboration. Sweatingly, Randy provides it.

Randy: He, er, has loved you, er from a long time ago and, you might say, a galaxy far away. Now he wants to try for a close encounter.
Matron: Then why doesn't he?
Randy: Ah well that's it, the shyness, you see – he's petrified in fear of a rebuff. I'm his intermediary. What shall I tell him?
Matron: If I agree to see him, only then will he expose himself to me?
Randy: You've got it in a flash.
Matron: And you have a daffodil in your hair. (Covered in confusion, he removes it as...) Well, Dr Firkin. I cannot of course guarantee to like your timid friend – much less dance the tango for him with a rose in my teeth. But I will see him. Thank you. Good morning.

He leaves. Matron, continuing her work, absently hums a bit of "Ah Sweet Mystery of Life... "

INTERIOR. CORRIDOR TO MATRON'S OFFICE. DAY.

Jim waits at other end. Randy approaches, deep in thought.

Jim: Well? I'm agog.
Randy: You're a sadist. To put me through that.
Jim: What happened?
Randy: I demolished her office. I lost my nerve. I told her Romeo is someone else. (Sigh) And for what I've done to the old bat, I feel like a piece of very mouldy cheese.

He looks at Jim in genuine contrition.

INTERIOR. WARD. DAY.

Charles, at the door, trying to look like he's here on legitimate business, is properly impressed by Two More of Dave's Girls, each kissing him goodbye. The entire Ward, with the exception of the happily scribbling Cecil, is, as usual, fully envious of the remarkable Dave. The bed formerly occupied by Bob now has another Patient. The Girlfriends leave, drifting past Charles as if he does not exist, their eyes bent on Dave to the last. Charles squares his shoulders and approaches Dave.

Charles: Excuse me, Mr Beaton...?
Dave: Don't you want...?

Dr Tinkle (Kenneth Williams) doesn't seem pleased to see former patient and student nurse Sandra May (Barbara Windsor) in Carry On Doctor *(1968).*

He indicates Bill, who's dozing fitfully. Charles shakes his head. Dave indicated him to sit. Charles does so. Charles sets a quiet, intimate tone.

Charles: This has nothing to do with medicine. You have every right to tell me to naff off.

Dave: I know.

Charles: You're the talk of the hospital. All these girls. You're amazing. And I'm frankly, desperate. (Plunge) Mr Beaton, I'm wildly in love... and I can't even bring myself to tell her... How? What? Will you tell me? What's the secret?

Dave: Well, I don't know...

Charles: Please, Mr Beaton. Please.

Dave: You know the old saying.

Charles: What's that?

Dave: Never introduce your doctor to a pal.

Charles: I won't tell, anyone. Honest. I'm desperate. Please. What is the secret?

Dave: The secret is... Moderation.

Charles produces pad and pencil, takes notes feverishly, starting now with:

Charles: Moderation...

Dave: You're attracted to a girl. Let 'er know it. Not too eager, not too casual. In between. Moderation.

Charles: In – between...

Dave: Buy 'er a drink. (Warningly) Not too sweet, not too dry.

Charles: Ah. Drink...

Dave: Ask 'er to your place. But not too anxious – and not too orf 'and.

Charles: ... orf 'and...

Dave: Your flat must not be too 'ot, not too cold. Not too much light but, likewise, not plunged in darkness.

Charles: ... plunged... yes... (Looks up from notes) She's at my place. Then what?

Dave: I'll give you an 'int. A woman is like a plant. So you have to...?

Charles: (Earnestly) Water her?

Dave: Dear oh Lor'... Talk to her. They love bein' talked to. Not too brainy, mind – and not too common. The objective is to ease 'er into your bedroom. Not too obviously – and not so roundabout it takes all night.

Charles: I see. That wouldn't do at all, would it?

Dave: No. It would not.

Dave eyes Charles in almost open doubt for a moment. But continues:

Dave: Now you 'ave to undress 'er.

Charles: Yes. Well. My gosh. Of course. (Gulp.) Er. How?

Dave: Well, not as if you're tearing off wallpaper – and not like you're unpeeling a rare fruit. Either extreme, when it comes to the brassiere, can be dangerous. The strap comes flyin' loose round the front and can 'it you in the eye.

Charles: (Taking notes still) "... 'it you in – the – eye..." Yes.

Dave: Finally – there she is.

In the Ward there is absolute hush and stillness. Every syllable of Dave's crash-course is getting breathless attention from all, including the now-awake Bill, and Cecil, his pen at last poised in mid-air, his dedicated writing halted.

Dave: On your bed. Nude, relaxed, willing, confident. She is ready.

Charles: ... Ready... (Looks up: dry-throated) Then what do I do?

Dave looks finally and keenly at him. Sighs.

Dave: Send for me.

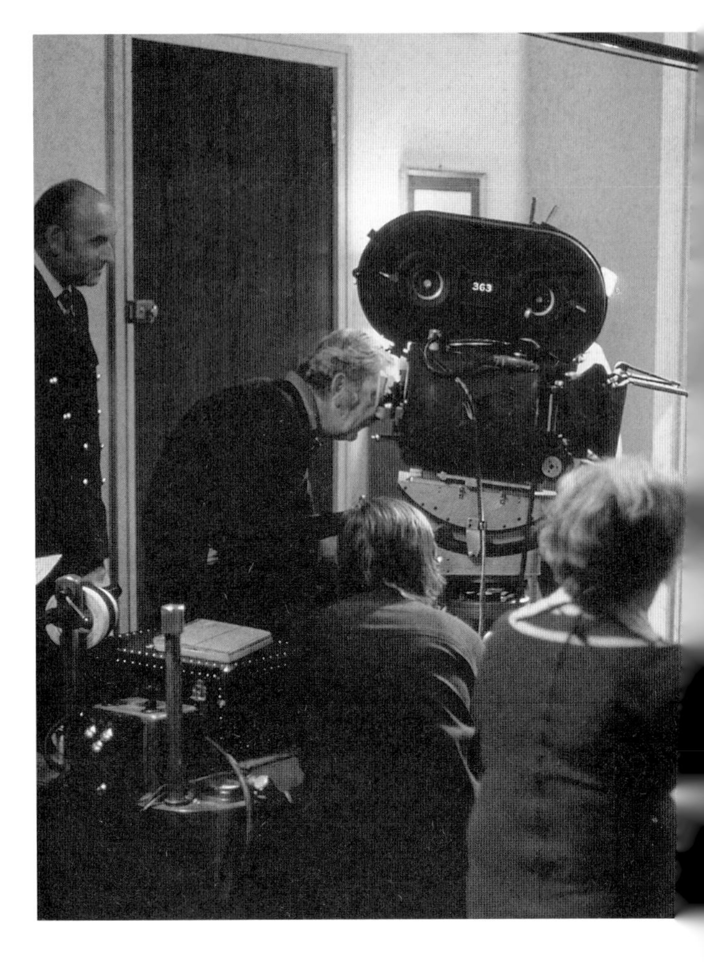

INTERIOR. WARD CORRIDOR. DAY.

Patsy: (keen as always) Yes, Sister.

She takes a file of papers from Sister and runs towards Main Corridor, dedicated, possessed.

Sister: We do not run, girl. That's how mishaps occur.

PATSY stops running, nods obediently, walks with dignity. At the corner, she collides with Vendor's cart. Perfect timing.

INTERIOR. MAIN CORRIDOR. DAY.

The cart slews around, its top surface of goods scattering immediately to the floor. The same movement sends Patsy spinning giddily and she sits on the floor, her papers flying. The force of the cart's move wrenches it out of Vendor's control. It crashes into a row of parked wheelchairs: he hits the wall, falls back, finds himself

Filming Carry On Matron *at the end of 1971.*

seated on the floor next to the dazed Patsy. The cart hits the opposite wall after it veers away from the wheelchairs. All its contents disperse as it overturns. One wheelchair, turning right around, rolls fast towards – Sister, who, frozen-faced, is at end of Ward Corridor, surveying the scene, catching and halting the runaway wheelchair. She looks at Patsy. Patsy looks back up at her from the floor. No suitable comment seems possible from either, as assorted shouts and orders and the rumbling of untended wheelchairs resound offscreen

INTERIOR. ACCIDENT AND EMERGENCY. DAY.

Body on trolley, concealed by sheet. Two feet stick out. Old Lady very distressed. Doctor extremely sympathetic.

Doctor: Take your time. Just tell me what happened.

Old Lady: He fell down dead. In the garden. Bending down, 'e was, to get a cabbage for our dinner.

Doctor: And what did you do?

Old Lady: What could I do? I 'ad to open a tin of peas...

INTERIOR. WARD. CORRIDOR. DAY.

Charles strides in, very determined, as Margot emerges from Kitchen. He grabs her by the elbows, reverses her into:

INTERIOR. KITCHEN. DAY.

Charles: (Setting fast pace) Moderation and the middle way be damned.

Margot: (Bowled over) This is not the time or place to talk politics.

Charles: It's high time I followed my own instincts. And this is as good a place as any. Stand still.

Margot: Let go of me, please.

Charles: Never.

Margot: Don't I have any say in this?

Charles: None. I think you've been waiting for me to say it all.

Margot: And what does "all" add up to?

Charles: This.

He embraces and kisses her firmly. She is dazed.

Margot: I'm on duty...

Charles: That's not what you say at this point in my dreams.

Margot: You dream about me?

Charles: Not any more. No need. (Final panic) Is there?

For answer, she kisses and dazes him.

Charles: Margot!

Margot: Charles!

Sister: (offscreen) Bingo!

ZIP TO:

Sister on the threshold. She couldn't be more genuinely pleased. Is positively beaming, thumbs up. Behind her, in Ward Corridor, Stella passes, urgent and determined.

Glamour girl actress and model Margaret Nolan playing maternity patient Mrs Tucker in Carry On Matron *(1972).*

INTERIOR. WARD. DAY.

Stella, ignoring the impressive sight of Dave with yet another Girlfriend, who's dreamily combing his hair, goes straight to Bill.

TWO SHOT Bill and Stella: He's astonished to see her.

Stella: Are you free?

Bill: No. I'm just off to practise for the marathon.

Stella: I mean you're not due for a treatment or anything?

Bill: No. Apparently all we can do is sit and watch this thing knit.

Stella: Just like your mother on our honeym...

She bites her tongue. He doesn't protest however, just looks curiously at her – a look she holds. In fact, from this point, they do not take their eyes off each other.

Stella: Bill, I was right about the divorce but only because I needed to be away from you to understand you.

Bill: You could have gone to your mother.

Stella: Be serious.

Bill: I don't think I dare.

Stella: Now I understand you. You're the sort who needs looking after – but you're no less of a man and an achiever for that. Churchill and Mozart were the same.

Bill: How does that help me? I choke on cigars and I'm tone-deaf.

Stella: Don't try to understand anything except – I've never stopped loving you.

Bill: I know. Even when you wished me dead it was only because I was so bloody miserable.

He takes her hand.

Bill: Stell. I've never stopped loving you either. I've lain here thinking of all sorts of women. But I'm no Dave. I've only ever wanted you.

Stella: (Taking his other hand) Who's Dave...?

Cecil: (To someone o.s.) Aaaaah. Told you, didn't I? It was just a lovers' tiff...

Bill and Stella are still linked, by hands and eyes. Dave's hair-combing Girlfriend is just leaving, blowing a final kiss to him. When she's out, Dave sighs, says, to the Patient opposite him, are looking at Bill and Stella.

Dave: That's all I want out of life – to be allowed to be a one-woman man...

INTERIOR. PORTER'S OFFICE. DAY.

Harry looks sadly at a wad of bank notes in his hand.

Harry: That's it. The last of our nicking money – and all our Premium Bonds besides.

Ted: An' I'm gettin' the stuff at a bargain price at that.

Harry: Four thousand rolls of loo-paper... I never thought to see me life's savin's wiped out like that.

He kisses the money goodbye and slaps it into TED's hand.

INTERIOR. WARD. DAY.

Sir Roderick enters, escorted by Sister, goes to Cecil.

Sister: Sir Roderick's taking a special interest in

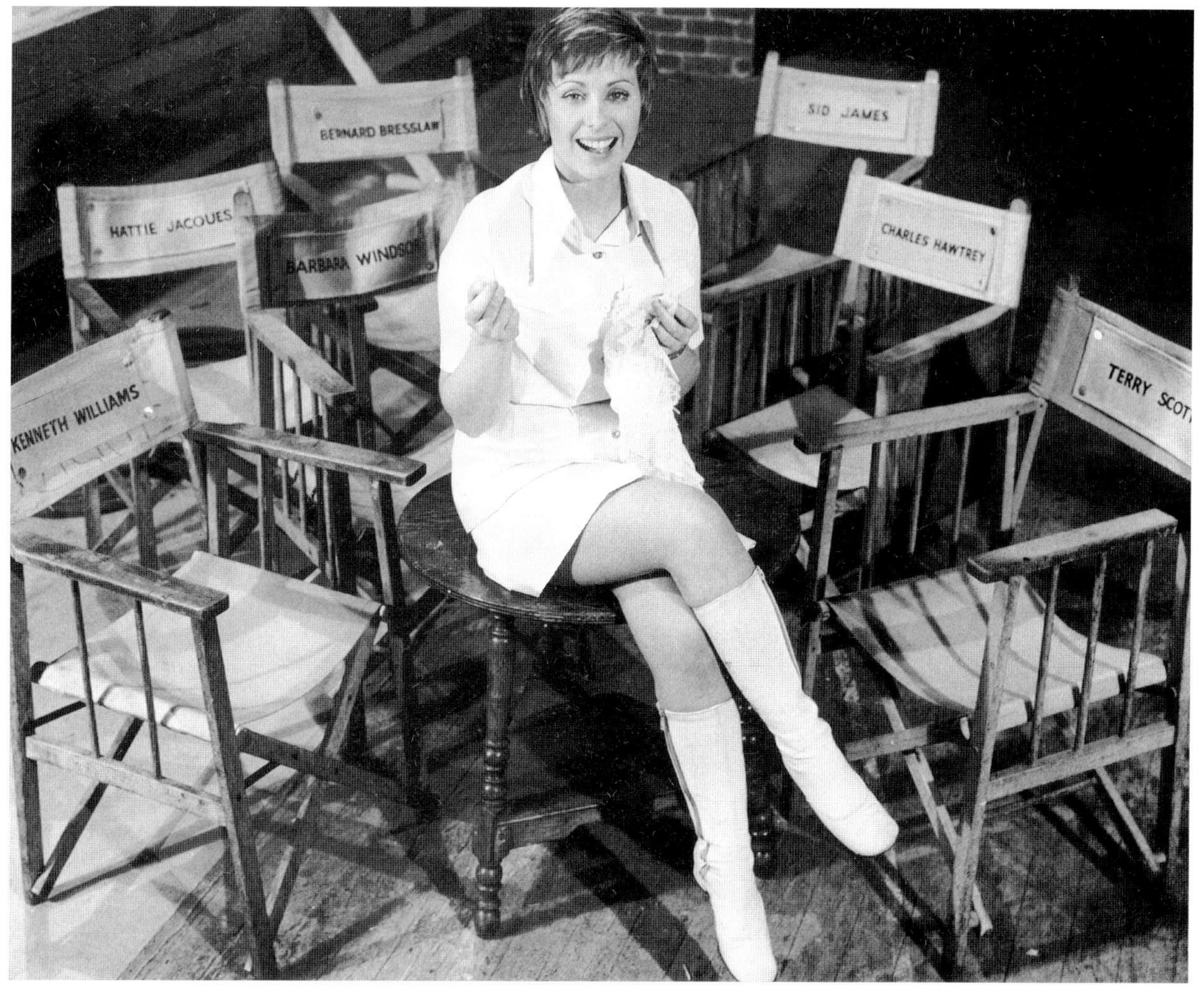

Valerie Shute played the pregnant Miss Smethurst in Carry On Matron *(1972) and is pictured here surrounded by the empty 'director's chairs' of the cast.*

your case, Mr Cholmondeley.

Cecil: How nice. Or is it because I'm in a bad way?

Sir R: Not at all. All tests are complete. There's no need for surgery.

Cecil: Oh goody-ho-ho.

Sir R: (Slightly taken aback) You've obviously been worrying too much...

Cecil: Oh yes-yes. About my fairies.

Sir R: (Pushing on)... and have a microscopic duodenal ulcer. It should respond to diet.

Cecil: And pills. A new pill! And you need my consent to try it. Because there may be side-effects. So I'll have to stay in a couple more days.

Sir R: How did you know?

Cecil: Fairy Lightfoot had to do that at the Sugar-Plum Clinic when she sprained her ankle.

Sir R: (Despite himself) How?

Cecil: Flying through the thunderstorm to warn the elves. You see, they'd just escaped from the pixies' farmyard.

Sir R: Who had?

Cecil: The Giant Cocks.
Sir R: (To Sister) Do you know what we're talking about?
Sister: He's a write...
Sir R: There's no need to insult the patient, Sister. I'm surprised at you.
Sister: Sir – he's a writer.
Sir R: Do I have your consent, sir?
Cecil: With all my heart, Honker. We'll be married at the little acorn church under the mushroom.
Sir R: Pardon?!
Cecil: (Tremulous) I can't help it. Those are the exact words at the end of one of my most touching tales. About two weeny-pigs.
Sister: Not bad actually. He let me read it.
Sir R: What's it called – "Hogshead Revisited"?
Sister: No., "Gone With The Grunt".
Sir R: The pill, the treatment. Do you consent to that, Mr Cholmondeley?
Cecil: Oh yes-yes.
Sir R: Excellent. It will calm you down – or it won't.
Cecil: Very fair.

Sir Roderick begins to turn away.

Sir R: (To sister) Full report on the effects. Regular observation.
Sister: Of course, Sir Roderick.

He halts, turns back to Cecil.

Sir R: Out of sheer professional curiosity and I know I'm taking my sanity in my hands – but – what was Fairy Lightfoot taking?
Cecil: Extract of sweetpea.
Sir R: Were there any side-effects?
Cecil: She grew a moustache and her wings clogged with fur.
Sir R: You've never had a story published?
Cecil: Not a syllable.
Sir R: (leaving) I wonder why...?

INTERIOR. SOLARIUM. DAY.

Toothless Old man sits comfortably – but looking gummily and longingly at a nice firm red apple on a plate on the table near him. Enter White Coat with carrier bag.

White Coat: Hello old-timer. Sister told me you've been and gone and lost your dentures.
Toothless: (Mumbling) Yemmm it'm a mubby muisance...

White Coat takes a set of dentures out of bag.

White Coat: Try these.

Toothless does. They don't fit. Shaking his head, he hands them back. White Coat gives him another set. In they go. And in they stay.

Toothless: (Radiant) Perfect! (picks up apple) I didn't know they had a dental department here. (Polishes apple)
White Coat: They don't.
Toothless: Oh? Where do you work then? (bites into apple)
White Coat: Mortuary.

Toothless, wide-eyed, stops in mid-bite, apple wedged in his teeth.

INTERIOR. WARD. DAY.

Another lover of Dave's, in smart Cowgirl outfit, is smooching single-mindedly with him. Enter Sister, straight to Cecil.

Sister: Just going off duty, Mr Cholmondeley. It's three hours since your first pill. Now, for my records, are you relaxed?

For answer, Cecil gets out of bed and tries to embrace her. She evades, nips round the centre table. As wholesome and innocent as ever, Cecil plays catch-you-if-I-can while:

Sister: Now, now, Mr Cholmondeley! Think of your little fairy-friends.
Cecil: Screw 'em.

He dives for her and falls on top of the table. While he's very temporarily out of action:

Sister: (Urgently) I want two able-bodied men...
Dennis: Why – isn't one like him enough for you?
Sister: Mr Harper – please help to control Mr Ch...

Cecil, grinning exultantly, slides off the table and makes another grab for her.

Dennis: Calm down, old boy.

Dennis grabs him. Cecil struggles – joyously, romping.

Cecil: But I love her.

Sister: (Exiting, shouting) What's it say on the label?

INTERIOR. WARD. CORRIDOR. DAY.

Margot and Patsy readying to leave as Sister, looking rather wild, flies out of the Ward. Margot is naturally nonplussed. Wide-eyed Patsy looks from one to the other as:

Margot: What?

Nothing is more irritating, when you are enmeshed in crisis, than to be asked "What?" when you seek assistance. Sister's look and tone reflect this desperate impatience:

Sister: The label, the label – what's it say on the label of Fairy Lightfoot's pills?

Margot: Fairy Li...? Oh. About what?

Sister: SEX!

Patsy: Oo!

Margot: Nothing, Sister. I read it with you – very carefully.

Sister: Well, just one's given him a side-effect that sticks out a mile.

Margot: He must be one in a million!

Sister: Not to me, he isn't. Get in there. Help calm him down. (Margot hurries into Ward) Nurse Furness! Call Sir Roderick. Tell him Mr Cholmondeley's getting an aphrodisiac reaction.

Patsy: Afra?... Afroo...?

Sister spins her round and shoves her towards phone.

INTERIOR. WARD. DAY.

Cecil is rolling on the floor with Dennis. Having marvellous time. Plenty of energy, but not an ounce of nastiness in him. Margot is hurrying to the two of them. Sister bounces in to help Margot. As the melee develops and moves, everyone JUST misses jostling Bill's traction-leg. He is petrified. Dave and Cowgirl embrace on, oblivious.

Director Gerald Thomas discussing medication and motivation for Carry On Matron, *with Kenneth Williams.*

EXTERIOR. MERCY STREET. DAY.

HARRY emerges from pub as Sir Roderick's Rolls Royce emerges from hospital driveway. Phone rings offscreen.

INTERIOR. SIR RODERICK'S ROLLS ROYCE. DAY.

Sir R: (Picking up car-phone) Yes? (Big reaction) Side-effect? What kind?

He jams on the brakes.

EXTERIOR. MERCY STREET. DAY.

Once again, road-crossing Harry is almost run down – and reacts as before.

Harry: What's-a-matter – ain't you got an...? (shrug) Oh yeh. I remember. You ain't.

INTERIOR. SIR RODERICK'S ROLLS ROYCE. DAY.

As HARRY continues slouchingly crossing road in front of it:

Sir R: (On car-phone – even bigger reaction) It's acting on him like a what, child?

INTERIOR. WARD. CORRIDOR. DAY.

Patsy: (on phone – importantly – and innocently) You know, sir – an aphrodic.

INTERIOR. WARD. DAY.

Between them, Sister, Margot and Dennis have managed to get Cecil up off the floor but he's still happily resisting, and also trying to kiss and fondle the girls.

Cecil: I love you all. Don't fight over me. Peace. Happiness. You'll all get your turn.

They try to propel him to his bed. Instead, thanks to his gleeful wrestling, they all fall on it, with squawks and grunts.

INTERIOR. MATRON'S OFFICE. DAY.

Matron, humming "Ah Sweet Mystery of Life", passes window, idly glancing out, suddenly returns in puzzled reaction to:

EXTERIOR. HOSPITAL. DAY.

Matron's window POV

Sir Roderick is actually running into the Hospital from his parked Rolls. Very tense and urgent.

INTERIOR. ENTRANCE HALL. DAY.

Soir Roderick and Matron, coming downstairs, almost collide.

Matron: What's up?

Sir R: I tremble to think.

He runs on. Astonished, she follows him.

INTERIOR. WARD. CORRIDOR. DAY.

Night staff (Night Sister, 2nd Night Nurse, Student Nurse arrive – and are scattered by Sir Roderick and Matron running in. They stare after this senior pair – actually and unprecedentedly running – as they charge on into:

Nurse: (Musing) You're not supposed to run...

INTERIOR. WARD. DAY.

Sister, Margot, Cecil, Dennis and now Patsy as well, tangled on and around Cecil's bed. With everybody still in motion, they variously become aware of each other as Matron and Sir Roderick run in and streak for Cecil's bed.

Matron: Sister!

Sir R: Mr Cholmondeley!

Sister: Matron!

Matron: (Faintly) The Regional Board...!

The thought stops her, briefly, and she leans for support against a bed. Bill's. Extra-terror from him re his traction-ed leg's chance now of being dislodged.

Cecil: (Calling to Matron) I love you!

Patsy: Oo dear!

Margot: (Goosed in the mêlée) Mr Harper!

Bill: Bottle!

And the Night Staff arrives in the doorway, goggling at the scene.

Night Sister: (To 2nd Night Nurse) Get him a bottle.

2nd Night Nurse: (To Student) Get him a bottle.

Student Nurse: Get him a bot...

She realises she has to get it herself.

And still Dave and Cowgirl follow their own interests. Cecil breaks free of restraint, rushes for Matron. She evades, turns, runs. Chase. Straight off, she bounces into returning Student Nurse who has the bottle knocked from her hand. Plastic, it falls and Bounces, to a faraway Patient, who catches it neatly.

During the following, therefore, the bottle is thrown from bed to bed, en route to the increasingly anxious Bill who also agonises over leg-jostling as people scrape, hairsbreadth, by his bed and the delicately-poised traction-outfit. He continues safe from dislodgment – but it's close.

Sir Roderick strides purposefully to resolve the situation. Swerving around the table, Matron bumps into

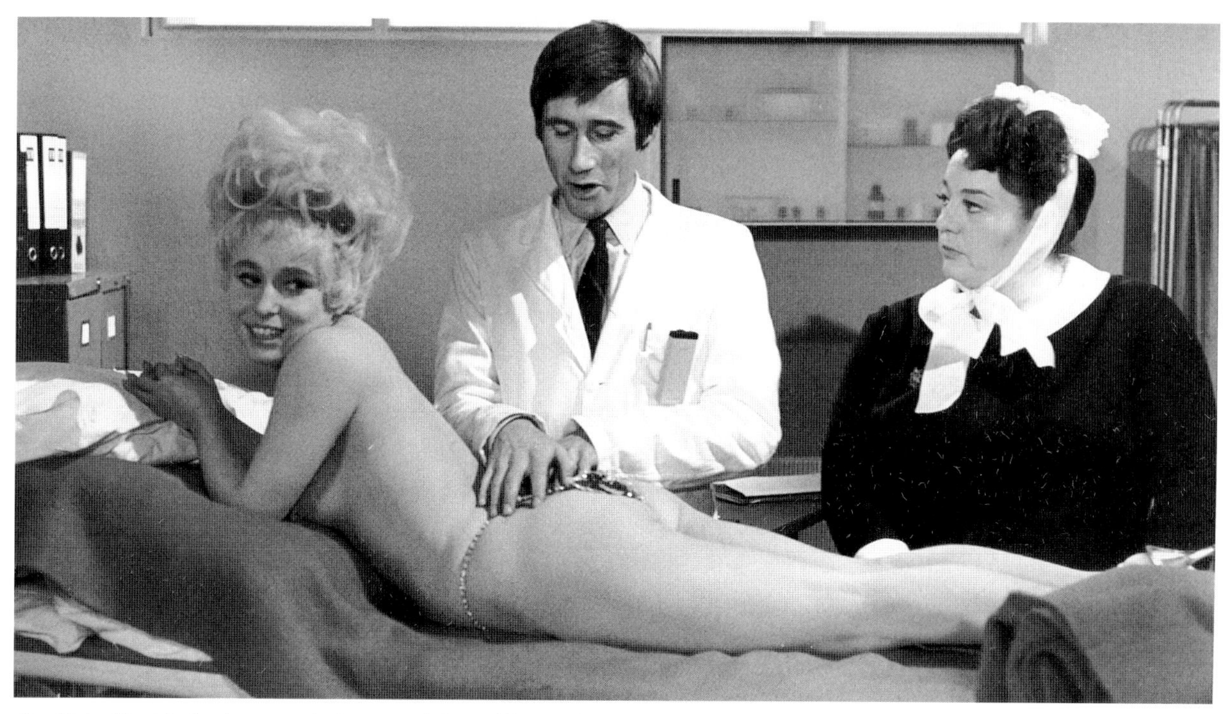

Jim Dale (Dr Nookey) gets to the bottom of the problem with Goldie Locks (Barbara Windsor) and Matron (Hattie Jacques) in Carry On Again Doctor *(1969).*

him. He bounces off her, on to Cecil's empty bed, and bounces off it, to disappear beyond.

Cecil: (catching Matron) My darling!

He swings her around and embraces her., The sight is so world-shattering that everything STOPS in sudden awed SILENCE and STILLNESS – including Sir Roderick rising groggily from bedside. The sole object in movement is the plastic bottle -finally flung across past the embraced couple – and avidly seized by BillL. His MOAN of anticipated relief breaks the spell...

... Cecil blinks, and his rampage halts as suddenly as it started. He withdraws from the embrace with Matron – with an intake of shocked breath.

Cecil: How dare you, madame – and me a respectable goblin?

Matron: It's all right, Mr Cholmondeley. My fault entirely. Now just get back to' bed...

Sister, Margot, Patsy: All dishevelled. Sister speaks, quietest, to them, in full admiration and example.

Sister: That's nursing. The patient is 'right – first – last – and all the time.

RESUME SCENE

Sir Roderick helps Matron escort the beweildered CECIL to bed.

Sir R: Easy there. The medicine was, to put it mildly, wrong for you.

Cecil: (Discovery) And I've been wrong about the fairies. I must try to write about real people – and their simple pleasures.

CLOSE-UP Bill – Hands beneath blanket, bottle not in sight.

Bill: Aaaaaaaaaaaah....

INTERIOR. CONSULTING ROOM. DAY.

Woman Patient: After I've been with my husband, why do I feel like I've got indigestion?

Woman Doctor: Maybe it is. Have you tried Andrews?

Woman Patient: Yes – and Bert's and George's. But it makes no difference whose it is.

INTERIOR. LECTURE ROOM. DAY.

Sir R: Specialise though we may, we must never lose sight of the basic human drives – sex and hunger. Gentlemen, you are the first to know that I propose to do a clinical study of both, in urban areas, and based at this Hospital. I go from here, at once, in fact, to apprise Matron of the project.

He leaves, bubbling with enthusiasm.

Jim: You didn't hear a word of that.

Randy: I've decided to see Matron.

Jim: And be her Casanova after all?

Randy: No. Tell her the truth, and apologise.

Jim: There's a good boy.

Randy: What was sir on about anyway? I'd better jot down some initials to remind me...

Jim: Sex and Hunger in Towns.

Randy: (Writing) S.H.I...

INTERIOR. MATRON'S OFFICE. DAY.

Matron: (On phone)... tea, today, definitely. Yesterday's coffee tasted like industrial waste.

IINTERIOR. CORRIDOR TO MATRON'S OFFICE. DAY.

Sir Rodrick enters jauntily at one end.

INTERIOR. MATRON'S OFFICE. DAY.

Matron writing in a beautifully-bound book with a lock on it.

Matron: (V.O.) (At writing-pace) "Dear Diary... I have decided that my 'secret admirer' is almost certainly a typical Firk by Dr Prankin".

Matron: Drat.

She scratches out and corrects the incorrect phrase, closes diary, puts it to one side.

INTERIOR. CORRIDOR TO MATRON'S OFFICE. DAY.

As Sir Roderick arrives and knocks on Matron's door...
... Randy appears at other end of corridor, dragging his feet. Grateful for the delay, on seeing Sir Roderick, he withdraws and awaits, round the corner.

Matron: (Offscreen) Come.

INTERIOR. MATRON'S OFFICE. DAY.

Enter Sir Roderick.

Sir R: I have no appointment, but...

Matron: Be seated.

Sir R: Too excited about – for one thing – sex.

He strides, eyes gleaming, brain humming. Matron glances at the diary – and catches her breath.

Matron: (To his back) It's you...? You? (to diary and herself) It's him – him! (to Sir R) Suddenly? Just like that?

Sir R: Oh no. I suppose I've had it in my mind for aye these thirty years.

Matron: Aye these...? (To herself, shock) Heavens. The St Vitus Day Dance, (Continued) nineteen - (Hastily) -whenever-it-was. That song... it's haunted me... They played... Ah yes... " Ah Sweet Mystery of Life..." (Controls palpitations) You were saying – sex?

Sir R: I need your co-operation.

Matron: I imagine so, yes.

Sir R: Goody-ho-ho! You can service me, then – with six nurses?

Matron sputters in total consternation.

Sir R: To share with the others, of course.

Matron: (Hoarse) What others??!!!

Sir R: The other four doctors.

Matron: Of all the bestial, male arrogance...!

Sir R: Oh no. You've got it all wrong.

Matron: I have?

Sir R: Of course. Two of them will be women.

Matron's speechless expression is now such that even he must halt in his striding for:

Sir R: I'm not making myself clear, am I? It's one of my sins.

Matron: (Faintly) The least, by the sound of it...

Sir R: Listen. You know me. Impulsive. Impatient. My ideas fall over each other, higgledy-piggledy and Gone With The Grunt. I'm sorry. I'll begin at the beginning. Right. Now. I want to set up a clinical study here on urban Sex and Hunger.

In view (left to right) Matron cast members: Bernard Bresslaw, Kenneth Cope, director Gerald Thomas and Sidney James, who are interviewed while playing cards during a break in filming.

Matron's hopes deflate. She looks, more than a little ruefully, at her diary.

Sir R: I could make do, at the start, with a staff of six Nur... What's the matter.

Matron: Nothing...

She closes the lock on the diary, quite tenderly.

Sir R: Yes there is. I know you, Matron Bullivant. And I haven't seen that look on you before.

Matron: Haven't you...?

Sir R: Not once in thirty...

His tone and pace change – softer, slower.

Sir R: Yes I have. Just once... There was - music... A hospital dance... Yes. That was it. Here. Mercy Street. Where we've been all our professional lives.

Matron: But none of our privates.

Sir R: We slipped away. Went for a walk.

Matron: In the graveyard.

Sir R: And I – I made a dead set for you. That music. What was it? From the dance, in the distance.

Matron: "Ah Sweet Mystery Of Life".

Sir R: You remember!

Matron: A Bullivant never forgets.

Sir R: Gad. To think you've waited thirty years to say that. Was it – worth it?

Matron: I don't know. But I'll tell you this: it beats your joke about Cohen's eggs.

Sir R: Do you regret the years slipping by? Concentrating solely on your career?

Matron: It's thanks to you I had a career. Remember? I wanted to give up nursing. Couldn't take the discipline. You encouraged me, that night to – Carry On.

(Bravely) I had my memories. One glamorous night in the graveyard. And – you?

Sir R: I've watched you grow – in all directions. And I always felt – yes, I had a hand in her success.

Matron: You're too modest. It was more than just a hand – but – may we? Dare we? Be done with memories – and look to the future...?

Sir R: Together – Millicent?

Matron: Roderick...

INTERIOR. CORRIDOR TO MATRON'S OFFICE. DAY.

Randy waiting at the corner. Matron and Sir Roderick approach, in silent contentment, looking at each other. In his anxiety, Randy doesn't notice this air about them at first.

Randy: Er, excuse me... (They halt) I have – something to tell you, Matron...

She comfortingly pats his hand.

Matron: I know you do, dear boy – and it doesn't matter – so don't bother...

Matron and Sir Roderick move on. She puts her arm through his. Randy gapes after them – realises – and grins in huge relief, and not a little sentiment.

INTERIOR. WARD. CORRIDOR. DAY.

Jim hurries in and finds Patsy in, of course:

INTERIOR. SLUICE. DAY.

Patsy: You shouldn't be here.

Jim: I couldn't sleep last night.

Patsy: Well you can't sleep here.

Jim: Why not? I heard you did the other day.

Patsy: Don't remind me. Why couldn't you sleep?

Jim: Guess.

Patsy: All right. Let's make a date.

Jim: Tonight?

Patsy: But I must be home by eleven.

Jim: I promise – in one piece, and good as new.

Patsy: (Disappointed) Oh. (Realises) Of course.

He steals a peck. Hurries out. Patsy day-dreams. SISTER sticks her head in, tells her off but not too seriously.

Sister: We need that stuff cleaned, not mooned-over. Carry On, Nurse. (Patsy merely sighs) Do I have to say Carry On Again Nurse?

Patsy comes to and works like a demon. Sister smothers a smile. Corridor wall-phone rings.

INTERIOR. WARD. CORRIDOR. DAY.

Sister picks up phone.

Sister: (On phone) Men's Surgical, Ward 4F. Sister... (Tense) Yes. Immediately.

INTERIOR. MATRON'S OFFICE. DAY.

Matron very tense. Door-knock.

Matron: Come.

Enter Sister, anxious.

Sister: What is it? You sounded terrible on the phone.

Matron: The Regional Board. It's meeting in special session. The decision will be made today. I'm going mad here, alone. I must be with someone when I hear...

Sister: I'll stay with you, of course.

Matron: (Conscience) To think – I've taken you away from patients.

Sister: Nurse Walton can cope.

Matron: (Agonised) What shall I do if they close Mercy Street...?

Sister: Don't think of it. Talk about something else. Anything.

They do – but in the same anxious, flat, taut tones, with the same unsmiling, dour, tormented expressions.

Matron: Let me see. Oh yes. I'm getting married.

Sister: Who's the lucky man?

Matron: Sir Roderick.

Sister: Congratulations. So you'll become a lady. I never thought it possible.

Matron: How's Nurse Walton coming along with that idiot Dr Murray?

Sister: He declared himself.

Matron: Why – couldn't he smuggle himself through Customs?

Sister: (Miserably) That's quite funny.

Matron: I hope Nurse Walton can still smile six

months from now. That Dr Murray has all the gypsy abandon of a lopsided truss.

Sister: Yes, he does look like he thinks the G-Spot's somewhere on a Dalmatian. But they'll be all right. And little Nurse Furness has a beau too.

Matron: Another Houseman I suppose. Honestly, sometimes I think their heraldic sign is a pair of trousers rampant over the Nurses' Home.

Sister: (Tragically) That's funny too.

Matron: So. Walton, Furness. Myself. All deliriously happy in love. And you?

Sister: Bugger-all.

Matron: Don't give up. Romance is in the air.

Sister: Soon, there may be nothing but air round here when they start knocking down... (Bites tongue) Sorry. I didn't mean to... The whole idea was to stay off the subject...

Matron: It's impossible. D'you think it'll be in the papers yet?

Sister: I'll run and get one.

She hurries to and opens the door. Harry enters immediately, tense. Matron rises, expectant, taut.

Harry: (indicating Sister) Er...?

Matron: It's all tight. (Sister closes door) You – know the result? Before the newspapers?

Harry: Through me mole.

Matron: And?

Harry: We've won.

Matron sits and does a whole number of controlled, emotional reaction. Head in hands, lip-biting, knuckle-gnawing etc..

Harry: It was a near thing.

Sister: That doesn't matter. We won.

The patients - Bernard Bresslaw, Sidney James and Frankie Howerd - revolt against the tyrannical Doctor Tinkle (Kenneth Williams) at the comic climax of Carry On Doctor (1968).

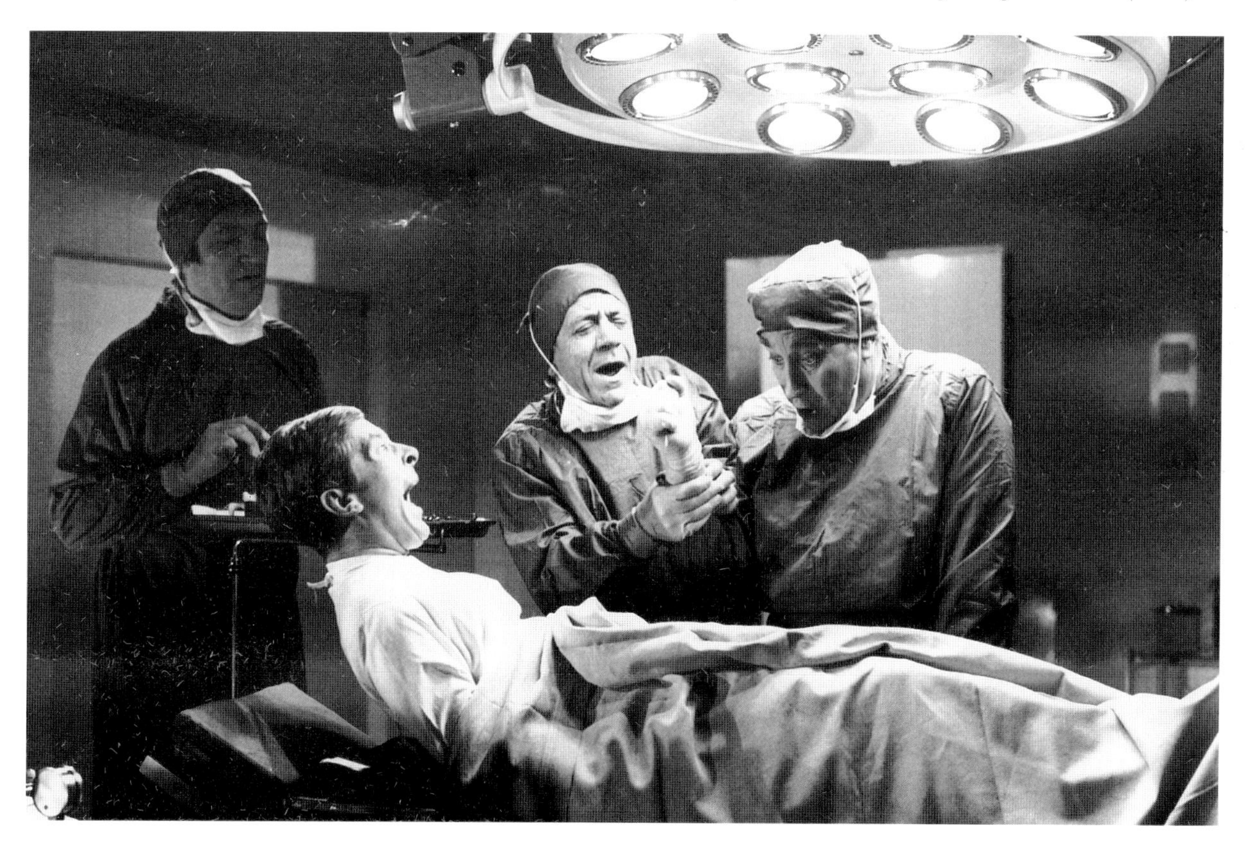

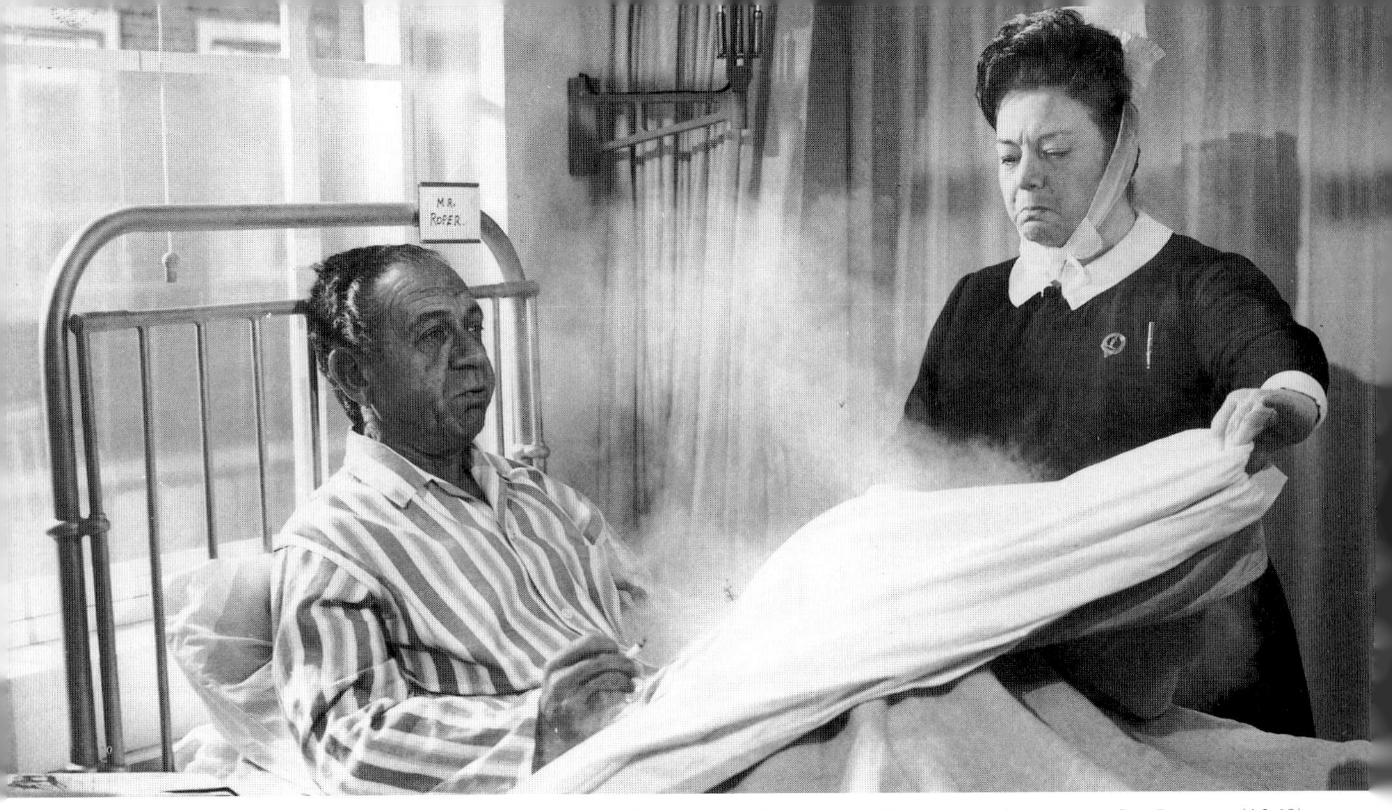

Charlie Roper (Sidney James) is caught smoking under the bed-covers by Matron (Hattie Jacques) in Carry On Doctor *(1968).*

Harry: Beggin' your pardon, Sister – but it do matter.

Matron and Sister look at him curiously.

Harry: Most of the Board was agin us. Then one man spoke up. 'E knows a Nurse 'ere. She'd just the other day told 'im, orf 'er own dear little bat, about Mercy Street trainin'. The Bullivant way. 'Arsh, 'ard, hagony – but it does the trick. Makes proud, responsible, super – that was the word – super Nurses. She swore she wouldn't want to be nowhere else but at good ol' Mercy Street 'Ospital...

Sister, affected, looks across to Matron.

Harry: (Offscreen)... even though Matron B seemed, lately, to be possessed by the spirit of a Foreign Legion prison-guard, there was no place like Mercy Street for this Nurse, he said.

Matron is deeply affected.

Harry: (Offscreen) That swung the votes over to us. They clapped 'im for five minutes. Gave 'im a standing ablution.

Matron: Of course, I can never thank him enough. But who is he?

Harry: Furness, Matron. 'E's a Mr Furness. Nurse Patsy Furness. Her dad.

Sister is openly and honestly astonished.

Matron: Thank you, Mr Drummond. (to Sister) I shall have to be harder than ever on her now – in case she even suspects how grateful I am that she unknowingly saved...

She breaks completely, and sits, weeping. Harry is mystified. Looks at Sister. She indicated him, kindly, to leave. He does so.

Sister is about to approach Matron, hand outstretched in comfort, when Matron, "recovered", suddenly rises, goes to window, looks out.

EXTERIOR. MERCY STREET HOSPITAL. DAY.

Matron's window POV

Favouring Sir Roderick's parked Rolls Royce. "Ah Sweet Mystery Of Life" heard, briefly.

INTERIOR. MATRON'S OFFICE. DAY.

MATRON still has her back to the uncertain Sister.

Matron: You're fired.
Sister: What?!
Matron: Fortunately, you have a better job to go to.
Sister: What? Where?
Matron: Mine. Here.

Sister is speechless. Matron turns.

Matron: It makes sense.
Sister: It makes me dizzy.
Matron: Consider. Who knows who'd take over from me if I hang on until official retirement? If I go now I can recommend someone who knows and loves the district. I know change has got to happen here. I'd rest easier knowing and liking who's making the changes.
Sister: All right. On one condition.
Matron: Name it.
Sister: That you never come back. Even as a patient.
Matron: Understood. Done.

They shake hands, but it almost at once becomes an impulsive and generous embrace. When they part, it is with mutually glistening eyes.

Matron: Any questions?
Sister: One. Why did you always insist on still being called Matron instead of Senior Nursing Officer as they call it now?
Matron: Because I could not get used to any of the new ways. Senior Nursing Officer! Matron! I ask you!
Sister: Goodbye, Matron...

She leaves. Matron looks at a certain photo on her desk. It has been present throughout, scrupulously unidentified.

Matron: Well? Did I do right?

PAN TO:
The photograph. It is of Hattie Jacques.

EXTERIOR. MERCY STREET. DAY.

Sir Rodericks's Rolls Royce emerges from Hospital driveway. The horn sounds at once and Harry is revealed having his routine heart-attack. As Sir Roderick sticks his head out of the car:

Harry: All right, Sir Cleverdick – you've proved you've got one so...
Sir R: I didn't stop you for that, Drummond. But to ask you something.
Harry: Oh? (Already shaking) Oo... What...?
Sir R: You know everything that goes on round here. Don't pretend you don't. Just tell me: why, for the past few days, has the hospital toilet-paper been marked Department of the Environment?
Harry: (Resigned) I might've known you'd be the one to notice. I've always said you've got eyes in yer...

POV FROM MATRON'S OFFICE WINDOW

To the halted Rolls Royce in the street below. Offscreen, in a piercing, confident soprano, Matron lets fly with a prolonged:

Matron: (Offscreen) Ahhhhhhhhhhhhhss-ssssssssssss-ssss...

PAN TO:

INTERIOR. MATRON'S OFFICE. DAY

Matron looking down fondly on her future happiness, continuing her triumphant song of joy:

Matron: ... weet Mystery Of Life. At last I've found you...!

THE END

FADE OUT

There can only be one matron to Carry On *fans – Hattie Jacques, seen here in a scene from* Carry On Matron *(1972).*

Acknowledgements
First and foremost our thanks and gratitude to Peter Rogers who continues to allow us to bring the rarest aspects of *Carry On* into the public domain. And to the inspirational Norman Hudis for continually proving that the daffodil really is the funniest flower of them all! Thanks to our great friend Jack Douglas for continued support and incisive memories. Our special thanks also to those fine actors and actresses who gave their all in the name of *Carry On* only to find their performances clipped in the wonderful scenes that make up this book. Our gratitude to Lofty Rice and the ever cheerful folk at the Pinewood Stills Department, Sian Facer at Carlton International and John Herron at Canal + Image for allowing us to constantly rummage through their boxes of photographs. Thanks to Jo Brooks at Virgin Publishing for ensuring *The Lost Carry Ons* was published on time. And our continued thanks to Pinewood Studios and particularly Steve Jaggs, David Rance and David Roalfe. We offer our posthumous thanks and respect to the most prodigious of *Carry On* writers Talbot Rothwell – this book is a testament to his, hitherto, uncelebrated and unheard comic writings. Finally to our respective loved ones who, after all these years, can still tolerate 'just one more' viewing of a *Carry On* classic for the umpteenth time…time for tiffin!